Book and Painting

THE HODGES·LECTURES

Book and Painting

SHAKESPEARE, MILTON
and the BIBLE

Literary Texts
and the Emergence of
English Painting

BY RONALD PAULSON

THE UNIVERSITY OF TENNESSEE PRESS
KNOXVILLE

Clothbound editions of University of Tennessee Press books are printed on paper designed for an effective life of at least 300 years, and binding materials are chosen for strength and durability.

Frontispiece: Plate 1. William Hogarth, *The Battle of the Pictures.* Etching. 1745.ic

Library of Congress Cataloging in Publication Data

Paulson, Ronald.
  Book and painting.

  (The Hodges lectures)
  Includes bibliographical references and index.
  1. Art, English.   2. Art, Modern—17th-18th centuries
—England.   3. Art and literature—England.   4. Ut
pictura poesis (Aesthetics)   5. Shakespeare, William,
1564-1616—Illustrations.   6. Milton, John, 1608-1674—
Illustrations.   7. Bible—Illustrations.   I. Title.
II. Series.
N6766.P36   750'.1   82-2769
ISBN 0-87049-358-2   AACR2

CONTENTS

PLATES

(beginning on page 170)

The Englishman eats roast beef and plum pudding, drinks port and claret; therefore, if you will be read by him, you must open the portals of Hell with the hand of Milton, convulse his ear or his sides with Shakespeare's buskin or sock, raise him above the stars with Dryden's Cecilia or sink him to the grave with the melancholy of Gray.

[Fuseli, Letter to Dälliker, Nov. 17654, in Eudo C. Mason, *The Mind of Henry Fuseli* (1951), 110–11.]

I. INTRODUCTION

English Painting and Literature

I recall a conversation with a colleague in the history department. We were discussing art history courses as a part of a British studies curriculum. He said, with only a trace of a smile, that he could conceive of a British studies program that omitted the subject of art altogether. "But not one that omitted literature?" I asked. "Literature and the law," he said, "—England's great contributions to European civilization."

The *book* of my title refers to the works of high literature that meant most to painters in England between 1700 and the early nineteenth century (I have already discussed some of the low, or popular, works and their impact in *Popular and Polite Art in the Age of Hogarth and Fielding).*[1] The importance of literature to painting in the western tradition does not need to be labored. It was the referent for most serious art from the Renaissance until the advent of what has been called "modernism." By some, in fact, "modernism" has been defined as the abandonment of the text, leading to the abandonment of external referents. In England the importance of literature was even greater than on the continent, or at least very different. There is a real sense in which English painting (that is, painting by Englishmen, not by foreigners who happened to reside in England) was a branch of literature rather than art.

Any account of English painting has to begin with William Hogarth. But even if we include his marvelous oil sketches and the passages of great fluency in all of his paintings, there is nothing of *primary* interest to describe in Hogarth (as compared to his continental contemporaries Chardin and Giambattista Tiepolo) that is purely pictorial. If he is measured against his greatest continental contemporaries in graphic terms, he will be found a second-rate provincial. If, however, he is taken into the company of his literary contemporaries—Swift, Gay, Fielding, Richardson, Sterne—and measured against the art *and* literature being produced on the continent in the eighteenth century, he will rank very high indeed. The appropriate response may therefore be to assimilate him to the literature rather than the art of the period and so to the methods of literary criticism, in the context of which he does make a great deal of sense and is of primary importance.

I suspect that this formulation may apply to a large part of English art as well as to Hogarth. I do not mean that Constable, Turner, and perhaps Gainsborough—the greatest English painters, at least two of which will stand against the greatest continental painters—are primarily verbal, for indeed their major contributions lie in portraiture and landscape; but that their art, however visual at the core (or in its most important aspect), persists in an English way to ask verbal questions, that their art is incomprehensible without a consideration of its verbal aspect, and that each painter was willy-nilly part of the Hogarth—or shall we say English, or perhaps Shakespearean?—tradition.

The great authorities for English painters therefore tend to be among the books, not among the paintings. Hogarth supports his palette (in his self-portrait in the Tate) on a pile of books, the works of Shakespeare, Milton, and Swift, and we know he read more deeply in Shakespeare than he studied the works of the old masters. In our own century Stanley Spencer read the works of Shakespeare and Milton and was satisfied with reproductions of Giotto's paintings in textbooks. (In one case he painted from Ruskin's description of a Giotto.) The word and the concept were privileged in various ways over the image in the act of painting. The image—which Hogarth conveyed through reproductive engravings and Spencer through the mechanical filling in of paint on a squared-off canvas—was more a product of invention than of the painter's hand. There were excellent precedents for the superiority of idea to execution in the High Renaissance, but to see where English painters excel one needs only compare subject paintings by English and French painters. The French ones are in general technically far more sophisticated as paintings but less resonant as imaginative constructs.

The explanation for this situation may lie in the fact that in the eighteenth century the great tradition of English literature, primarily poetry, was second to none. I do not think anyone would say the same for English painting. There was not—before Hogarth—anything that could be called a native tradition of painting in England. The "Englishness" of English painting[2] refers to the fact that before the rise of Reynolds and artists who drew on Italian sources, it tended to assimilate itself to the indigenous, flourishing tradition of the written word rather than to the graphic tradition; and this was at least in part a reaction against the totally un-English, foreign nature of so much of the English graphic heritage—not only painters who came from Switzerland, Flanders, and Germany, and musicians from Italy and Germany, but even kings who were Norman, Welsh, Scottish, and German. Before Hogarth (and his father-in-law Sir James Thornhill), the notable painters in England had been Holbein, Rubens, Van Dyck, Lely, and Kneller, all foreigners representing alien cultures.

Only the writers were unequivocally English, and so the medium of the English language was the one pure, undefiled source. The eighteenth century was a time when Englishmen delved into their national origins, which often took the form of adapting popular, simple, and local forms of art. One reason for George III's undiminished popularity despite ministerial incompetence and disasters at home and abroad was that he was the first native-born English king in nearly half a century, and another that he exalted in his own person the simple, rural English virtues. The pride of nationalistic Englishmen was lodged in their own past, particularly as reflected in the true national art, poetry and the drama: in the traditions of Chaucer-Spenser-Milton-Dryden-Pope and of Shakespeare-Jonson-Congreve. Shakespeare's plays—comedies as well as tragedies and histories—were a yardstick by which other judgments were made, partly at least because they tended to be exceptions to every "foreign" rule, value, and assumption about high art.

The English tradition of painting opened with Hogarth, the first artist of English descent to achieve an international reputation (largely through the wide distribution of his engravings). It continued with Reynolds, in his own way as literary as Hogarth but far more concerned to assimilate English art to continental traditions, and then went on to those eccentric illustrators Blake and Fuseli (though another foreigner), to the formal innovators Turner and John Martin, and straight through the nineteenth century and the Pre-Raphaelites, the decorators of the Houses of Parliament, Frith and Maclise, to Watts, Egg, Mulready, and Waterhouse, and in our own century to Sickert, Stanley Spencer, and Francis Bacon—to Michael Andrews and David Hockney. When Hockney does a series of etchings he calls *The Rake's Progress* and paints a large colorful version of Hogarth's tiny engraving *Satire on False Perspective,* he is drawing attention to this aspect of his English heritage.

This book, in short, is going to be about some verbal (as well as verbal-to-visual versions of) structures that impressed themselves on English painting. The texts I have chosen to study are obvious and need no explanation: the works of Shakespeare, Milton's *Paradise Lost,* and the Bible, with a glance at Cervantes' *Don Quixote.*

My omissions are more problematic. The *Iliad* and *Odyssey* spring to mind. They served as Pope's substitute for an epic of his own. He translated them, making them poetically and politically normative texts for his own time. They also served as subject for many history paintings, beginning with the series painted by Gavin Hamilton in the 1760s.

Hamilton's combination of the literary text of Homer and the graphic text of Poussin (in particular his *Death of Germanicus*) showed artists how to structure a certain kind of picture of multiple responses to a dead and transfigured object. Or perhaps Hamilton only found in Homer and Poussin a vehicle for his and his contemporaries' concern with transcendent subjects (the death of a hero at the moment of victory or the death of a bird in a luminous scientific experiment) in an imminent world, England in the 1760s. In France, Jacques-Louis David learned from Hamilton's precedent, and a great tradition of painting followed, centered on the morally and spiritually ambiguous act of revolution against constituted authority. No major English art can, however, be said to depend on Homer's text itself in the way it does on the story of *Paradise Lost*.

The *Aeneid* was the epic that carried most weight with the writers of the Restoration and the first half of the eighteenth century. Pope's *Iliad* was seen largely through the text of Virgil's *Aeneid*, whose plot concerned the transfer of a society from the smoking ruins of one city to a new land, with a conforming protagonist *(pius* Aeneas) who defends social values against private ones (the love of Dido). It can be argued that the *Aeneid* and Aeneas' mission were Milton's model for *Paradise Lost* with the negative transference of empire by Satan played against the positive relocations of Adam in the Redemption of the Second Adam, Christ. Certainly the kind of heroism idealized in *Paradise Lost* was closer to that of Virgil's Aeneas than to Homer's Achilles—who reappears in *The Aeneid* as the antagonist Turnus and in *Paradise Lost* as Satan. *The Aeneid* itself, however, had little effect upon the artists, who were not ready for its subject until later in the century, by which time Aeneas was being replaced as a hero by Achilles or Odysseus (of whose journey Aeneas' was a variant). At the time when the *Aeneid* might have shaped their thoughts English artists were still painting portraits and only wishfully aspiring to such an elevated subject, or turning to its Christian equivalent. The safest subject they could manage at the time was the lower, more accessible one of *Don Quixote*, a poor-man's Achilles whose humble adventures permitted them to represent contemporary and sometimes local detail while retaining Achilles' heroic intentions. When they attempted high flights they simply copied the Venetian artists who were repeating stories of the Greek and Roman gods and goddesses.

Gods and goddesses raise the subject of Ovid, who in his way was as important as Virgil for Pope and the poets (even for Swift). For the landscape poets Ovid was essential, because landscape—at least in England—seems to have needed the myth of metamorphosis to join the human and natural elements, the staffage and the landscape proper, in order to keep landscape in line with history painting. The other poetic models for landscape were Virgil's pastorals and georgics—and primarily the latter—filtered, of course, through a tradition of graphic representations by Claude Lorrain, Gaspar Dughet, and Nicolas Poussin. Were I to extend these chapters to include the subject of landscape painting (in more than the glancing way I do in Chapter IV), I would have to discuss these poetic models. The literary problems connected with landscape painting are, however, a subject to which I have devoted a separate monograph.[3] One phenomenon we shall witness is that at the opening of the eighteenth century the prominent, the viable genre, was the portrait, which even determined much about the nature of English history painting; whereas from 1760 onward, at the peak of portrait greatness in the works of Reynolds and Gainsborough, this genre was gradually superseded by landscape. Gainsborough's figures were soon lost in their landscape backgrounds, and by the end of the century landscape had been raised in practice, if not yet in theory, to first place in the artistic hierarchy. History painting was assimilated to landscape painting as it had earlier been assimilated to portraiture, before being dropped as no longer necessary.

Some influential works—Bunyan's *Pilgrim's Progress* for instance—are secondary-magnitude literature in the sense that an artist can be said to get what Bunyan offers him straight from Bunyan's source, the Bible. On the other hand, when we discuss the Bible, we should bear in mind that *this* New Testament, this typological relationship between Old and New Testaments, was probably to some extent read through the mediation of Bunyan's immensely popular books. For English painters the tradition of Protestantism represented by Bunyan was read into the story of the apostles Peter and Paul in the Raphael Cartoons, almost as well known to them as Bunyan and the Bible. I might also have discussed the works of Dryden, Swift, and Pope which gave a satiric edge to the art of the period, especially to Hogarth's earlier work. I shall, in fact, show how it was Samuel Butler's *Hudibras,* the English equivalent of *Don Quixote,* that unlocked for Hogarth the secret of how to illustrate Cervantes' paradigm of illusion and reality. Certainly Samuel Johnson's thought influenced Reynolds, as Burke's did a multitude of history painters and landscape artists. We shall encounter references to these, remembering that the mutual influence of contemporaries or near-contemporaries is far too large a subject for this short study.

The literary works I am dealing with were all models that carried certain kinds of authority—aesthetic, religious, or nationalistic. In important ways they impressed themselves upon the graphic forms of English art in the eighteenth century, and have continued to do so into the twentieth. It is also clear that in so far as they *im*pressed high culture stereotypes, they *re*pressed other matters—popular or low-culture games, pastimes, certain kinds of labor, aspects of sexuality, and to a large extent children, blacks, whores, kitchen utensils, natural functions, and the like. In other words, high art, and by the eighteenth century in England, high literature too, embodied particular shapes and formulations, but also particular omissions or subtractions from everyday experience. Shakespeare was unique in being both a high culture object and (when unpurged by critics and bowdlerizers) capacious enough to include all manner of things, high and low.

It is also obvious that while the great works of literature carried authority and established some general mind-sets, they were chosen and used by artists for the artists' own particular purposes. These purposes could be high or low. I am reminded of the woman overheard to say as she left the theater after a performance of Shakespeare's *Antony and Cleopatra:* "Yes, and the funny thing is, exactly the same thing happened to Monica."[4] This is essentially the way English artists used Shakespeare, just as it is probably safest to say that they built on their own early works more significantly than on the work of any other artist they seem to be borrowing from.

There was a degree of mutuality in the relationship between artist and Shakespeare or Milton. The basic questions in the case of each artist are what happens to Shakespeare when he is illustrated? and what effect does Shakespeare have on these artists in their independent work that is not Shakespeare illustration? How do they leave their mark on Shakespeare, and how do Shakespearean forms, themes, assumptions, and structures leave their mark on painting? I suspect, for one thing, that these fictions or structures carried more normative weight and authority at the beginning than at the end of the century, and indeed at the beginning than at the end of the individual artist's career.

On the other hand, "literature" often meant more than a literary text to these painters. It could also mean the text apprehended through graphic equivalents—for example, the Bible through the paintings of Michelangelo or Raphael. "Literature" has to be taken to be a much larger concept than the printed text.

This book began as the John C. Hodges Lectures delivered in October 1980 at the University of Tennessee, Knoxville. The three lectures focused on "Shakespearean Painting" but also drew on the Miltonic and Biblical influences. Although the whole book could still, without too much distraction, be called "Shakespearean Painting," I have recast the lectures into separate chapters of Shakespeare, Milton, and the Bible, and the interrelation of the traditions in the work of Blake, Fuseli, and Turner. Because he is the most representative of English artists and because I know him best, Hogarth has been used as my chief example in the earlier chapters. I begin, however, with the influence of Cervantes' *Don Quixote,* a work which was neither English nor unequivocally high art. It served as a mediator for English painters who wanted both to produce high art and to represent what was uniquely native English. The initial question is therefore about the nature of illustration, and throughout I shall be referring to "illustrations" of Shakespeare and Milton. I do not, however, want to give the impression that this is in any sense a study of book illustration. It is about the main tradition of English figurative painting, which is from Hogarth to Fuseli, Blake, and Turner.

Graphic Equivalents for Verbal Texts

The 1714 edition of Alexander Pope's *Rape of the Lock* is a good example of the relationship between literary and graphic traditions as they focus on the illustration of a text. It seems pretty certain that Pope supervised the illustrations by Louis du Guernier for this, the first five-canto edition of the *Rape.* The case for his personal involvement begins with the fact that his contemporary agreement with the same publisher (Lintot) for his *Iliad* translation contained the clause that decorations will be produced "by such Graver as the said Alexander Pope shall direct and appoint"; we know that he did interesting visual things with the printing of his later poems, in particular *The Dunciad* (1729 edition), and that he was studying painting with Charles Jervas at this time. We also know of the active assistance given by Swift and other writers to their illustrators. Morris Brownell's researches (as well as Elias Mengel's) have removed any doubt we may have had that Pope was master of a graphic vocabulary apart from a verbal.[5]

Robert Halsband's recent book on illustrations to *The Rape of the Lock* has filled in the context.[6] From research into the book trade Halsband has gleaned the interesting fact that while very few poems were published with illustrations in this period (six in the decade 1704-14), in the year 1714 alone there appeared Garth's *Dispensary* (seventh edition), Gay's *Shepherd's Week,* and Pope's *Rape of the Lock,* all illustrated by du Guernier; Boileau's *Lutrin* was reprinted with the illustrations appended in 1712, and a religious work of Edward Young also appeared with illustrations. With the exception of the Young work, these all have in common the fact that they were illustrated and that they were mock-heroic poems. It is just possible that the rash of illustrated books was merely due to the availability of du Guernier, or to the precedent of the *Lutrin*'s success in 1712, but it may also be that there was thought to be something inherently illustratable about poems in the mock-heroic mode.

Halsband points to the example of Belinda's bed transformed by du Guernier into a military tent in the illustration for Canto I, which corresponds as a graphic equivalent to the martial metaphor of the poem, in which a card game is described in terms of epic combat; and to "the massive pillars (their pedestals enormously enlarged)" of the palace facade in the illustration for Canto II, as a mock-heroic equivalent.[7] The search for this sort of equivalence is a game any illustrator might have found attractive and amusing to play.

Such graphic equivalents are, of course, crude compared to the subtle nuances of Pope's verbal text. But the illustrator may also produce equivalents for what is *not* specified in the text. The most suggestive example, it seems to me, is the illustration for Canto II, Belinda's ride down the Thames to Hampton Court Palace (pl. 2). How is an artist to illustrate Belinda's "painted Vessel"? He could, of course, copy a contemporary boat of the sort on which such young women did travel on the Thames. Halsband informs us that these were barges, with a rowing crew but no sails. The sort of boat du Guernier depicts, with sails (stipulated in Pope's text), did occasionally appear on the Thames, but these were usually freight boats. After that, the artist might turn to literary precedents: Cleopatra's barge, with its burnished prow, and so on, would be one; and this would have had graphic equivalents of its own. For an Englishman, however, Shakespeare's Cleopatra would be the first text brought to mind because Belinda could be seen as a sort of Cleopatra and the poet describing her another infatuated Enobarbus. This would have suited Pope's intentions in his text.

Another graphic alternative (the one Halsband sees) was more readily available to a satirist: the Ship of Fools, in graphic versions such as the illustrations for Sebastian Brandt's *Narrenschiff*. Du Guernier has shortened Belinda's boat to a stubby shape that resembles some Ships of Fools.[8] My point is merely that Belinda's boat might alternatively have been visualized as a Noah's Ark, as an ironic Journey of the Magi (like the one in the Clark Art Institute), or perhaps even as Christ's boat on the Sea of Galilee. Belinda on the Thames might have been based on Raphael's Cartoon *The Miraculous Draught of Fishes,* with Belinda (her eyes "Bright as the Sun," "the Rival of his Beams") in the position of Christ. In any of these cases, the visual convention adds a metaphoric dimension. There is no word in Pope's text that says Belinda is traveling

10

on a Ship of Fools. But there *is,* we see after looking at the illustration, a sense in which she is doing just that.

The illustration in this case produces a discontinuity, a deviation from Pope's text. The graphic language is simple and uncomplicated—and vivid—by contrast with the words. It simplifies the text. But because it appears with the text, the illustration augments it, adding another dimension of which Pope cannot have disapproved, though he would not have allowed it into the words of the poem itself. He would not have said it himself, but he did not mind an illustrator saying it, in precisely the way he added pseudonymously *The Key to the Lock* which imposed an overt politico-allegorical interpretation on the delicate comedy of his poem. The illustration becomes a part of Pope's whole process of revision (vs. Addison's determination, Pope reported, to "never alter anything after a poem was once printed"): Pope adds the new cantos, the illustrations, *The Key to the Lock,* Clarissa's speech, and so on, each an additional aspect of his poem. An illustration is, in this sense, a characteristic addendum to a Pope poem—and probably to many other eighteenth-century works that function on the same additive principle as Pope's *Rape of the Lock.*

The frontispiece (pl. 3) goes further, however, introducing an unacknowledged or even suppressed part of the textual meaning. Belinda as Venus with her mirror, a reference to a long iconographical tradition of *Vanitas,* merely underlines the verses on Belinda's toilet. But, as Halsband argues, her exposed leg connects her with a traditional image of lustful woman, conflating vanity and licentiousness in a single image. Belinda cannot be *lustful* in Pope's text, though she can have a lover's image lurking in her heart.

The figure of the satyr writes in boldface the sexual component that is discreetly, playfully implicit in the poem. Something unmistakably a satyr's leg was also exposed beneath the drapery of Belinda's dressing table in the illustration for Canto I, and two satyrs remain in the headpiece to the poem printed in the 1717 *Works.*

The Rape of the Lock is about rape—about the domestication or Ovidian metamorphosis of satyrs into beaux, of instinctive behavior into ritual through the conventions of polite society. Pope never gives us more than an allusive gesture to this effect, as in the broken china or, at its most overt, in the line about "hairs less in sight," or in the displacements of the Cave of the Spleen (which the illustration does not pick up). In the illustration, however, he can make explicit what he could not in his text. And yet the satyr still contains the delightfully ambiguous status of signifying—according to context—either of its senses, animal lust or (and the two are not mutually exclusive) the operation of satire.

11

(A satyr serves the second purpose in Hogarth's frontispiece to *Hudibras* and his last *Beggar's Opera* paintings).

An illustration can either underline meaning in the text or educe meaning that was implicit or unacknowledged, even perhaps repressed by the poet. Pope's *Rape* demonstrates the problem which is most obvious in the case of Dickens' relationship with his illustrator Hablot K. Browne ("Phiz"). Whatever Browne may later add of his own, Dickens originates and sets up the illustrative assumption. This is the use of Hogarthian emblems to make clear—i.e. visual—his meaning, or certain parts of it he wants emphasized. What Phiz does as well, however, is to expose the aspects that Dickens is repressing in his text—as in *The Old Curiosity Shop,* the fantasy of the older man trying to seduce the young girl. A good example is the phallic shape and behavior of Quilp in the illustration, who is shown pushing through doors and windows with his tall narrow hat, and ends drowned and washed up on the shore next to some piles which give him, by optical illusion, the most spectacular displaced erection in all art.

Browne is exposing precisely those folk aspects that Dickens wished most to keep in the background of his text. We can see Browne either as Dickens' id, with the function of his illustrations "to emphasize embedded sexual nuances," to "emphasize the unruliness of the energies unleashed by Dickens' imagination,"[9] or as self-appointed critic, with his illustrations deconstructing or subverting Dickens' ostensible gentility. For it is precisely in *The Old Curiosity Shop* that Dickens begins to combine satire and sentiment not only in his text but in his combination of illustrations, by dividing them between George Cattermole and Browne (and later between Browne's own comic and "dark" styles). Whoever was responsible, the illustrations bring out the parts that are repressed in the text, developing the representation (in the Freudian sense) that is covered by symbolization and sentimentalization. Is this Browne's insight, or did Dickens instruct him to do precisely this, in the same way that Pope probably had his illustrator introduce the satyr with which he did not want to mar his own text and be himself associated?

We can draw one important conclusion that will apply in a general way to the rest of our examples: Truth is graphic, exposure is visual, as in drama where the concealments of words are eventually swept aside by a collapsing screen, a falling curtain, which reveals the truth. Even when the seeing is metaphorical, when Oedipus is blinded, the image of insight is visual. Browne's illustrations for *The Old Curiosity Shop* point toward the role of the camera in Lewis Carroll's art: the repressed material in both his text and in Tenniel's illustrations emerges in Carroll's photographs.

This is not to say that the exposed latent truth is any more valid than the manifest one, or that one cancels the other, but only that they interact in interesting ways. For example, *Gulliver's Travels* (1726) was another book, like *The Rape of the Lock,* in which the author had a hand with the illustrations. More than almost any other satire of the period, *Gulliver's Travels* raises the issue of how the illustrator represents the satirist's most powerful attribute, his style. Should the illustrator imitate Swift's deadpan style or the horrible reality he projects? Should he show us the action the way Gulliver sees it or the way Swift sees it? Swift himself may have contributed a comment through one illustration, the frontispiece. For when *Gulliver* was reprinted in the collected edition of Swift's *Works* in 1735 he had George Faulkner (the publisher) replace the frontispiece of the 1726 edition, which showed "Captain Lemuel Gulliver," with another. This one, labeled "Splendide Mendax," shows a figure who is posed, and with a very similar face, as the figure was on the frontispiece of volume one of the *Works,* a portrait of Dean Swift in clerical bands. As you turn from volume 1 to volume 3 you notice the resemblance. It looks as if Swift is offering us a visual association of himself and Gulliver, his fallible, misanthropic persona; but it is also a sophisticated acknowledgment of any author's Gulliverian lies in a work of fiction.[10]

Don Quixote *and the Tradition of Comic Illustration*

What then do we mean by illustration, and what are the various possibilities of the relation between illustration and text? What do we mean by comic illustration? And how is this different from the moral or satiric tradition of graphic art that we associate with the first original mode of Hogarth's English painting, "modern moral subjects"?[11]

In Renaissance art as in book illustration the imitated was essentially a written text, assisted of course by objects in the external world, the art tradition of representation, and the artist's own sensibility. The artist's dropping of—or dispensing with, or dissociating himself from—the "text" is a major development of post-Renaissance art, a part of the larger transition from fidelity to the imitated text to fidelity to nature (or the fiction of this fidelity) and ultimately "self-expression" in one of its many forms. With the illustration-painting, as with book illustration, there were always the alternative possibilities of conveying information, merely providing repose or distraction from the labor of reading, developing some aspect of the meaning that was of significance to the artist or his patron, or showing how this particular painter would illustrate this particular text. But a normative element from the world of imagination rather than the real world always remained: the written text.

Book illustration was one of the ways artists in the eighteenth century made their break from great subject, great style, and great patronage. This was, in Joseph Burke's words, "the underground channel by which traditions of *istoria* were kept alive in England at this period when the supply of patrons willing to give over the walls and ceilings of their mansions to grandiose decorative painting was a dwindling one."[12] Through the agency of book illustration an artist could introduce other, more immediate or contemporary texts than those relied on by the history painter. A Poussin painting refers to, or imitates, a text of Ovid or Virgil (or a complex composite text), as well as those visual precursors who are themselves illustrators of one of these or some other related text. By contrast, a Hogarth could shift his attention from Homer, Virgil, or the Bible to Cervantes, Molière, or even Samuel Butler, and thence to his real interest, which was the contemporary scene, England in the 1720s or 30s. With Cervantes and Butler the artist with satiric inclinations had a text that opened up the possibility of the mock-text, a way of juxtaposing the heroic, the romantic, the plainly fictional with the contemporary commonplace. Illustration is as clear a case as exists of literature influencing art, for as literature broadened and dealt with different and more contemporary subjects, and used new strategies of communication, the artist was drawn to develop, or found a sanction through illustration for developing, the same concerns graphically. Hogarth and his tradition are inconceivable without *Don Quixote, Pilgrim's Progress,* and the works of Defoe, Butler, Swift, and Gay.

Hogarth's own progress was from the particular text on the opposite page in the illustrated book to the large independent engraved illustration for *Don Quixote* and *Hudibras* that assumes the text in the viewer's mind and reminds him by a few lines and references underneath. Then he moved on to the general text, a criminal or spiritual biography beside his life of a harlot, or beside his life of a rake both spiritual biographies and his own earlier progress of a harlot. He might include or imply yet other kinds of progresses and lives, sometimes using scenes from the Bible which act as ironic commentaries. Perhaps recalling those imaginary texts projected by Cervantes behind *Don Quixote,* Hogarth implies a non-existent history painting prior to his reproductive engraving and, prior to that, some literary text or other (connecting himself with series of the engraved reproductions of history by Raphael, Poussin, and others). Both painting (except for a small oil sketch of his own) and literary text were, however, only assumed. The actual text illustrated was something seen and experienced—this was another part of the Hogarthian fiction—and imagined by the painter himself. This last point is important because the assumed *other* in every Hogarth "history" is an immediate experience of life in London, containing recognizable portraits and places, beyond the imitation of literary or graphic texts. It represents (as in his subscription ticket *Boys Peeping at Nature)* a lifting of the veil or skirt of Nature to have a personal look at what is underneath.

Hogarth turned his engraved image into another form, the best model for which is not the illustration but the emblem. He adapted literally the structure of the Renaissance emblem in which the visual and verbal are closely related, the meaning (or reading) emerging through an interplay of the title, the motto, and the visual image; sometimes he even added a prose commentary or verbalization of the meaning of all three. If there is a text prior to the emblem, it is known only to the artist, and the reader's duty is to reconstruct it by inference. In other words, the emblem is not merely illustrating a device (motto), a known adage, or an apothegm; it may use one or more of these commonplaces *(topoi)* as its raw material, both visual and verbal, but it does so in order to produce a total image that is more than the sum of its parts, that is independent, problematic, and to be deciphered.

D.C. Allen has pointed out the relation of the *Emblemata* of Alciati to the *Tabula Cebetis,* "the prototype of that major Renaissance literary-artistic invention, the emblem."[13] Alciati's emblems appear just one generation after the first printing of the *Tabula,* with its simultaneous description and explanation of the visual symbols. In the emblem each viewer is the equivalent of Cebes, the versifier or commentator of the emblematic image, who educes the meaning from the metonymically or metaphorically-related objects in the picture, silently or not so silently supplying the words. This meditation is itself materialized for Hogarth's progresses in later printed commentaries like those of Rouquet, Lichtenberg, Steevens, and the Irelands—in each of which there is so close a cooperation between object and reader that the reality of the object is in the transaction rather than strictly speaking in itself: ultimately in the interplay of viewers talking out their interpretations together.

In short, what emerges as the Hogarthian "comic history" or "modern moral subject" is not an illustration that completes a text but an image that offers a visual substitute, with its own more or less materialized implied verbal text. The one interprets a text; the other projects its own text. This is not to deny that there is, inevitably, something of a prefigured text as complicated in its way, only more fragmented, than the "Virgil" or "Ovid" imitated by Poussin. The mock-heroic painting, for example, may presuppose (like the mock-heroic poem) scenes and figures in the *Aeneid* juxtaposed with known contemporaries like Thomas Shadwell and their known plays or poems. In *A Harlot's Progress* (pl. 36) the ratio of contemporary reference (Mother Needham, Colonel Charteris, his rape trial of 1730, and other facts of that year) to the heroic past (allusion via composition to a classical or biblical prototype) is relatively high, which explains Hogarth's heavy reliance on various reading structures—objects of a high denotation, parallels and contrasts between these or between known and unknown figures—in order to make the third element, his own invented text or the record of his personal observation of the life of a harlot in London.

Even when an artist like Hogarth is "illustrating" a text, he is probably using that text to convey his own concerns. We must nevertheless distinguish his illustrations from the emblematic structure that was his contribution to English art.

By the "comic" tradition of illustration, in the largest sense of the term, we do not mean "what makes you laugh," for much of the illustration of comic writing (for example, Cervantes and Molière) was not in itself comic; it merely represented the action described in a comic text. This sense of "comic" is a concern with the low or commonplace, the unheroic or untragic, and ushers in the main concerns of progressive painting in England in the eighteenth century. But what then is a comic illustration? Obviously it must be amusing either in itself, in its own terms, or in combination with the text.

The small illustrations Hogarth made for Samuel Butler's *Hudibras* (probably c. 1721, but published in 1726) will serve as an introductory example: they were simply copied from an earlier set (1710) but transformed by Hogarth into comic images. The Hudibras of the 1710 edition is a deformed little old man going through the paces indicated by Butler in his verses; Hogarth, by his play with gesture and facial expression, his grotesque exaggeration and his wavering line, turns him into a creature who is funny-*looking*.

But a second person is necessary, for although comic illustration, throughout the century, will be largely indicated through grotesque exaggeration alone, something happens when a contrasting figure is added. In Hudibras' encounter with the lawyer, Hogarth changes the latter from a perfectly normal person (in the 1710 plates) into one as

16

corrupt in a bored way as Hudibras. Two kinds of distortion are related. On the other hand, in "Hudibras wooing the Widow" (pl. 4) the second figure is normative or, perhaps better, a detached observer to Hudibras' deeply involved (passionate, hypocritical, foolish) action. Hudibras' gesture of wooing is expressively comic in itself, but to be understood it requires the patient widow to whom it is made.

One book above all others, *Don Quixote,* served as a vehicle for the development of comic illustration. The illustrator could, to begin with, introduce the contemporary English settings he really wished to represent and the humble events of everyday English life. What *Don Quixote* embodied was the essence of comic structure, the incongruous. It was constructed on a combined intellectual and formal incongruity, which was to organize much of eighteenth-century comic writing and art, setting both Hogarth and Fielding on their respective ways. This was an incongruity between the aspiration or illusion of a Don Quixote and the reality of his surroundings, between the image of a knight-errant with his heroic steed and the tall, bony, decrepit old shapes of both Quixote and Rosinante; and in formal terms between these lanky shapes and the short, earthy, well-fed shape of Sancho, amid inns, herds of sheep, and windmills.

In the 1720s both Hogarth and John Vanderbank made illustrations for the Spanish-language edition of *Don Quixote* sponsored by Lord Carteret, an ambitious piece of book-printing that was trying to live up to elegant editions of Racine and Tasso and emphasize Cervantes' status as classic rather than comic author.[14] Vanderbank, whose obsession with the subject led him to continue painting scenes from *Don Quixote* for the rest of his life, used Cervantes as a way of delineating the congenial subjects denied him by the decorum of history painting. He substituted an English for a Spanish milieu, but the only comic shape allowed was the figure of Sancho. Both he and Hogarth felt constrained to juxtapose Quixote and Sancho not as comic extremes but as ideal and real; Quixote wears a dignity quite at odds with the reality around him.

Hogarth's Quixote images are far more elevated than his small *Hudibras* plates, in which cheap printing and a popular audience allowed him a freer rein. "The Adventure of Mambrino's Helmet" (pl. 5) contrasts the heroic figures of Quixote and Rosinante (a surprisingly well-formed horse) with those of the shaggy donkey and cringing barber. The effect is pathetic rather than comic. However, Hogarth also introduces a larger contrast between the encounter itself and, at a great distance, the round figure of Sancho on his roundish mule merely watching, two quiet observers from another world. Hogarth has not only made the point nicely but suggested something of the difference in shape as well as distance and attitude. One possible element of a comic incongruity then would seem to be an audience or observer of some sort who is set off against the adventure in which the comic hero is caught up.[15]

Only in "The Curate and Barber disguising Themslves" (pl. 6, a scene which Vanderbank did not choose to illustrate) did Hogarth find a more congenial subject. The costuming of these unprepossessing figures, and the juxtaposition of the antlers above the inn door, the chamber pot on a shelf, the coat of arms, and the mirror in which the barber regards himself, broach some of Hogarth's own central themes: these can be summed up as the comedy of masquerade.

Decorum seems to have limited the extensive use of such detail to large independent *Quixote* plates like those of C.A. Coypel imported from France (1724). Hogarth made only one such independent illustration for *Don Quixote*, and this followed the interests explored in the "Curate and Barber." However, as if unwilling to sully the Don's dignity, he chose a scene involving the delusion of Sancho (pl. 7). Here a group of various outlandish characters are participating in a scene of plainly unheroic action. The regally-designated Sancho, who cannot however hide his Sancho-ness, shown amid regal food and service, in what is clearly a palace, is nevertheless starving. The court physician prevents his eager hand from lifting a single morsel to his mouth, the waiters withdraw the plates, and one courtier uses the tablecloth (which is supposed to hold food) to stifle irreverent laughter. Sancho, who is himself playing a king, is in the midst, unknown to himself, of play-acting at his expense. As a witness to the whole charade, a fat woman laughs outright. If Hogarth had continued a set of illustrations on this scale, we can be sure he would have included "Don Quixote and the Puppet Show": he alludes more than once to Coypel's illustration of the scene, borrowing from it the figure of Sancho, the amused bystander to madness.[16] Such scenes carried the authority of Coypel's popular series, but the difference is instructive. Coypel's plates are expressive too, showing a wide variety of comic response but within the conventions of French art, which means of a fairly rigid decorum. The figures are only as expressive, we might say, as comic actors on a stage; whereas Hogarth's figures exist in a purely graphic realm of the grotesquely comic.

The next stage of development can be seen in Francis Hayman's illustrations for Smollett's translation of *Don Quixote* of 1755.[17] Taking Chapter 16, concerning the adventures in the inn, Hogarth had illustrated the scene of the wounded Quixote being covered with poultices by Maritornes and the innkeeper's wife while Sancho watches. The comedy, such as it is, rests in the almost unpleasantly deformed figures working on Quixote, and perhaps also in the juxtaposition with San-cho's quiet observation, which seems to be Hogarth's version of the Quixotic situation. Hayman, however, has taken the later scene in which Sancho finds Maritornes, who is fleeing from Quixote's deluded embraces, in his bed (pl. 8). "There was the mule driver [Maritornes' jealous lover] pounding Sancho, Sancho and the wench flaying each other, and the landlord drubbing the girl; and they all laid on most vigorously, without allowing themselves a moment's rest."[18] Hayman has chosen to portray slapstick action, which allows for violent move-ment, exaggerated postures, and facial distortion that goes beyond a scene of stasis or mere formal contrast. But it is also noteworthy that he has chosen the moment just prior to the passage quoted: the innkeeper is not yet quite involved in the struggle but only an interested bystander, holding up his candle to observe the combatants. (His figure is com-plemented by the completely uninvolved figure of the sleeping man on a nearby bed.) Hayman initiates the tradition of comic illustration that goes straight to Rowlandson, who in fact copied his illustration (pl. 9). Rowlandson has merely simplified (by omitting the sleeper) and ex-aggerated the violence and put the bed covers over Maritornes in order to make explicit the fact that her place of concealment was in bed with Sancho. This is as much a part of Rowlandson's personal subject matter as the costuming and role-playing were of Hogarth's.

Hayman as well as Hogarth avoids the central scene of the chapter, in which Quixote himself wrestles with Maritornes, thinking she is Dul-cinea (to which the struggle with Sancho is only a postscript).[19] This scene involves a psychological comedy which Hayman is quite incap-able of transmitting, but it is the one that Hogarth develops in his large *Hudibras* plates, where he has a less high-minded hero to deal with. Hudibras, the second-hand Quixote, a genuinely low character, allows Hogarth to develop not only the formal contrasts that Cervantes set in motion but also the intellectual and moral ones, which grow into the allusive structures concerning the wit of mingled objects and milieu that lead to his "comic history paintings," and that explore comic possibili-ties far beyond anything in the tradition of comic illustration per se. The play begins with the contrasting shapes of Hudibras and his squire Ralpho but goes on to the juxtaposition of different kinds of reality, different sources of imitation, different texts and interpretations of the text (or of individual words within the text).

The basic problem, which Hogarth solved only indirectly, and no one else came close to solving, was how to illustrate *Don Quixote*. Here was the story of a mad old man who reads too many romances and sets out to be a knight errant in a time when there are no more knight errants. He therefore attacks windmills, thinking they are giants and herds of sheep thinking they are armies. How does an artist represent the story of a madman? How does he represent illusion?

When Hogarth illustrated *Don Quixote* itself, he did no more than show a relatively idealized Quixote attacking contemporaries, who therefore tended to come out looking more sympathetic than Quixote, and the humor was produced by the comically-uncomprehending point of view of the sober surrogate for the reader, Sancho. I do not know why Hogarth was unable to conceive of the solution in his Quixote illustrations—even in the one large plate, which turned out to be Sancho's illusions rather than Quixote's. The relatively small format may have allowed for no more than he gave us. Perhaps by the time he made the Sancho Panza plate he had already solved the problem and did not want to return to it. The answer is probably that the solution was more available in the English *Don Quixote,* Butler's *Hudibras,* which was a political vision, a satire with immediate local interest. For here we can see the transition from the small illustrations, which were more or less copied from earlier illustrations, to the larger plates, the size and format of the series of engravings after eminent history paintings—of the Raphael Cartoons, Sir James Thornhill's *Life of St. Paul,* Laguerre's *Marlborough's Victories,* and *The Life of Charles I.* Given this format, what Hogarth does is find a graphic equivalent for Quixote's delusion, and he locates it in the sweeping baroque forms—readily available in engravings—of heroic painting.

He places Hudibras, looking like the small misshapen figure he is, hump and all, in the midst of a group of rustics carrying out a Skimmington (pl. 10); but he depicts them in the forms and poses of the procession of heroic revellers in Annibale Carracci's *Marriage of Bacchus and Ariadne* (pl. 11). The specific choice was appropriate: what better heroic parallel for a Skimmington, in which the mock husband and wife are carried in procession, than a Bacchus and Ariadne? Ariadne, jilted by Theseus and picked up by Bacchus, is here replaced by the scold and her probably cuckolded husband. But, more important, the coruscating forms of the baroque become the graphic equivalent of Quixote's madness. And this model can then serve Hogarth for placing his own contemporaries, who are also Quixotic in their poses of heroic folly (sometimes of Biblical figures) in the *Harlot's* and *Rake's Progresses* and *Marriage à la Mode.*

The exaggeratedly baroque and baroque-classical compositions act as reflections of Hudibras' heroic interpretation of what is in fact low. If

Hogarth had chosen to illustrate in the same way the scene in which Quixote embraces Maritornes while thinking she is Dulcinea, he would presumably have conveyed the psychological comedy by embodying the scene in the style of the Carracci. From the emblematic title page of *Hudibras* onward, he introduces us into a world of illusion and fantasy which is the context or medium of Hudibras' crazy actions. Far beyond the comic situation, this becomes an exploration of moral illusion and reality. In a way the whole world of the English Civil War is an unheroic one, seen in both its gross reality and the illusions of heroism projected by the combatants and those who remembered and sentimentalized it. Hogarth's plates, like the poem they illustrate, are about a specific political situation whose repercussions were still felt in the England of the mid-1720s.

These large independent plates also contribute the complex sense, which Hogarth of all his contemporaries grasped best, of a page of mixed engraving and type with intricate relationships between words and images. Each plate is his reconstitution of the poem itself, in his own visual terms. In "Hudibras Sallying Forth" (pl. 12), the overtones are of a heroic progress, with the knights dominating the picture space, haughtily posing in the middle of a balanced heroic composition (the house to the right was in fact added late to emphasize the balance); and these are contrasted with the grotesque shapes of the quixotic pair. The idea of an admiring crowd has been reduced to a pair of rustics and a dog who respond in their different ways to the heroic progress. Hogarth is literally illustrating only the lines (which he prints beneath his plate) "Then did Sir *Knight* abandon Dwelling, / And out he rode a Colonelling" (I.i.13-14) and the following lines which describe Hudibras and Ralpho, but he includes the general lines (I.i.1-2 and 9-12) which set the scene for the satire, and illustrates them too in his own characteristic way. "When *civil Dudgeon* first grew high, / And Men fell out they knew not why" (I.i.1-2) refers in Butler's poem to upheavals both physical and political, to the King and Parliament, the High Church Anglicans and Puritans, and so forth. But Hogarth transforms "high" into the size and position of the two figures, Hudibras and Ralpho, in relation to the rustic spectators; and "Men fell out they knew not why" is dramatized in the literally falling fruit baskets and the figurative falling out between the two rustics. The latter is a result of the farmer's awe of the heroes; he backs into his wife's table, spilling the produce, for which she blames him; and so indeed he will never "know why" they began their quarrel. In a domestic metaphor Hogarth projects a small tableau of the country, its produce, its simple tenants, and its civil war, caused in fact by the grandiloquent gestures of heroic fools.[20]

The next two lines—"When *Gospel-Trumpeters,* surrounded / with long-ear'd Rout, to Battel sounded"—refer of course to the Puritan soldiers (the "Roundheads") and their habit of cutting their hair short, and imply an accompanying bestiality: they are a pack of curs. Hogarth reduces the "Gospel Trumpeter" and the "long-ear'd rout" (mob) to a barking dog with extra-long ears, who is trying to "rout" or re-route— or disperse—the two knights rather than herald or support their advance. "And Pulpit Drum Ecclesiastick, / Was beat with Fist, instead of a Stick" are Butler's own translation of the ecclesiastical podium of the Puritans into a military drum, on which the preacher beats a call to arms. This Hogarth translates into the rustic's liquor keg, suggesting that ecclesiastical words are the ranting of drunkards, the pulpit an intoxicating place, and so on (based no doubt on a reading of Swift's *Tale of a Tub*).

The lines are reprinted under the design to allow a comparison between verbal and visual texts, in effect serving as part of an emblematic riddle to be solved by the viewer. With Butler's text in mind, the viewer goes from the lines quoted to the visualization and back again. Each stage, as Hogarth reveals his own interpretation of Butler's words, produces an incongruity or metamorphosis which should amuse. Indeed Hogarth's transformation is so thorough that another text is projected forward which is read emblematically out of the constituents of Butler's text, Hogarth's quotation, title (motto), and image—which is now the subject of a whole new construct put together by the viewer. And in this intellectual play, I would argue, lies the comedy of Hogarth's *Hudibras.*

The heroic baroque forms serve a second function, which is indissolubly related to the mimetic: to render the representation of contemporary English reality respectable—to elevate it. For Cervantes' *Don Quixote* was taken as a paradigm by the artist who had two quite incompatible desires: to paint idealized history as the art treatises told him he should and to represent his own local, contemporary country and culture. For the writer *Don Quixote* served as the paradigm for the transition from similar literary forms—the epic, the romance—to the novel, which was the important new form to emerge in eighteenth-century England. The vehicle in both cases was the "mock-heroic" mode, which included the heroic and the realistic in the same frame, one as figure and the other as ground.[21]

Quixote the protagonist allowed for a two-sided image of reality, which can be either the delusion of madness or the ideal against which a fallen world is exposed and judged. The radical ambiguity of this protagnoist led to alternative interpretations and alternative characters. One was a sick madman who has become infatuated with an idea he regards as the ideal, usually by reading too many of the wrong books (romances). This figure is not himself evil, but through his obtuseness he reflects evil: these are the knaves he meets on his journey as well as the authors of those books that turned his head in the first place. As he appears in Swift's satires, Quixote becomes the madman who tries to remake the world in his own image. As Butler's Hudibras, his madness has more than a tinge of hypocrisy, and his windmills and herds of sheep are innocent English country folk whom he takes for agents of the devil (i.e. King Charles I). In either case, the message of the satire is the futility of his mad quest, demonstrated by the catastrophes that befall him when he brings his heroic delusion into conflict with the world of ordinary objects and people.

But this figure, the madman, can also slip over into the reverse, a victim of the hard realities of the world that he is idealistically trying to change, and thereby unconsciously expose the knaves and fools who make life miserable for him. As many of Cervantes' eighteenth-century imitators realized, Quixote can be turned into the satirist as knight-errant, the ruined exemplar of an earlier and better age. These inter-pretations all appear in *Don Quixote* itself and lead to figures as different as Hudibras and Fielding's Parson Adams, Richard Graves' Geoffrey Wildgoose and Sterne's Walter Shandy—the Quixote seen respectively from the Augustan and latitudinarian points of view. The mock-heroic mode itself offered an ambivalent view of contemporary life, which could easily tilt either way. When Quixote is beaten by the mule driver for manhandling his whore Maritornes, whom the deluded knight-errant takes for a fair maiden come to test his virtue, we see one man being punished for his crime against reality, but we also see a second man, beating him up, whose only standard is reality. Satires, novels, and paintings based on these assumptions begin as both a criticism of a false ideal, which, if practiced now, would lead men to attack innocent folk with lances, and a criticism of the real world in which the true ideal is unattainable. The unreal is attacked because it is unreal—and delusive, misleading, or capable of manipulation by hypocrites; the real is attacked because it is real and has usurped the place of the now unreal ideal. But both are *portrayed*. Don Quixote makes possible the mimesis of the commonplace as well as the ideal, in a particular juxtaposition.

This was the literary form that was available to writers and artists in the early decades of the eighteenth century in England, and it served as the basis for a provincial English art—one which wished to be free of

Italian and French academic rules but did not quite dare, and so incorporated the ideals along with the contemporary reality, which it criticized and celebrated simultaneously. It was thus a form that was liberating for the writer or artist: the character of Don Quixote and the structure of his travels offered Englishmen a way to deal with the subject of an individual in his shifting but less than happy relations to the demands of society, while retaining the safe escape valve of comedy.

This was a fiction that served not only Fielding but Hogarth and contributed to the new forms of fiction both invented. It was a fiction that worried the critics who were trying to formulate comic theory: for here was a comic butt with whom one sympathized as much as one ridiculed him.[22] It was also a fiction in which the artist tended to see himself—or alternatively his instructors, the authors of the art treatises—as a romance-deluded knight who has been placed in a real, unidealized, eighteenth-century London and must cope with this situation. There was, I suppose, a natural association between the artist and his protagonist.

The English artist, I am suggesting, has something in common with the protagonist who emerged in the novel—the man or woman who aspires to the idealized life of romance (literary, historical, heroic, aristocratic) and thereupon sees reality distorted through those aspirations. This life, with its code, aspirations, and way of thinking is contrasted to the protagonist's real world and true self. Cervantes shows that the romance world is an evil insofar as it represents a cramping of one's own nature, a madness that sees giants where there are only windmills, or a code of manners that is inappropriate to the particular man who aspires toward it or to the particular time in which he lives. But it can also be a good insofar as it represents a corrective to the petty forms of the present, man's natural instincts that have been fettered by the customs of society, a higher reality revealed by some divine madness, the worlds of imagination and poetry, or even the true reality beneath the deceiving appearances of the world and the ideal world we fall short of. In the Quixote fiction we have the whole range of eighteenth-century art and literature from Swift and Pope to Hogarth and Fielding, and from them to Barry, Fuseli, and Blake.

II. SHAKESPEAREAN PAINTING

CHARLES DE GAULLE [asked to name the foremost masters of the European spirit]: "Dante, Goethe, Chateaubriand."
INTERVIEWER: ". . . What of Shakespeare?"
DE GAULLE: "European?"[1]

Shakespeare and the Englishness of English Art

Shakespeare to some extent *was* England and dominated its art as well as its literature in the years in which English painting emerged. It is fair to say, however, that at the outset of the century he dominated the minds of the painters more than of the poets. Although even Pope dutifully produced his edition of Shakespeare, he was hardly a Shakespearean poet (at least in the same powerful sense in which he was a Miltonic poet). The artists, however, felt so keenly the subservience of visual images in England, and their own lack of a native tradition, that they turned to the literary text as all they had. Pope, after all, had Spenser as well as Milton and Shakespeare to choose from. The painter had no one in his own field.

What Shakespeare represented at this time was an absence of paradigms, a freedom from rules and close classical imitation—in every way the opposite of French literature and painting, and so of the norms held up by the Restoration and early eighteenth century to its writers. He was a terribly ambiguous figure, tempting but dangerous in crucial ways. He represented English literature, as opposed to Latinate, Frenchified, Italianized literature—something as pure, provincial, and politically significant as the English Bible and the English countryside.

The simplest way to see what Shakespeare meant to English painters in the eighteenth century is to take a retrospect from the climactic enterprise of Shakespearean illustration at the end of the century: Alderman John Boydell's *Shakespeare Gallery*. In 1787 Boydell, the enterprising printseller, spoke to a group of artists that included West, Romney, Sandby, and George Nicol (the printer) and told them that

> he should like to wipe away the stigma that all foreign critics threw on this nation—that they had no genius for historical painting. He said he was certain from his success in encouraging engraving that Englishmen wanted nothing but proper encouragement and a proper subject to excell

in historical painting. The encouragement he would endeavor to find if a proper subject were pointed out. Mr. Nicol replied that there was one great National subject concerning which there could be no second opinion, and mentioned Shakespeare.[2]

Here we have the factors that brought Shakespeare to the fore: the privileged status of history painting, still the top of the academic ladder in art; the turning to English national heroes and subjects; and the doing so through the wide dissemination of engravings.

In his preface to the 1789 catalogue of the *Shakespeare Gallery*, Boydell introduced the second aspect of the problem of painting Shakespeare:

> Though I believe it will be readily admitted, that no subject seems so proper to form an English School of Historical Paintings, as the scenes of the immortal Shakespeare; yet it must be always remembered, that he possessed powers which no pencil [i.e. paint-brush] can reach; for such was the force of his creative imagination, that though he frequently goes beyond nature, he still continues to be natural, and seems only to do that which nature would have done, had she o'erstepped her usual limits—it must not, then, be expected, that the art of the Painter can ever equal the sublimity of our Poet.[3]

By the poet, Boydell means the words of Shakespeare's text and, by implication (since Shakespeare was the poet of nature), nature itself. Indeed, how *does* a painter try to match the sublimity of Shakespeare? Boydell has the conventional—and practical—answer of the painter of the time: "The strength of Michael Angelo, united to the grace of Raphael, would here have laboured in vain—For what pencil can give to his airy being, 'a local habitation, and a name'?" It was, however, precisely Michelangelo and Raphael who did give to Shakespeare a "local habitation." Or at least one solution for the painters who had been to Italy, guided by the theories of the *P.R.A.* Sir Joshua Reynolds, was to find visual equivalents of Shakespeare's sublime words, characters, and actions in the figures of High Renaissance painting, roughly contemporary with Shakespeare's drama (and so a historical as well as stylistic parallel).

This was by no means the procedure Hogarth had introduced when he related Hudibras to the baroque style of Annibale Carracci. Hogarth's response was, to say the least, ambivalent. The baroque forms were his representation of the now-dead past, of Hudibras' illusion as well as his own rueful attempt as an artist to elevate low materials. James Barry, avoiding discrepancies, seeks a graphic equivalent of Shakespeare's blank verse by giving Lear and the dead Cordelia the monumental forms of High Renaissance history painting, and using the general composition of a Pietà (pl.13). Although the figures have been moved around a bit, he seems to have in mind the Carracci *Pietà* now in the National Gallery, London (pl. 14). (Fuseli illustrations for the same scene are even more blatantly based on *Pietàs*.[4]) Cordelia, in short, is Christ, and Lear is Mary the Mother—an echo that seeks to evoke something of the pathos in Shakespeare's scene.

When James Northcote illustrates the burial of the little princes in the tower from *Richard III,* he draws upon the forms with which Caravaggio represented the *Entombment of Christ* (pls. 15, 16). On the other hand, when Benjamin West illustrates the madness of Ophelia, he places her and Laertes before Claudius and Gertrude, the king and queen, seated on a dais (pl. 17). This sort of scene calls for the evocation of the Raphael Tapestries of the Lives of the Apostles (known to Englishmen through engravings but especially through the physical presence of the Raphael Cartoons in the Royal Collection). Raphael provides a scene in which figures of conventional authority are related within an orderly architectural setting to figures of some higher authority—whether St. Paul showing his power to the proconsul (pl. 32) or poor mad Ophelia demonstrating her higher wisdom before a corrupt Danish court. In this painting by West, and in Northcote's representation of Richard III fawning hypocritically on the little princes before murdering them (pl. 18), what originality the artist possesses (once he has found his graphic equivalent in Raphael) goes into the faces. Northcote, who may be drawing on coronation scenes or some other model of a group portrait, puts all of his imaginative power into the hypocritical expression of Richard and the various other expressions of princes, York, Hastings, and the Lord Mayor.

Boydell saw in a commonsense way that in England the conflict lay between history painting and the most flourishing indigenous genre, portraiture. As he wryly observes:

> foreigners . . . have said, with some severity, and, I am sorry to say, with some truth, that the abilities of our best Artists are chiefly employed in painting Portraits of those who, in less than half a century, will be lost in oblivion—While the noblest part of the Art—HISTORICAL PAINTING—is much neglected.

When the Boydell Shakespeare paintings and engravings began to be seen, it was the opinion of some critics that the best parts were the portraits—the character of the faces—which were the most "English" part of the compositions, some would have said the most "Shakespearean." The critic of the *Gentleman's Magazine,* for example, wrote that "the beauty of many of the heads, considered separately from the figure to which they belong seems intuitively to indicate their proceeding from a school chiefly attentive to portrait painting."[5] I think that a viewer today will respond to that comment. Not the derivative compositions, not the often shaky knowledge of anatomy, but the vivacity of expression in the faces carries the only interest in those miles of paint-covered canvas executed for Boydell.

For, as T.S.R. Boase noted, the two approaches to Shakespeare employed by English artists consisted of, on the one hand, the Italianate and on the other the native tradition coming from Hogarth through Hayman, men who had worked at Vauxhall Gardens or the theaters, most often at book illustrations, but had never traveled abroad.[6] One was a tradition that sought a level of decorum equivalent to their bardolatry in the high style of Italian art, and the other that emphasized Shakespeare's unique Englishness.

This second group—or part of it—also started out as artists who made a living painting portraits. Reynolds was, of course, himself a portrait painter and used history painting as a way of elevating his portraits. But the painters I am referring to produced small conversation pictures that were often theatrically-oriented. In England Hogarth's *Beggar's Opera* (1728, pl. 21) is the originary case, but he did many small non-theatrical group portraits as well. These painters offered an alternative to the employment of High Renaissance painting as their model; and that was the actual stage production, which was part of the portrait-painting tradition through conversation pictures, which included also in Hogarth's case his "modern moral subjects" of the 1730s. (A very simple, typical example is John Zoffany's portrait of David Garrick and Mrs. Pritchard in *Macbeth* from 1768: pl. 72.)

Paintings of the theater represented the first phase of Shakespearean illustration in eighteenth-century England. But by the time of the Boydell project it was felt that English painters should rise above their native origins in the mere copying of stage productions with contemporary actors and actresses playing the Shakespearean roles. The *Public Advertiser* of 6 May 1789 wrote along this line:

> There was some reason to fear that our painters [of the Boydell Shakespeare Gallery] would have sought for and gathered their ideas from the theatre, and given us portraits of the well-dressed Ladies and Gentlemen [of the stage]. . . . There was some reason to fear a representation of all that extravagance of attitude and start [sic—probably "art"] which is tolerated, nay in a degree demanded, at the playhouse. But this has been avoided; the pictures in general give a mirror of the poet. . . .

As the quotation suggests, this was a pitfall that was not entirely avoided. I suppose some people may have feared that the English quality of Shakespeare illustration was being replaced by a foreign. This would have been Hogarth's opinion, though in his own practice he discreetly mixed the sense of Shakespearean staging in London of the 1720s and 30s with the graphic vocabulary that any painter must draw upon, which included details from Renaissance paintings transmitted in engravings.

The works of neither the Hogarth nor the Boydell generation were pure. One of the most interesting of the Boydell illustrations, Joseph Wright of Derby's *Tempest* (pl. 19), for example, simply fits Shakespeare's cast into one of his own familiar cave-mouths, looking out onto open water, moonlit or sunlit. Hogarth's version of *The Tempest* in the mid-1730s (pl. 29) pulls in both directions—to the public area of recognizable iconography from the great tradition of European art and to the private area where Shakespeare serves as a vehicle for his own personal experience. W.C. Fields' explanation of why he read the Bible so avidly ("Looking for loopholes") explains pretty well how most of us read, and this proves to have been the case with the illustrators of Shakespeare as well.

One inference we may draw is that "Shakespearean" for Englishmen could mean either a specific stage representation of a play or those powerful Shakespearean words—so powerful that they can only be approached through the graphic forms of the most highly-respected continental painting. But aside from this privileging of the stage, the impact of Shakespeare on English art consisted of a general feeling, some assumptions, and a frame of mind rather than specifically visual structures—or verbal for that matter. Herein lies the contradiction between the need for representing a stage performance and imitating High Renaissance painters like Michelangelo and Raphael. Hogarth, for example, or Fielding would have realized that Shakespeare, were *he* to have used a Michelangelo, would have done so to subvert or demonstrate the unfittingness of the parallel. Hogarth emphasizes the fact by making his scenes theatrical, often indicating stage conventions, and suggesting that the references are themselves to stage effects.

Shakespeare's structures, in short, offer a sanction for certain ways of thinking but do not offer the sort of parallel and autithesis that Englishmen of the Restoration and eighteenth century were taught to revere. They rewrote Shakespeare's plays to give them more symmetrical pairings of characters, more symmetrical and formally-satisfying, less ambiguous endings. When Shadwell added a male contrast to Miranda in *The Tempest* (a man who has never seen a woman), he was joining an illustrious tradition that included John Dryden and Nahum Tate. Milton, I hope to show, contributed plots and formulations of the sort Dryden and Tate sought, whereas Shakespeare contributed, above all else, the desirability of *not* formulating.

The hostile Voltaire can start us out on a list of Shakespearean characteristics as they seemed to the eighteenth century, beginning with his insularity—the inapplicability of his art to other nations than the English: "The reason is obvious; real merit will be sought after by all nations; a people whose drama, music and painting were adapted only to their own taste, and exploded by every other polite nation, could not justly flatter themselves with having the gift of good taste."[7]

If we subtract some of Voltaire's own provincialism, we see that he does draw attention to an insularity of English-Shakespearean assumptions, of which we can still read in a recent *TLS* article. Shakespeare "is supremely outside the classical canon" (or tradition), and "there is an extraterritorial quality to his work, an apartness from the tradition at the centre, systematic, Hellenic-Christian, political, overtly philosophical . . . ."[8] Voltaire's Shakespeare offered an ethos suitable for the provincial, the outsider, the questioning systemless mind, who builds a criticism into every affirmation; and not for the artist who sought assimilation with the continent.

Voltaire clarifies his views on Shakespeare in another essay: "It seems as if nature took pleasure to unite in the head of Shakespeare all that we can imagine great and forcible, together with all that the grossest dullness could produce of everything that is most low and detestable".[9] It is this mixed quality—the disorderly lumping together of the admirable and the squalid, the great and the low—that Voltaire cannot understand; and that in the Boydell Shakespeare project led Reynolds and James Barry to paint one kind of scene, and Robert Smirke another, and William Matthew Peters another—and which only perhaps Fuseli was able to represent in anything like its variousness. In general, the tragedies and Roman histories draw on the Italian, the comedies and some English histories on the native tradition.

Voltaire, whenever he launches into another attack on Shakespeare, complains about the co-presence of "scenes so perfectly beautiful, and passages so very full of the great and terrible," with "those monstrous farces" such as the grave-digger scene in *Hamlet* or "the idle jests of Roman shoemakers and cobblers" in *Julius Caesar*.[10] And what these amount to is the violation of "taste" and the "remotest idea of the rules"—the unities, especially of tone.

> It seems that up to now [he writes at his most positive in *Lettres sur les Anglais*] the English have only produced irregular beauties. . . . Their poetical genius resembles a closely grown tree planted by nature, throw-

30

ing out a thousand branches here and there and growing lustily and without rules. It dies if you try to force its nature and trim it like the gardens of Marly.[11]

Here is Horace Walpole's response to those critics like Voltaire, for whom Shakespeare's "mixture of buffoonery and solemnity is intolerable":

> Let me ask if his tragedies of Hamlet and Julius Caesar would not lose a considerable share of the spirit and wonderful beauties, if the humour of the grave-diggers, the fooleries of Polonius, and the clumsy jests of the Roman citizens were omitted, or vested in heroics? Is not the eloquence of Antony, the nobler and affectedly unaffected oration of Brutus, artificially exalted by the rude bursts of nature from the mouths of their auditors?[12]

It is the mixing of both tones, which he associates with "bursts of nature," that to Walpole is the Shakespearean Element. De Quincey's comic relief or Robert Penn Warren's "Mercutio Element," or what I believe contemporaries felt as a freedom to mix modes, Walpole thought of as "touches [that] remind one of the Grecian sculptor, who, to convey the idea of a Colossus within the dimensions of a seal, inserted a little boy measuring his thumb." In this passage Walpole is explaining his own procedure in *The Castle of Otranto* (1765). The setting off of terror by comic relief in the gothic of Walpole and Radcliffe had been, earlier in the century, in the novels of Fielding, the richness of incident and the refusal to produce paragons instead of "mixed characters." Both were "Shakespearean."

Nikolaus Pevsner's "Englishness" of English art sees what Voltaire is describing in the largest sense as the fact that "English art in nearly all ages escapes the system"; that "it even escapes the accurate dating by style which is the art historian's ambition." Indeed, to submit English art to system—that is, to continental categories of history painting, landscape, and so on, or even of high and low style—would be "losing in truth and in richness what could be gained in order and in lucidity."[13] In a sentence Pevsner has summed up the principle of English art whose authority was to be found in, above all others, Shakespeare.

The eighteenth century's version of Pevsner's formulation was to see Shakespeare as the poet of nature rather than art. Samuel Johnson offered the classic statement when he wrote in the 1760s those well-known words, "his drama is the mirror of life"; "Shakespeare is above all writers, at least above all modern writers, the poet of nature; the poet that holds up to his readers a faithful mirror of manners and life."[14] (Pope before him had written that *"Homer* himself drew not his art so immediately from the fountains of Nature.")[15] This was the

Shakespeare who is an irregular genius, an "original," whose complexity overrides rules and formal structures, the author of things finely observed: men and manners, talk and thought, sentiment and passion, which can be summed up as aspects of "nature" as opposed to "art."

First, Johnson points out, was the failure of his characters to measure up to the ideal types: Menenius, a Roman senator, can also play the buffoon, and Claudius, the usurping king of Denmark, can also be a drunkard. In the second place, this is the mixing of tones and genres—which Johnson was almost the first to recognize as the essence of the tragicomic form, that is comedy but comedy that nevertheless engages matters of great significance in a problematic way. In Shakespeare's practice, this takes the form of plots and fictions that can go either way, into comedy or into tragedy, until, by a kind of irony, the ending is willed to be comic (and therefore remains ambiguous). Fielding employs this kind of ending in *Amelia* if not in *Tom Jones;* the Austen novels, in particular *Pride and Prejudice* and *Mansfield Park,* perhaps also *Emma,* close in this way.

Another sense of "nature" is "character"—the strong personal lineaments (stimulated by climate and the eating of roast beef) the English thought distinguished them from their continental counterparts. "Character" in fact stimulated artists to yoke Shakespeare with the English portrait tradition, the one genre in which it was felt English artists excelled. The importance of "character" in Shakespeare's plays, elaborately developed in 1777 by Maurice Morgann in his remarkable essay on Falstaff, is the sense of a life extending beyond the limits of the rules, the unities, and even the frame of the play, the literary text (or canvas). Writing a kind of criticism that would eventuate in Mary Cowden Clarke's *Girlhood of Shakespeare's Heroines,* Morgann nevertheless drew attention to an important characteristic which connected Shakespeare with a number of strands of art and literature in the eighteenth century:

> . . . those characters in *Shakespeare,* which are seen only in part, are yet capable of being unfolded and understood in the whole; every part being in fact relative, and inferring all the rest. . . . And very frequently, when no particular point presses, he boldly makes a character act and speak from those parts of the composition which are *inferred* only, and not distinctly shewn. This produces a wonderful effect; it seems to carry us beyond the poet to nature itself, and gives an integrity and truth to facts and character, which they could not otherwise obtain: And this is in reality that art in *Shakespeare* which, being withdrawn from our notice, we more emphatically call *nature.*[16]

Morgann not only associates this ambiguous extension of character with "nature," he draws the obvious conclusion—that was beyond most of his contemporaries, perhaps even Johnson—that this is the Shakespearean art which we have become accustomed to calling nature. It is a conception of art in which the road in a landscape does continue beyond the picture's frame and the men and women in portraits do have body parts not shown and lives and relationships that extend in all directions, in time and space—in which this quality of a work of art is more important than the formal structure of the figure in relation to the ground, the subject in relation to the frame.

What happens when nature is thus extolled over art, and Shakespeare is the great model of the power of nature? Hume's words "Nature is always too strong for principle" could be the motto of the Shakespearean tradition in England, at least up to the time of the Boydell Shakespeare Gallery, and perhaps demonstrated there as well. One notices also less concern than, say in France, with aesthetic wholes. The Shakespearean problem, that has dominated English art and made it a battleground of literary and art historians (and literary critics), is how to reconcile the need for form in art with the need to respect contingent reality? How to shape an art object by creating pattern without falsifying life? Shakespeare automatically enters the picture when one tries to isolate the sense of form we detect in anything from a Hogarth to a Stanley Spencer, or the aesthetic principle that explains the absence of what the art historians call architectonic structure in painting. This follows, I believe, from the Shakespearean (not just the "literary," vide Voltaire) notion of form as a violating of unities, a breaking of the frame, a density of incident, a psychological richness, spilling over and piling up and moving about in time and space which amounts to a reliance on psychological complexity over formal coherence. For all its intensity of focus, Richardson's *Clarissa* is the great eighteenth-century example that first comes to mind.

As Voltaire shows, this sense of form evolves in the context of the French, the Racinian notion of form, which is not only a powerful simplicity and unity but also an emphasis on both the characters' seeing and being seen composed in simple pictorial forms (and in the play's imagery of sight). This Racinian composition the English tradition at any rate more commonly associates with painting than with writing or staging. As Voltaire's words about the gardens at Marly suggest, the contrast is summed up in the French opposed to the English garden. One has a strong external impression of visual unity and simplicity; the other offers the spectator an experience of moving about, a "pleasure of Pursuit" (Hogarth's term), within a maze—which Addison described so well in *Spectator* 476, on method:

33

When I read an Author of Genius, who writes without Method, I fancy my self in a Wood that abounds with a great many noble Objects, rising among one another in the greatest Confusion and Disorder. When I read a Methodical Discourse, I am in a regular Plantation, and can place myself in its several Centers, so as to take a view of all the Lines and Walks that are struck from them. You may ramble in the one a whole Day together, and every Moment discover something or other that is new to you, but when you have done you will have but a confused imperfect Notion of the Place [i.e. of the whole]; in the other, your Eye commands the whole Prospect, and gives you such an idea of it, as is not easily worn out of the Memory.[17]

In *Spectator* 477, the next paper, he describes gardens in terms of poetry and painting: makers of parterres are epigrammatists and sonneteers, makers of bowers and grottoes and cascades are romance-writers, Wise and London (the gardeners) are heroic poets, and he himself composes in the pindaric manner, running "into the beautiful Wilderness of Nature, without affecting the nicer Elegancies of Art." It is, of course, significant that Addison equates writing, methodical discourse, and English landscape, but more that he describes the experience of reading his own writing as "walking in a Labyrinth of my own raising, not to know whether the next Tree I shall meet with is an Apple or an Oak, an Elm or a Pear-tree." Addison is acknowledging in himself the quality I am trying to describe as Shakespearean—and he finds its greatest sanction in the eighteenth century in Shakespearean drama. While some would associate this quality with mere muddle, he is associating the English natural garden with genius, as opposed to the over-cropped, over-geometrized French garden. Johnson is probably thinking of this passage when he uses the same metaphor in his "Preface to Shakespeare, 1765," calling Shakespeare a "forest in gratifying the mind with endless diversity."[18]

The point is not that nature is preferred to art but that the relationship between nature and art is understood to be one of extreme contingency. In the case of Shakespeare this problem arises in various forms, for example in his absolute ruthlessness toward the fates of innocent characters (Ophelia, Cordelia, Desdemona). Johnson could bear to see *King Lear* only with Nahum Tate's ending. In the same way Hogarth's treatment of his Harlot and Rake, of Tom Nero and the characters of *Marriage à la Mode* was not followed by Fielding and the other novelists who followed him in so many other respects (with the single exception of Richardson in *Clarissa)*.

On another level contingency appeared to Johnson and the other eighteenth-century critics in Shakespeare's word play, a reliance on puns that amounted to an uncertainty of cohesion in the relationship between word and sense or word and thing. When Hogarth (pl. 37) has a sword (being carried out of a room under the arm of the Harlot's young lover) serve also by a trick of perspective to "stab" her elderly keeper in the back, he is creating a pun. When Turner signs a painting with a duck he is punning on his own middle name Mallord, and when he puts a hare near the ruins of Battle Abbey he is punning on the name Harold Harefoot, the king who was killed near the Abbey at the Battle of Hastings. One need ony recall Hazlitt's remark, applied to Turner, that Shakespeare took the greatest delights in his "conceits" and "some artists among ourselves have carried the same principle to a singular excess."[19] These "conceits" are acknowledgments of both the power of words and the arbitrary relationship of word and thing.

Shakespeare, as Johnson and other critics saw, was on the brink of a realization that divine analogizing can be carried to the point where anything can be related to anything else, and so the whole system will appear arbitrary—an insight the eighteenth century found hard to swallow and which Johnson attacks in his essay on Abraham Cowley.The conceit—the pun or the catechresis—showed an awareness of the centrifugal nature of words in relation to things, as well as an attempt to acknowledge it by violently yoking together the most heterogeneous materials, whether words and things or things and things.

How do we reconcile "mirror of nature"—privileging nature over art—and the "conceit," the punning word-play? The pun shows precisely the insecurity of art in its rendering of nature and plays with its failure: as for example in anamorphic art, another popular form of Shakespeare's time. Although Pope himself was as witty as any poet, it was a wit attached—like Milton's—to Satan and the fallen world, presupposing difference and disunity. Officially Pope was *for* judgment over wit, as was Hogarth. If one wanted to be in a tradition of wit *and* nature it was to Shakespeare he had to turn—not to the notorious cases of Donne, Cleveland, and Cowley. Under Shakespeare's copious mantle, poet or painter could be natural and witty because he was talking about nature itself.[20]

I am ready now to make a series of propositions concerning "Shakespearean" painting. The first is that linguistic forms and painting are basically different in this way: poets are aware of the ultimate mimetic discrepancy between their words and the objects in nature they represent or to which they are supposed to correspond. They begin with the knowledge that words are arbitrarily assigned to things. But painters, even when they are copying other paintings rather than the object in nature, are (in Gombrich's terms) "making and matching."[21] They see a continuity between the object in nature and their representation of it.[22]

Obviously literary painting was a main tradition of Renaissance art and so carried within it the problem of discrepancy in so far as its subject was ideal or imaginary. But English painting from Hogarth to Blake and Turner shows an awareness of the contradictions—the problems—in painting itself, as well as in pictura-poesis painting, that goes beyond anything dreamt of on the continent. Blake presents and explores the discrepancy between word and image, and Turner shows his awareness not only of this discrepancy but of the more basically painterly one between material paint and the immaterial, aerial sunlight that is the object of the landscape-painter's representation.

Hogarth's Falstaff

I have said that there was a general movement in the eighteenth century for writers and artists from fidelity to the imitated text to fidelity to something called "nature," and that the Shakespearean text was thought of as one form of "nature." In the case of Shakespeare one of the things "nature" might be was a stage representation of the Shakespeare play. Shakespeare offered an alternative to a literary text in the appearance of living people on a stage performing his plays; or, as Lance Bertelsen has put it, "not a text, but a contemporary event generated by the interpretation of a text."[23] This means that the graphic models an artist uses to illustrate his literary text can be replaced, or at least augmented, by the direct representation of something seen. Or as Francis Bacon said, "Those who determine not to conjecture and guess but to find out and know . . . must consult only things themselves." Pevsner notes of the "Englishness of English Art," that it is always the experience of a thing rather than the thing itself that concerns the English artist, who fills a position in relation to his subject either as an observer, an eye registering something, or as a teacher-preacher, who adds to the rendering of observed life a moral lesson.[24]

By the 1750s and 60s David Garrick, the great actor-producer, was taking advantage of this fact by advising and sometimes employing painters (Francis Hayman, Benjamin Wilson, and John Zoffany) to represent him on his stage performing in plays by Shakespeare and others. The intention was to publicize and immortalize his productions. We know that he wrote specific advice and instructions to Francis Hayman on what scene to choose and how to represent it in the cases of *Lear* and *Othello*. Garrick advised him to follow the Garrick production of *Lear* for the poses but the literary text for the inclusion of the Fool, who was at that time omitted from stage productions. Garrick shrewdly sought a diplomatic merger of the stage and literary traditions, but Hayman chose to omit the Fool and follow exactly the *seen*—and in that sense perhaps more real—Lear, even though his illustration was to accompany the printed text.[25]

Bertelsen also shows that in one case at least Garrick's staging directly influenced history painters. His composition of the tomb scene in *Romeo and Juliet* (the version of the play in which Juliet awakes after Romeo has taken his poison but before he has died, allowing for a final embrace) involved an intensely-lit inner stage set off from the dark rectangle of the outer stage. The scene was copied by Benjamin Wilson in a painting (Yale Center for British Art), transmitted in a mezzotint of 1753, and then adapted by Wright of Derby as his characteristic scene-within-a-scene in paintings like *A Hermit studying Alchemy* (1771-72) and *Virgil's Tomb* (1779). One suspects that other Wright paintings also benefited by contact with conventions of stage lighting.

These are interesting and important facts. But questions remain: What are the graphic sources behind the stage representations of Garrick and other theater managers? And then what does the painter bring to his representation of the stage production from other graphic sources? How much of Garrick's production itself is derived from Hogarth's paintings of the stage in the late 1720s and his engraved series of stagelike scenes (with inset scenes and pictures) of the 1730s? How much do either Hogarth's or Garrick's scenes owe to the staging of Gay's *Beggar's Opera* or the Drury Lane *Henry IV,* and how much to Raphael's Cartoons or the history paintings of Poussin—as later Loutherbourg's sets (also made for Garrick) were derived from the landscape paintings of Salvator Rosa and Gaspar Dughet?[26] The exact relationship is now impossible to establish: Hayman's illustrations may draw on graphic material that was *not* in Garrick's staging. Even his *Lear,* closely following Garrick's stage performance as it does, may owe more to art than mere conventions of drawing.

The best we can do is look at an example for which some documentation does exist and which has the advantage for us of having opened up the subject. Hogarth is the artist—by all odds, the important figure here as in so many aspects of the creation of the English tradition of painting. He more than any other artist tried to represent the national, the local or provincial English tradition of painting. He was the first English artist to show that Shakespeare's plays and in particular those dealing with English history could be used as the basis for an English version of history painting—and was thus the original inspirer of Boydell's Shakespeare Gallery, as he was of Boydell's successful dissemination of prints. For Hogarth also saw that the way to prove his point about English history painters and the subject matter of Shakespeare and

English history was to reach the largest possible audience with his images. It was fitting that Boydell, in 1790 as the Shakespeare Gallery was launched, bought Hogarth's copperplates from his widow's estate and issued them under his own imprint.

Hogarth's written statements about his art leave no doubt that he treated his subject as if he were a playwright: "my picture is my stage, and men and women my players, who by means of certain actions and gestures exhibit a dumb show. . . ."[27] His "modern moral subjects" of the 1730s and 40s were series of six, eight, or twelve engraved plates, divided into scenes with a beginning, middle, and end, not only in the series of six but implicit in each of the plates. While the art treatises had already made the connections between history painting and stage representations, Hogarth carried the possibilities further and more explicitly than any other artist, and with greater awareness of the implications.

Shakespeare was by all odds his favorite dramatist. Shakespeare of all writers had, Hogarth writes, the "deepest penetration into nature," and it was from nature that Hogarth educed his own theories of form, beauty, and moral instruction. In his *Analysis of Beauty* (1753) he wrote up the results of his empirical search for "examples in nature," and he repeatedly called upon Shakespeare for support. Shakespeare, says Hogarth, sums up "all the charmes of beauty" in the words "INFINITE Variety," and he cites Enobarbus' lines on Cleopatra—"Nor custom stale / Her infinite variety"—which he says describe "Cleopatra's power over Antony."[28] Nature, beauty, and now variety: these are the crucial terms for Hogarth, and most of the citations of Shakespeare relate to variety; but we should not forget that it was Cleopatra's "power" that Hogarth believes Enobarbus is describing in his "infinite variety." What we notice most of all about Hogarth's use of form—the large rococo element in his form—is that it never serves a total architectonic purpose; rather it breaks into local units that only direct the eye from one part of the picture to another, producing a structure for reading a complex moral plot and influencing or exerting power over the "reader."

Hogarth began his career as a painter with two stage representations, which can be dated, in origin at least, from two sketches apparently made in the theater on paper from the same pad. One was of Shakespeare's *Henry IV, Part 2,* and the other of John Gay's *Beggar's Opera* (pls. 20, 21).[29] I have no doubt that Hogarth painted these at just this time because he saw the theater as the distinctive English contribution to art, especially in the 1720s when it seemed threatened by foreign operas and entertainments of the sort Gay was satirizing in *The Beggar's Opera* (and Pope at exactly the same time in *The Dunciad*).

The drawing of *Falstaff examining his Recruits* even retains a vestige of the stage curtain, omitted in the painting. It is worth noting that in the *Beggar's Opera* paintings Hogarth made it absolutely clear that he was painting a stage production—and indeed a play that was about play-acting, a metaphor of "life as a stage." In the Falstaff painting he moves one step closer to the later scenes from *The Tempest* (pl. 29) and *Richard III* in which he attempts to raise stage representation of Shakespeare to the status of history painting, a balance between what was seen on the stage (Garrick, for example, remains a portrait) and the heightening of history painting.

The scene represented is III.ii., in which Falstaff and Bardolph come to Justice Shallow's country residence in Gloucestershire to impress (the technical term was "crimp" in Hogarth's time; Shakespeare calls it "pressing") recruits for the war against the rebels, and with Shallow and Silence witnessing, Falstaff examines the local citizens who are being crimped. And then, when Shallow and Silence are out of earshot chatting with Falstaff, Bardolph accepts bribes from two of the recruits, passing on the word to Falstaff, who then announces his decision to reject the two who had bribed him and enlist the others who had not, regardless of their physical condition.

Hogarth has conflated these scenes into one action, with Bardolph passing the bribe to Falstaff behind his back. The bribing citizens are on one side, the honest ones, being crimped, on the other: Shadow, a "half-fac'd fellow" in gaunt profile, and Feeble, the "Woman's tailor," behind him. It is characteristic of Hogarth to join two or more moments, two or more actions, suggesting before and after as well as the pregnant present.

The production Hogarth saw opened at Drury Lane Theatre on 21 February 1726/7, the first one of this play since 1722. It was performed again on 25 February, 14 March, and 9 September, and then not again until the autumn of 1728, on 18 October and on 3 and 30 December. The play he saw was Thomas Betterton's adaptation, *King Henry IV or the Humours Sir John Falstaff,* which cuts out many of the scenes unrelated to Betterton's protagonist Falstaff (making Hogarth's scene IV.iii., not III.ii.).[30] Betterton's alterations of the text were primarily in the direction of creating a vehicle for himself as Falstaff.

I don't think there is any compelling argument for Hogarth's having seen or represented one performance rather than another. He may well have seen more than one.[31] It would only be of some interest to know in which order *The Beggar's Opera* and *Falstaff* were painted. We know that the first *Beggar's Opera* painting (W.S. Lewis, pl. 21) was done shortly after the opening on 29 January 1727/8, because of the quick succession of versions Hogarth produced between then and 1729. The *Falstaff* painting is clearly signed and dated 1730, but this probably only means that it was delivered to its purchaser or declared finished on that date. The style is closer to that of the early *Beggar's Opera* paintings than to the paintings of 1730. It is only a question of when Hogarth began to transfer the sketch to canvas, and how long it took him to declare it finished. (There is evidence that it was not easy in those years to pry a painting away from him.[32]) I would guess that the sketch was made at one of the performances in the autumn of 1727 or the autumn of 1728. The stage curtain in the drawing, however, is a sign that he began in both cases to think of the performance on a stage; and this might suggest that his development in the two paintings was from the explicit to the implicit stage performance.

In any case the cast was the same for all of these performances, and the salient point is that Hogarth is painting a group of actors playing these roles, or—in the *Falstaff*—absorbed into the roles, since he does not, as in *The Beggar's Opera,* indicate the transitional stages between on and off stage, between actor and spectator. Falstaff is played by, and is a portrait of, John Harper; Shallow is Colley Cibber; and Silence is Josiah Miller. All of these, as it happens, also appear on the showcloth in Hogarth's *Southwark Fair* painting of 1733, which represents a copy of a print by John Laguerre. The faces and figures can be compared.[33] Hogarth's painting, in short, is a group portrait of these actors playing the Shakespearean roles.

The painting fits into the genre of conversation picture Hogarth painted over the next few years, between 1728 and the mid-1730s. This was a small group portrait of people involved with each other in a psychological relationship of some sort, often with a strongly theatrical tone. It is easy to see how Hogarth, with his training in Vanderbank's and Thornhill's academies, saw a close connection between history painting as portrait groups and as *l'expression des passions* (that important category of history painting examined by Le Brun and others). He began to paint history as portrait groups, and (I suspect with the sanction of Shakespeare) as comic history groups. His own comic histories of the next two decades could be regarded as the equivalent of Betterton's *Humours of Falstaff* in relation to Shakespeare's *Henry IV*: he retained the comic incongruities and omitted the high-sounding speeches of the polite characters, though not the memory of them.

It was Jonathan Richardson, who also advocated the use of theatrical conventions for history painting, who attempted to raise portraiture to a parity with history. He promulgated the idea that "history painting records the great actions of the past, portraiture the men who conceived and executed them," and this doctrine in its least useful manifestation urged an Englishman to surround himself in his house with moral exempla in the form of portraits of ancients and contemporaries, friends and ancestors, idealized as heroic virtues. Richardson had a great influence on Reynolds, and probably on Hogarth as well, who simply applies the doctrine to portrait groups rather than single figures. Hogarth's point is that in a situation of psychological tension he catches the human face at that pitch of contortion in which it becomes as it were a caricature of itself—and only in this sense (he would insist) is he a caricaturist. For example, a hypocrite is obviously beyond the power of the artist's brush; a foolish or wicked mind may lie beyond a handsome face. But it is likely to betray itself in expression when excited by passion. In this sense Hogarth's conversation pieces and his "modern moral subjects" could be taken as a series of portraits—a sub-portrait genre—or as a portrait-history of the sort Reynolds was to paint in the 1750s, but with the emphasis on history rather than portraiture. Hogarth as well as Reynolds demonstrates that portraiture—face-painting, the expression of faces as well as the gestures of hands and bodies—remains the dominant mode of painting in England in the first half or two-thirds of the century. There is, of course, no inconsistency between this tradition and the essential Shakespearean genius for showing "character." As the century drew on, it was "character" and the variety of characters and their expressions in his plays that set off Shakespeare from all other writers.

In the case of Hogarth's *Falstaff,* whether the stage blocking came first or the conventions of conversation pieces, he finds a close equivalence between the two forms. Falstaff's gesture, for example, is roughly equivalent to the gesture of the host who, in Hogarth's conversation pictures, is binding together (as a good host should) different groups of his guests, or his guests and his family, into a single "party" (pl. 57). The composition, however, derives from one of his *Hudibras* illustrations of 1726, *The Committee* (pl. 22), which shows the Parliamentary rebels around a table, squabbling together, trying to rule England, and at the same time being informed of what is going on outside in the street—the Burning of the Rumps (of beef, and in effigy, of themselves, the Rump Parliament) at Temple Bar. The verses illustrated begin:

> And now the Saints begin their Reign
> For which th' had yearn'd so long in vain
> And felt such Bowel Hankerings,
> To see an Empire all of Kings.

Hogarth's scene, in this case, is related to a popular print called *The Committee,* a graphic equivalent more appropriate to this particular passage of Butler's satire than the baroque history painting he used to illustrate *Hudibras and the Skimmington*. But to this scene of power usurped by clods and riffraff, "an Empire all of Kings," Hogarth adds the conversation picture host, Falstaff, and moreover gives him a gesture (different from the one in the directly-observed sketch) that derives from the God of Michelangelo's creation of Adam or from Raphael's God creating the sun, moon, and stars—and makes Falstaff the "King" figure lacking in *The Committee*.[34]

One thing is certain: Hogarth sought out this scene in Shakespeare and in the *Henry IV* plays. Of all the scenes he could have chosen, he chose only this one. And he portrayed it so as to show the culpability of Falstaff, the man in power. We need only compare it with Hayman's versions of the same scene, of the 1760s, which play primarily on the comic contrasts of bodily shapes (pl. 23).

Hogarth was aware of this Falstaff. In *The Analysis of Beauty* he uses Falstaff to illustrate the idea that incongruous forms make us laugh, as when Falstaff says *"stand before me boy I would not be seen* to his little page when the lord Chancelor was passing by, and again *this sighing and grieving blows a man up"*—to which, he adds, Hudibras and Don Quixote "afford many seeming confermations." He refers to the visual effects of stage performance, and adds that Butler and Cervantes in their verbal texts "afford" confirmation. As he says, "it is plainly the Inconsistency and mixture of incompatible matter that causes involuntary laughter" (p. 180). The second reference is to Falstaff's reply to Hal's query, "How long is't ago, Jack, since thou sawest thine own knee?" "A plague of sighing and grief!" replies Falstaff, "It blows a man up like a bladder" (Pt. I, ii.iv.). In the jovial Falstaff's gaining weight from sorrow Hogarth sees a humorous "inconsistency," a "mixture of incompatible matter," which amounts to the incongruity of the knight's size and his sly fabricated fantasies about it.

But Hogarth does not use this Falstaff in his painting. He turns instead to the theme of power and justice. Characteristically (again anticipating Morgann) he adds to the expression of the faces and the gestures of the bodies the objects on the walls, the possessions that characterize their owners or the figures who stand in contiguous relationship to them. The target directly above the figure of Falstaff (with bow and quiver of arrows) is no doubt Hogarth's emblem of justice—straight on the mark, a bull's-eye. There is also a picture on the wall overlooking the action: it shows the Gloucester Giant or some such local hero from the past. (The tree and the small man must be there to establish scale for the other, much taller man, who seems to be holding a longbow.) Perhaps he is a memory of Double the archer, whom Falstaff and Shallow remember from the heroic past. Certainly he is the English yeoman who stands in overwhelming contrast to the ragtag recruits whom Falstaff has "pressed."

We must now relate Hogarth's Falstaff to his other Shakespeare representation of 1727-28, an engraving of *Henry VIII,* which shows Cardinal Wolsey in the process of falling from favor—or plotting to keep from falling (pl. 24). Colley Cibber's production of *Henry VIII* had opened at Drury Lane on 26 October 1727 (the *Henry IV,* recall, was played on 9 September) and enjoyed a long run, partly because the coronation scene duplicated the recent coronation of George II. Hogarth's engraving, however, is political rather than illustrative of a performance of the play—although it may also have been that. He had begun to issue fairly blatant anti-Walpole cartoons from December 1726 shortly after the founding of the opposition newspaper *The Craftsman.* On 18 November 1727, less than a month after Cibber's *Henry VIII* opened, *The Craftsman* drew attention to the resemblance between "The Character of this ambitious, wealthy, bad *Minister,*" Cardinal Wolsey, and Sir Robert Walpole.[35]

The *Beggar's Opera* painting presents a Macheath who resembles contemporary portraits of Walpole. While Peachum was also associated by Gay with Walpole, the Macheath association was based on two factors, both of them implicit in Hogarth's paintings: his association with more than one "wife," Molly Skerrit as well as Lady Walpole; and the dismissal and sudden reappointment of Walpole at the accession of George II. Macheath is shown between his two "wives" Polly and Lucy but in prison, from which prison and sentence of death he is reprieved at the end of the play by the play's venal author. The same issue was stressed in the engraving of Henry VIII and Cardinal Wolsey. Wolsey was also, of course, one of the bad clergymen Hogarth portrayed in his works; one of whom appears in *The Punishment of Lemuel Gulliver* (earlier in *The South Sea Scheme),* misadvising the king, and later in the first and last plates of *A Harlot's Progress.*

In this context we may see the other representation, *Falstaff examining his Recruits,* as the portrayal of the bad judge and also the bad adviser who is turned away by Prince Hal upon his accession. In this particular context, we can return to the imperious gesture Hogarth has given Falstaff—of Michelangelo's God the Father creating Adam—and suggest that it is employed to recall the remainder of the Falstaff story, in particular his relationship to Prince Hal in the scene back in Part 1 in which he plays the role of the king:

> *Prince.* Do thou stand for my father, and examine me upon the particulars of my life.

Falstaff. Shall I? content: this chair shall be my state, this dagger my
sceptre, and this cushion my crown.   (Pt. I, IV.iv.)

Hogarth recreates this scene, itself a parody of the true scene between
king and subject, at an even lower remove in Shallow's house, and the
viewers then fill in this aspect of the Falstaff story, thereby pointing
toward the end of the play and his rejection by Hal, now King Henry V.
(There were differences as well as similarities. Falstaff was friendly with
the Prince of Wales before his accession, Walpole not. But then of
course the Walpole-Wolsey analogy was only approximate too: Walpole like Falstaff was dismissed by the new king, Wolsey by the old.)

We then recall the other associations of Falstaff, with Doll Tearsheet
and with conviviality, and we may suspect that Hogarth also chose him
because he shared these characteristics with Walpole. The anti-Walpole
Craftsman of 29 July 1727 quotes the scene in which Falstaff plays the
king and describes himself in flattering terms, ending with the words
"Banish plump Jack, and banish all the world."[36]

Among other things, I take this as evidence that Hogarth probably
made his drawing of the scene from *Henry IV, Part 2,* following the
September 1727 production, perhaps with the *Craftsman*'s words of 29
July in his ears (and not following the production of October 1728).

A final fact is that some time after the death of George I the Great
Seal, returned by the Chancellor of the Exchequer at the king's death,
was melted down. Walpole received the new seal on 15 August 1728,
long after he had been reappointed, and some time after that he had the
superseded matrix converted into a salver, as was the custom. He hired
Hogarth to engrave it—a great honor for an engraver. This was in all
likelihood a bribe, for Hogarth's references to Walpole became very
discreet thereafter. The paintings of *The Beggar's Opera* and *Falstaff*
were unusual among his paintings of those years in that neither was
engraved, that is publicly-disseminated.

The Hogarthian use of the political analogy is altogether characteristic (of him and of his time, for example of his friend Fielding), but so also
are the prolepsis and analepsis that extend the significance of the scene
to a beginning and an ending which will close off the action of the play
itself, and that reach far beyond the immediate conflation of examina-
tion, bribery, and judgment we first noticed in the gesture of Falstaff's
hand behind his back. Hogarth here, and in his later independent series
(especially *Marriage à la Mode),* is very close to the "Shakespeare"
Maurice Morgann was to explore in his essay on Falstaff in 1777 in that
he extends the life of his fiction beyond the frame of the canvas, as
beyond the proscenium arch of the stage setting, in all directions.

Let me mention one more way, I believe the most important, in which he extends life outside the limits of the particular scene. In the early months of 1728/9 Hogarth sketched and painted another scene, closely related to the *Falstaff*, and presumably deriving from it (from the sketch if not the painting). This was the meeting of the Committee of the House of Commons that was investigating the cruelties of Bambridge, the warden of the Fleet Prison (pl. 25). The gesture is different and the figures are not parallel to those in the Falstaff, but the human relationship to which this scene draws our attention is precisely the same.

The *Hudibras Committee* showed a bunch of fools in power around a table. The Shakespeare scene showed a group that could have drawn some echoes from the *Hudibras* scene, since it too is a bunch of fools in power. But the *House of Commons Committee* shows the situation of the dishonest warden confronted by the honest prisoner in front of an audience (a chairman, Oglethorpe-Shallow, and MPs). Here Hogarth has drawn upon Falstaff the dishonest impresser of soldiers, imperiously "choosing" two while accepting a bribe from behind his back and excusing two others. The innocents are being condemned and the guilty (the bribers) freed. How far the notion of the dim-witted audience consisting of Shallow and Silence carries over to the members of Parliament we can only speculate.

It is possible that the Falstaff scene was only a preparation for the *House of Commons Committee* or scenes like it which follow. For the basic situation is a Hogarthian, not a Shakespearean one. In the painting he adds a prison background that was not present in the panelled conference room where the hearings took place. The image in fact relates to Hogarth's own youth spent in the Fleet Prison and its environs, while his father was imprisoned for debt.[37] This relationship between the prisoner and the warden, as between the innocent and the guilty, with an audience of supposed judges, or respectable spectators, was a basic structure of Hogarth's progresses of a Harlot and a Rake: for example, when the poor Harlot is threatened by the warder in prison. She is always surrounded by people who are ostensibly more respectable, but in fact far worse, than she.

Walpole and Falstaff were both charming as well as corrupt figures— as Pope's remarks in his *Epilogue to the Satires*, Dialogue 1 (1738) attest, as do some of Fielding's in his *Champion* (1739-41). I do not mean to suggest that Hogarth loses sight of these complications, but it is probably significant that when he alludes to Falstaff in his writings it is to associate him not with himself but with the *other*: for example, with the critics who, when confronted with his theory of the Line of Beauty, were puzzled "till it came to be explain'd but then indeed they all knew it before as well as falstaf knew the prince when he was robd upon gads hill."[38]

Hogarth's Falstaff is close to Morgann's, who combined youth, suppleness, wit, and vigor with an old, corpulent body—a figure quite different from Don Quixote, thin, ascetic, blindly heroic in the face of an unheroic world, with the reality principle embodied in his short pudgy companion Sancho. Falstaff is all conformity but with some awareness of his shabby complicity. Hogarth shows him taking his bribe with little care for concealment. If Hogarth's heroes (with whom he does seem to associate himself) are Quixotes, intense desirers of illusion at odds with the world in which they find themselves, his villains may owe something to Falstaff.

In *The Denunciation* (pl. 27) and *The Christening* (pl. 28), the paintings of 1729-30 that mark the transition from conversation picture to "modern moral subjects" (both were engraved), this figure appears as Justice de Veil and Orator Henley. Even Henley, whose sin is only concupiscence, is threatening in the context of bad clergymen and magistrates, officials who impose sanctions upon supposedly less-respectable, helpless people. At his least threatening, this figure appears as the leering reader of *The Sleeping Congregation* (1738) ogling a pretty young girl's bosom. No, Hogarth's Falstaff is not Morgann's jolly self-ironist; he is closer to Blake's Urizen—a judge with the power and the will to send men to their deaths, assuming a blasphemous pose of fiat lux.

Let us go back a step. One structure shared by *The Beggar's Opera* and *Falstaff examining his Recruits* is that of choice—one of the most repeated structures in novels and poems, part of the stage business in Gay's play, and a central topos in Hogarth's prints. In Hogarth's time, choice—in religious terms, a Protestant, a very Miltonic concept—was still pictorially embodied in the Choice or Judgment of Hercules (see pl. 31), about which I have written at great length elsewhere.[39] Macheath is engaged in supposedly choosing between his two wives, as Falstaff is supposedly choosing between suitable and unsuitable, healthy and unhealthy recruits. Hogarth introduces this commonplace of his own age into the Shakespearean situation where it does not fit and stands out as an alien, indeed a personal form. Later in the century, as the first plate in the *Boydell Shakespeare* volumes, Shakespeare himself is shown choosing between Comedy and Tragedy. In none of these cases is the protagonist choosing: Macheath wants both wives, Falstaff has accepted a bribe which settles his choice for him, and Shakespeare cannot choose because he is equally good at both (a fiction used earlier by Reynolds in his *Garrick between the Muses of Comedy and Tragedy*

46

of 1762 [pl. 71]). The Harlot also, in a different way, is refused a choice: the clergyman representing Virtue has turned his back (to seek Walpolian preferment), while the bawd representing Vice is vigorously arguing, as Virtue is supposed to be doing, supported by two seconds. At bottom all are corrupt, emphatically contemporary Hercules situations, and I suspect that Hogarth's aim is to make his spectator "choose" in a way denied to his characters, but also to see the undermining of that great classical and Protestant paradigm, choice.

Falstaff, however, is not a false Hercules choosing between vice and virtue, but a judge—a Solomon, the other side of the Hercules-choice topos—and so an anticipation of de Veil choosing between the two versions of the story of the pregnancy, Henley officiating over a baby who is either this lover's or that husband's. The shifting versions of the myth are all too evident, and they hinge on the interchangeability of choice and judgment, of defendant and judge—issues that were of great personal importance to Hogarth, who later included what is surely in some degree a portrait of his father in the scene of the Rake's imprisonment in the Fleet Prison.

But Falstaff remains on the side of the wicked judge as chooser, not of the defendant—the Harlot, the Rake, and so on. In Hogarth's Bible paintings he changes his emphasis from the situation of the Choice of Hercules in which the young anti-Hercules is powerless to choose to that of the Judgment of Solomon in which the figure of power represents Solomon-like equity—a cold reason that cuts the property in question exactly in half; in which the figure of power is in a position to destroy both, or to render injustice to one party, and does.

I think it is easiest to see Hogarth's Falstaff as the first of the false judges, the pseudo-Solomons, who are pitted against the pseudo-Hercules, who derive from Don Quixote and are Hogarth's protagonists, either deluded or stupidly innocent. These are the Don Quixotes who sometimes appear in the Choice of Hercules situation, who being Quixotes always choose for the illusion against the reality and suffer for it at the hands of the Solomons. The reference begins as a personal one but is generalized as Hogarth merges Shakespeare with Milton and Cervantes.

It is worth noting that Hayman's *Falstaff examining his Recruits*, made for the 1740 Hanmer edition (another version, exhibited at the Society of Arts, 1754, pl. 23) was probably a self-portrait. It seems likely, if we can believe the Hayman anecdotes, that he identified himself with Falstaff.[40] When Zoffany included Hayman in his portrait group of the Royal Academicians (1771-72, London, National Portrait Gallery) he painted him in the same pose from Hayman's Falstaff.

Hogarth's Tempest

Hogarth's second Shakespeare painting was *A Scene from "The Tempest"* of the mid 1730s (Lord St. Oswald, pl. 29). At first sight, the *Tempest* painting seems to be quite a different case from the *Falstaff*. As Robin Simon has shown, it unmistakably draws upon Shakespeare's text rather than a contemporary production.[41] Hogarth's Caliban, for instance, does not derive from stage tradition, which seems to have given him a bearskin and long shaggy hair, but from Trinculo's questioning images:

> What have we here? a man or a fish? dead or alive? A fish: he smells like a fish. . . . Why, thou debosh'd fish. . . . Wilt thou tell a monstrous lie, being but half a fish and half a monster. (II.ii.)

Hogarth shows him with web feet (which Simon thinks would have made it difficult for him to walk on stage) and scaly legs and a strange fishy protuberance that might correspond to Trinculo's remark that Caliban has "fins like arms!"

Hogarth has also ignored the stage tradition of his time, which until 1746 was based on the operatic version of 1674 adapted by Thomas Shadwell from the stage adaptation by Davenant and Dryden. In the opera there was not even a scene corresponding to the one Hogarth paints. But there were added sisters for both Caliban and Miranda, and to match Miranda the girl "that never saw man" there was a young man named Hippolito "that never saw woman." It is not surprising that Hogarth should avoid the operatic version, since that was what *The Beggar's Opera* (Gay's play and Hogarth's paintings) as well as *A Harlot's Progress* and Hogarth's other early works were against, wishing to replace foreign operatic entertainments, including decorative history painting by the Italians, by a true English product. Since there was no native stage tradition that served for this play, Hogarth was forced back on the literary text itself.

He chooses Act I, scene ii, the first meeting of Ferdinand and Miranda, which also includes Prospero to introduce the two parties and to hover over the scene as playwright-magician. Hogarth paints Prospero in the role of one of those host figures in his conversation pictures; and though in a remote setting, the size, scale, and situation are also still those of a small conversation picture. It does not compare with the huge Biblical paintings Hogarth made in 1736-38 for St. Batholomew's Hospital. By this time, however, the context is not the early *Wollaston Family* but a contemporary conversation like *Lord Hervey and his Friends* (Lord Bristol), a witty, somewhat fantastic pastoral scene with the protagonist showing something—a plan in this case— to someone else with retainers around him, some in bizarre poses.

Perhaps the more exact parallel is with the "modern moral subjects" Hogarth had finished between 1730 and 1735, *A Harlot's Progress* and *A Rake's Progress*. The most noticeable feature of these series is the imposition of details and compositions from the tradition of High Renaissance art, in particular Biblical scenes. The Rake is posed—or is posing, actor-like—as Christ in a Pietà, just as the Harlot assumes the posture of Mary in a Visitation and an Annunciation. To convey the sense of Shakespeare's scene Hogarth draws upon the iconography of the Bible, much as in the modern moral subjects, though here he does not have to worry about the possibility of blasphemy or antithetical references, and the allusion is even more overt.

The story is Miranda's, the woman who has never seen a man, with her aged father Prospero behind her and a lamb nearby; and Hogarth gives her the color of the Virgin Mary and a pose roughly like that of Mary at the Annunciation.

Ferdinand's most emphatic question to Miranda is about her virginity: "my prime request, / Which I do last pronounce, is, O you wonder! / If you be maid or no?" "No wonder, sir," she replies; "But certainly a maid." This situation might find its graphic equivalent in representations of the Annunciation, a scene Hogarth had used ironically to show the apprehension of the Harlot in her shabby quarters after a night of prostitution—hardly any longer a maid. But Ferdinand is not given the cross-armed pose of the angel in Annunciation scenes but rather the prayerful hands of one of the Magi come to pay homage, in a scene of conventional manger-like architecture. Ariel in this case becomes one of the heavenly angels floating overhead—and, I suppose, Caliban his diabolical opposite.[42] In Shakespeare's text Caliban is off stage at the moment gathering wood for a fire; Hogarth shows him having returned bearing his wood.

The heightening is appropriate and neatly accomplished. Nevertheless, it is hard to forget the use to which Hogarth had put the Virgin Mary and the Biblical echoes only three or four years before. I rather suspect that he may, among other things, have produced a painting here that answered some of the questions raised by that much more problematic and original series, *A Harlot's Progress.*[43]

I must pause to mention a few more biographical facts before proceeding. The *Harlot's Progress* had established Hogarth's financial security, his reputation as an artist to reckon with (though not yet a serious history painter, despite his arguments about modern history-painting), and had presumably cemented a reconciliation with his father-in-law, the painter and his earlier mentor, Sir James Thornhill. Thornhill, the artist of the immense history paintings at Greenwich Hospital, as well as their divine equivalents in the cupola of St. Paul's Cathedral, was the premier English artist of Hogarth's youth. When Hogarth eloped with his daughter Jane in 1728, just after completing the *Committee of the House of Commons* painting (Thornhill, an M.P., had secured Hogarth access to the committee and perhaps a commission), he and Lady Thornhill had been appalled and disowned the errant couple. Hogarth was as yet unproven.[44]

These facts bear some relevance to the scene Hogarth has illustrated. Remember that Ferdinand is summoned by Prospero after being saved from the shipwreck: Ferdinand recalls "Sitting on a bank, / Weeping again the king my father's wreck," and he repeats more than once the paramount fact that his father has drowned ("my drown'd father," "the king my father wreck'd"). Hogarth, you will recall, had a father who had spent some years in prison, and emerged a ruined man to die a few years later, in 1718. In the early 1720s Hogarth met Thornhill and fell under his spell—a spell we can recognize not only in the influence the older painter had on his art,[45] but in Hogarth's defense of him long after his death and his Quixotic need to follow in Thornhill's footsteps as English painter, as Serjeant Painter to the King, and even perhaps as knight.

Prospero at this point picks up Ferdinand and introduces him to his daughter Miranda, with whom Ferdinand immediately falls in love. But Prospero says, aside,

> They are both in either's powers; but this swift business
> I must uneasy make, lest too light winning
> Make the prize light.

He therefore tests Ferdinand, accusing him of treason and attempting to turn him into another wood-toting Caliban. Ferdinand, outraged, draws his sword, which Prospero's magic prevents him from raising.

> *Mir.*   O dear father,
> Make not too rash a trial of him, for
> He's gentle and not fearful.
> *Pros.*   . . . Put thy sword up, traitor;
> Who makest a show but darest not strike, thy conscience
> Is so posess'd with guilt: . . . .
> *Mir.*   Beseech you, father.
> *Pros.* Hence! Hang not on my garments.
> *Mir.*   Sir, have pity;
> I'll be his surety.
> *Pros.*   Silence! one word more

Shall make me chide thee, if not hate thee. What!
An advocate for an imposter! hush!
Thou think'st there is no more such shapes as he,
Having seen but him and Caliban: foolish wench!
To the most of men this is a Caliban
And they to him are angels.
Mir.   My affections
Are then most humble; I have no ambition
To see a goodlier man.

"Come on," says Prospero; "Obey . . . ," and of course Ferdinand does carry out such menial tasks for Prospero as gathering wood.

I think we can now see one of the reasons Hogarth has chosen this scene, just as twenty years later (1759) he told the story over again in terms of the story of Sigismunda, her father Tancred, and her lover Guiscardo (pl. 30). That was supposed to be a portrait of Jane grieving over the death of her mother, but Dryden's version of the story in his *Fables* (cited by Hogarth) differs from any earlier version in having Sigismunda and Guiscardo not merely lovers despite her father's disapproval, but married. Sigismunda's father Tancred sequesters her, but she falls in love with a young man

Of gentle blood, but one whose niggard fate
Had set him far below her high estate:
Guiscard his name was called, of blooming age,
Now squire to Tancred, and before his page. . . .[46]

The story unfolds of their secret courtship under Tancred's eyes, their elopement, and their discovery by the angry father, who kills Guiscardo and sends his heart in a goblet to Sigismunda, who fills the goblet with poison and drinks.

If the story of his childhood in prison was one plot or myth Hogarth could not escape from and kept retelling, another was the story of the boy who is adopted by a second father, presented with his dazzling daughter, and then denied her because he has not lived up to expectations. Prospero as Joseph, the aged husband, is appropriately confused with Prospero as the magician, stage-manager, artist, poet, and God-the-Father. Prospero, demonstrating his "so potent art" (as he calls it), is accompanied by his staff and his book—which he will at the end break and sink. (I do not want to claim that Ferdinand resembles Hogarth's self-portrait, but it cannot be said that he does not.)

Given Prospero's insult that Ferdinand is only a Caliban in relation to other men and that he is being condemned to carry on Caliban-like errands, it is not unseemly that Caliban should be included. Hogarth presents him as an emblematic threat to the marriage, crushing underfoot one of a pair of linked doves (a detail which should be contrasted with the manacled dogs of *Marriage à la Mode*, 1, and the two courting dogs of *Rake*, 5—and indeed, the doves at Venus' feet in *The Analysis of Beauty*, 1). This complex of associations also suggests why there is a connection, however strange, between Hogarth's *Tempest* and the imagery of the anti-Mary in his *Harlot's Progress*. We can relate the scene as well to the situation of the daughter mediating between her father and her interloper lover: Polly trying to reconcile Macheath and Peachum, Lucy trying to reconcile Macheath and Lockit, which becomes in *The Tempest* Miranda trying to reconcile Ferdinand and Prospero (Jane-Hogarth-Thornhill)—which then becomes, about the same time as the *Tempest* painting, the pretty wife mediating between the artist and the disorderly or threatening outside world in *The Distrest Poet* and *The Enraged Musician* (1736, 1741). But under this gestalt we may detect another that involves the rival father and son contending for the young woman: Peachum and Macheath separated by Polly, Lockit and Macheath separated by Lucy, in *The Beggar's Opera* paintings (and, as we shall see, Satan and Death separated by Sin in Hogarth's Milton painting).[47]

Among other things, as Hogarth makes clear, Shakespeare is the writer who will accommodate any appropriation and still survive unscathed. Peter Conrad has put this very nicely: ". . . the generous forbearance of Shakespeare welcomes distortions like this and can turn them to perceptive account—the more the illustrator outrages the plays, the closer he is likely to approach their own audacity".[48] But as to the method employed, I should mention at least the possibility that the Nativity parallel was conceivable in a stage production of *The Tempest* (though not one Hogarth could have seen before undertaking his painting). As Gay in *The Beggar's Opera* clearly blocks out Macheath standing between his wives in a "Choice of Hercules" pose (II.xiii), he may also be alluding to a Judas kiss when Jenny in this way signals the constable to arrest Macheath in the third act, and the opening of that act may have been laid out as a Last Supper with Macheath filling the central position (compare Hogarth's *Harlot*, 6, PL. 41). With this sort of allusion at work in Hogarth's engravings, it is not unlikely that Garrick employed similar devices in some of his productions.

Certainly the depth of reference, the multiplicity of the psychological and intellectual levels, though it has common precedents in Renaissance painting, is in the case of Hogarth a Shakespearean phenomenon with a strong dramatic authority. The formal structure of a Hogarth painting is for purposes of "reading," of guiding the spectator's eye toward cognition of various different sorts, whereas most painting in the Renaissance tradition used form for primarily architectonic purposes.

Shakespeare and Hogarth share a profound ambiguity, a refusal to settle for either/or choices and the firmness of a single gestalt, which begins with an undermining of settled assumptions and ends with an irrational inconclusiveness of the sort I have described as Shakespearean tragicomedy. These are the important assumptions I have referred to as deriving from Shakespeare, and they undermine the more normative structures that were being offered by the other great literary models, Milton and the Bible. The authoritative, decisive, even prescriptive structures are in those works, as we shall see in the next chapter, but the attitude toward them (which asks to take them with a grain of salt) comes from Shakespeare.

As G.K. Hunter has shown,[49] conventional Shakespearean illustration (whether in books or paintings) has tended to be constructed on visual oppositions of good and evil, light and dark, male and female, left and right, which betray the essential nature of Shakespeare's own literary structures. Shakespeare's scenes and plays progress from contrast to various senses of association and identity, as characters who are initially opposites gradually reveal their affinities. Quite different from the illustration of Shakespeare, however, is his influence on English art.

The question is whether the use of contrast is indigenous to the mode of graphic art. In England at any rate it is more likely the product of the other great literary alternative to Shakespeare's plays, Milton's *Paradise Lost* with its oppositions of good and evil, past and future, light and dark, and so on. This is the allegorical mode that takes over Shakespearean painting with the Boydell enterprise, sacrificing the essential interplay of character with other characters as human beings and sacrificing also the interplay of role and actor, of literary figures and contemporary portraits. It is less likely but also perhaps a possibility that the artist-illustrator tended to choose the first phase of the Shakespearean structure because he could only (as an artist) represent one moment, and so chose the moment of polarity rather than the later complicating and resolving action. If this is so among illustrators of Shakespeare, then we can conclude that it was Hogarth's genius to show the contrast *and* its dissolution within the same picture.

As a coda I should add that the third and final subject Hogarth painted from Shakespeare was a departure from the two earlier: this was a portrait of Garrick in the role of Richard III, which had launched the great actor on his career.[50] It was life-size, a portrait heroicized, on a monumental scale, and in the setting of English history. From this scene, painted in 1745 (Liverpool) and immediately engraved, can be traced the great portraits of Reynolds in which contemporary Englishmen are made to seem gods, heroes, or Shakespearean protagonists. I do not regard this portrait, impressive as it is, as a totally representative Hogarth painting. It is an operatic aria as opposed to the Shakespearean grouping that most fully characterized Hogarth's paintings. It is, in Hogarth's terms, a return to the full-length Van Dyck, Lely, or Kneller portrait, which he had replaced with the conversation picture based on theatrical conventions. But it was probably this painting, more than any of his others, that opened the way to the academic Shakespeare painting of the 1760s and after, and to the general maintenance of "character" if not portraiture in a context of rather conventional compositions.

III. THE BIBLE

Michelangelo and Raphael: The Graphic Tradition

The Bible was a text known to all classes and types of Englishmen, to representatives of low and high culture, of the subculture as well as the dominant culture. The Bible bore an authority equaled by no other text, and—unlike the Shakespeare or Cervantes of that time—it carried with its verbal text a very long tradition of commentary. This commentary was both verbal, in the form of annotation and even oral tradition, and visual. The painter approaching the Bible, either to illustrate it or to draw upon its authority and strength for his own original painting, had a powerful graphic tradition available to him. The Bible, unlike Shakespeare and Cervantes, offered visual paradigms. Or rather, whereas the Shakespearean text offered the opportunity to copy directly what was happening on stage, the Bible offered the artist the intermediary of a graphic tradition to imitate. It was possible to copy this tradition without even thinking of the literary text itself and to assume meanings in the graphic versions that might (by this time) be independent of the literary.

With the Bible, therefore, we begin to witness the imprint of high art on English painting in the eighteenth century. The whole tradition of Renaissance art, Italian as well as North European, was of course available in engravings, to be bought in London print shops. For history painting Raphael was the most revered authority, until toward the end of the century Michelangelo began to contest him for first place. By that time Reynolds, who finally in his last presidential discourse acknowledged his primary allegiance to Michelangelo, had long employed as model for *his* history paintings the simplifications of Raphael's Madonna and Child compositions. For his portraits he used historical compositions reminiscent of these Madonna-Child paintings or of Michelangelo's single figures around the Sistine ceiling.

The graphic precedents for Biblical stories came from the same artists. For the whole story there were the Michelangelo paintings on the Sistine ceiling and the Raphael designs on the arches of the Vatican Loggia—the so-called Michelangelo and Raphael Bibles. They related in their different ways the Old and New Testaments. Both continental and English artists relied on these. In England, however, the Old Testament was summed up in Rubens' baroque image of Solomon/James I on the ceiling of the Whitehall Banqueting House, and the New Testament in the Raphael Cartoons at Hampton Court Palace.

In England the tradition of history painting was based partly on the strain developed by Poussin out of Raphael's Tapestries of the Lives of the Apostles, and partly on the historical accident that put the original Cartoons for the Tapestries at the disposal of English artists. Because of Charles I's good taste and the luck of timing that saved the Cartoons from the sale of his collection during the Commonwealth, Englishmen found that the one monument of Renaissance art available to them without traveling to the continent was this climax of High Renaissance style, the great model of European history painting. The originals were accessible at Hampton Court Palace and engraved reproductions were even more easily accessible in London printshops. As we have seen, even when Shakespeare was illustrated for Boydell, the Raphael Cartoons remained a primary model for certain kinds of scene. For Biblical illustration, they remained authoritative. Their presence, however, made it even more difficult for a serious English painter to escape the need to distinguish himself in the line of painting they exemplified.

There was always at hand a second, an alternative model for history painting. This was Rubens' ceiling of the Banqueting House, another product of the connoisseurship of Charles I. The differences between Rubens' ceiling and Raphael's Cartoons were crucially important. Rubens' panels were baroque and operatic in their illusionism, Catholic and monarchical in their politics, a series seen unfolding upward and away from the viewer as if ascending into the sky. Their subject was the sovereign; they presented an allegory of divine right in which the court is the center of patronage, the perspective is from the royal point of view, seen properly from the throne with the king implicitly on a vertical axis connecting him with the deity Himself. The king's father, James I, is portrayed thrice, twice in the bestowal of a divine fiat lux and once in the process of apotheosis, and in any case as total source of interest, power, and beneficence.

The florid iconography is from the Old Testament with James I related typologically and analogically (as he had made clear he wished to be) to King Solomon. James's learning and supposed wisdom are related to Solomon's by the use of the twisted columns of Solomon's Temple in one panel and by the composition of a Judgment of Solomon in another:[1] a story twice illustrated by Raphael (in both the Stanze and the Loggia) and equally authoritatively by Poussin (Louvre). James/Solomon is shown passing judgment on two women, England and

Scotland, both of whom claim as their child the infant between them, the young Great Britain produced by the accession of the Stuart James I.

The Mantegna *Triumphs of Caesar* (or Mantegna Cartoons as they were often erroneously called because of their proximity at Hampton Court Palace to the Raphael Cartoons) were equally visible, but their influence on English painters was less direct. The form is processional, the figures are moving toward the left, burdened with a great variety of objects (mostly loot), and the center of it all is the figure of Julius Caesar. The Triumphs were the sort of monarch-oriented structure that found its English apotheosis in Rubens' Banqueting House ceiling. Everything emanated from Caesar, as in Rubens's designs it does from James I, though in a horizontal rather than vertical direction—a Renaissance-humanist rather than a baroque direction.

Neither of these king-oriented programs caught on for the English artist of post-1688 in the way that the Protestant-oriented stories of Raphael's *Life of the Apostles* did, with their discrete scenes of human interaction and horizontal progression through spiritual conversion of the self to the conversion of others. The Rubens, however, was a model for the decorative history painting that was undertaken in England from the Restoration of the Stuart Charles II onward, and in Hogarth's time not only by his father-in-law Sir James Thornhill in Greenwich Hospital, but by foreign rivals like Pellegrini, Amigoni, and the Ricci.

Antonio Verrio's apotheoses of royalty at the Restoration were more modest than Rubens' because of the altered political situation, but they were still forceful and flamboyant. As Parliament grew stronger, the decorative painters moved out from the capital to decorate the seats of the great noblemen. Verrio covered the walls and ceilings of Burleigh House with mythologies linking gods and Englishmen, and Louis Laguerre painted the story of Caesar (including his assassination) on the walls of Chatsworth, the seat of a nobleman who saw the crown as one element in a constitutional construct that includes a senate (Lords and Commons) and asks the king to remember this. Both Verrio and Laguerre decorated chapels with paintings of a New Testament subject, Christ healing the Sick, an exemplum of the virtue of charity which was to serve as the basis of much English church art in the eighteenth century—art which avoided the excesses of the baroque Catholic tradition by turning to the sober paradigms of Raphael. Laguerre painted on the walls of Marlborough House in London (for the duke and his duchess) murals of the battles of this great nobleman and national hero. These scenes are documentary. In the place of gods and heroes are panoramas of warfare in the war of the Spanish Succession.[2]

Although not too much should be made of the fact, there is an interesting slippage in some of these paintings that will become significant in the hands of an Englishman who was a contemporary of Swift and Pope, the self-conscious skeptic Hogarth. I refer to the fact, ignored by Rubens and I am sure unnoticed by Charles I's courtiers, that the two women England and Scotland who contest the child Great Britain and are reconciled by the monarch James I are in the Biblical story prostitutes. There is also the fact that Laguerre painted the victories of Marlborough by adapting compositions of the victories of Louis XIV at Versailles. I am sure he did this as a time-saver; he lacked the vigor of imagination to create anew. But someone carrying the two sets of engravings could have had fun at the expense of the Duke of Marlborough—unless, of course, the duke was in on the joke, which was in fact at the expense of Louis XIV, and Laguerre was another English ironist.

My point is that no one noticed such anomalies until they were pointed out in the 1730s by Hogarth, that "Shakespearean" artist of "nature's" unavoidable superiority to art. The aim of High Renaissance art, as Sidney Freedberg has put it, was "to achieve a harmony of regular, clear, and proportionate relations that is not evident in nature and, at the same time, to assert that this harmony pertains to an existence which is compellingly true."[3] This idealism was plainly something that English artists, brought up on the works of Shakespeare and other English writers (both poetic and political), could not countenance and still talk about "nature." So long as they accepted art as a closed system between patron and painter, questions of slippage did not arise. So long as they looked at the Whitehall Banqueting House ceiling from the perspective of the royal presence, in the way it was painted, they saw from the point of view of Solomon, the patron, and the high culture itself. But as soon as they separated themselves from the commissioner of the paintings they began to notice the discrepancies. And this, of course, was what began to happen in the late seventeenth century as Parliament and Court and as artist and patron drew apart.

The historical development of English art can be charted in time from Rubens' royal ceiling to Verrio's mythologies, to Laguerre's contemporary scenes of the duke's battles (and their relationship to the royal allegories of Louis XIV as Alexander the Great) as reportorial battle scenes, and thence to Hogarth's burlesque version of these battles in his *March to Finchley* (1750) or his fourth *Election* painting (1754) which echoes the battle on an arched bridge in one of Laguerre's *Battles of Marlborough,* which echoed in turn Rubens' *Battle of the Amazons*

(Munich). Hogarth's procedure here—and perhaps the whole trajectory of English painting—is analogous to Shakespeare's juxtaposition of Caesar and the shoemakers and cobblers. The possibility of seeing through the mask of royal authority was raised in a number of Shakespeare's plays, and the mental assumptions remained at hand for an original painter.

In one sense English painting from Hogarth to Reynolds and on to Fuseli, Blake, and Turner—that is, the tradition of history painting—was a story of self-conscious play with heroic motifs. We would have to begin again with Hogarth's version of Sebastiano Ricci's *Diana* (c. 1714, Burlington House) in *Strolling Actresses dressing in a Barn* (1738), or of the *Bacchus and Ariadne* (of Ricci, but even more of Annibale Carracci in the Farnese Palace in Rome) in *Hudibras meets the Skimmington* (pls. 9, 10). The relationship was a deflationary one, which in the hands of Reynolds could be inflationary as well as merely playful, but was again deflationary in Fuseli, Blake, and Turner.

What I have been outlining is a model based on Old Testament or Greek or Roman mythological motifs, which served for English artists as an anti-model. For most Englishmen the Old Testament carried associations, as in the Rubens ceiling, of monarchy, the Law, and (for Hogarth at least) Shakespeare's Shylock and his bond. Classical myths carried associations of lascivious behavior and arbitrary justice at the hands of fickle, self-centered deities. The Raphael Cartoons, however, offered a positive alternative because they embodied all the opposing New Testament values, which were more closely in line with the English Protestant tradition, and were increasingly glorified in the aftermath of the Glorious Rebellion of 1688 and the Protestant Succession.

The total structure of the Bible stories in the Sistine Chapel tells us a great deal about the different modes of narrative discourse available to a graphic artist. These sequences were all known through engraved copies which reduced the tremendous spatial effect of the Sistine to segments of paper, but which conveyed however weakly some sense of the original spatial structure. The basic contrast was between vertical and horizontal movement in space. The vertical movement of the Michelangelo paintings was upward into the lateral series of Old Testament scenes of the Creation, the Fall of man, and the second Fall and Flood, and so to the need for Christ's Redemption. These panels grew upward from the altar end of the Chapel, one out of the other, ending in the drunkenness of Noah after the Flood, and unfolding at the four ends into spandrels of providential intervention in the affairs of men, the Old

Testament narratives that foreshadowed Christ's mission of salvation: Esther and Haman, Moses and the serpent, Judith and Holofernes, and David and Goliath.

These narrative segments devolved downward into the sculptural figures (in a scheme adopted from the design Michelangelo had worked out for the tomb of his Sistine patron, Julius II): large brooding sculptural Ignudi, putti who decorate the Prophets' thrones, terrified or dazed but ignorant Ancestors of Christ, and the huddled bronze-colored nudes within spandrels. These were punctuated and dominated by the gigantic seers, the Old Testament Prophets and Sibyls of classical antiquity who do know that mankind is going to be redeemed. Below these was a row of popes in niches, and below them was the series of rectangular panels of the parallel lives of Moses, who freed the Chosen People from slavery in Egypt, and Christ (whom he prefigured) the Redeemer of mankind from the slavery of sin. Latin inscriptions originally ran above the paintings (and were published in 1513) underlining the relationships between Old and New Testament, between the Kingdoms of Law and Grace. Raphael's Tapestries, telling the parallel stories of Sts. Peter and Paul, were originally intended to hang lower on the walls, below the Old Testament images of Michelangelo and the parallel lives of Moses and Christ by Botticelli, Perugino, and others. If Moses was the precursor of Christ, the popes were his vicars, making a further reference down to the first vicar St. Peter in the Raphael Tapestries.

The Sistine Chapel was arranged rather like the projected decoration of the Loggia di Psiche in the Villa Farnesina, in which the episodes that took place in the heavens were on the ceiling, and the earthly episodes were to be illustrated on the walls in tapestries. All of these stages are represented by Michelangelo as an unbroken continuity in time before, during, and after the Redemption, but the supporting sculptural figures on the vertical axis are the crucial feature. They represent different stages of knowledge of the Redemption, but also a range of identity and difference, a descending order of similitude which bridges the gap between God and man and supports the Redemption in its second aspect, the Incarnation. Temporally they are a spiritual history of mankind, spatially a chain of degrees of Incarnation connecting the Fall with the Redemption. Even the narrative on the ceiling is related to ontological categories: God creates the universe, creates man who then creates sin, and so requires the Redemption of Christ. The story of the Fall therefore unfolds along the level ceiling representing the need and promise of Redemption, foreshadowed in the corner spandrels showing Old Testament divine intervention in types of Christ: on one side Judith and David are related to Mary and Christ; on the other Moses with the serpent is a sign of God's covenant and a prefiguration of Christ; and the complex of Esther/Mary, Ahasuerus/God, and Haman crucified prefigures Christ's Incarnation—the worst of men embodying God's providential design for his creation, connecting him to the best, as the first is connected to the second Adam.

I have gone into such detail with Michelangelo's part of the Sistine Chapel because this was the ultimate model for Rubens' ceiling of the Banqueting House, and it was also the ultimate model for the free spatiality of Blake's paintings and illuminations of the Bible story. When I return to Blake it will be necessary to keep this structure in mind, and to contrast it with the one that dominates English painting in the interim, that of the Raphael Tapestries/Cartoons.[4]

As a series, the Raphael Tapestries moved along the wall horizontally, not vertically overhead like the Michelangelo ceiling, and produced a model reading-structure in secular (or popular) rather than divine (or royal) time. Each panel was a planar composition, enclosed, delimited, constructed on a single-point perspective, box-like—the antithesis of the infinite recession and exfoliation of the ceiling paintings. And yet if the Cartoons told a chronological story that evolved in human time, they were both diachronic—a straight narrative in time—and synchronic in that they related Paul to Peter at each stage of their travels, as these were related in turn upward to the lives of Moses and Christ.

The subject of the Raphael Cartoons is conversion—initially a vertical relationship, but thereafter a horizontal one, of one human being to another. It is a social relationship within history, which serves as the base for the divine relations above that descend to Moses-Christ, and thence to the figures on whom their effect is felt in their rectangular scenes, Peter and Paul, and finally to the humans standing on the floor of the Sistine Chapel. They—or we—are at the bottom of the ontological ladder of Incarnation, horizontally related to the scenes in the Tapestry, as further witnesses to the actions: one final circle of response to the words of Peter and Paul by the human beings whose own salvation is at stake. (Michelangelo's Last Judgment finished the scheme, painted on a different plane from—at right angles to—the depiction of Incarnation-Atonement-Redemption-Conversion.)

The different relationships of the spectator to the ceiling and to the Tapestries distinguish the two kinds of history painting. The first, essentially rejected by English artists (as we shall see, rejected by Thornhill himself), is the infinitely recessed painting that places an insurmountable gap between the spectator and the protagonists (even the Ignudi, Prophets, Ancestors, and other viewers) of the scene. The second, portrayed roughly on a level with the spectator, includes the spectator within the composition not as an upward-aspirer—in Blake's Gnostic terms a human with a spark of godhead in him desiring reconciliation with the One—but as a human witness to human actions.

In the Sistine Chapel even the stories of Moses and Christ were out of reach, above the spectator's head; only the stories of the human apostles were at eye-level, and constructed with witnesses to the apostles' actions but with gaps for the spectator to fit himself into. For example, Elymas is blinded by Paul, reacted to by the proconsul who is thereby converted, and both are reacted to by the bystanders (pl. 32). By placing a closure around the bystanders, the Tapestries/Cartoons cut us the spectators off as participants, relating us to the witnesses rather than the protagonists, and so making us detached observers and judges.

These panels represent a model for history painting in which the heroic action is seen at a little distance, framed, placed, and related to other realities. It is neither something from which the spectator is separated as by a gulf or in which he is simply absorbed or immersed. It is never in doubt that they are crafted tapestries or paintings on the wall. And in this respect, they represent principles of theatricality that are distinct from the painted staircase or balcony of the country house with men and women represented as if looking down on us—or from the tomb sculpture in which a figure of Death seems to emerge at ground level from a real door to take the spectator as well as the figure on the monument. The difference is between a spectator to someone else's drama and an actor who participates in the drama and is still in the privileged position of a courtier, a patron, or even the royal presence itself in the Banqueting House. The experience of the Cartoons is less personal, more detached; it involves a moral choice or decision and not the empathetic ecstasy expressed by the patrons in their galleries above the estatic St. Theresa in Bernini's Cornaro Chapel.

The particular interplay of spectator with a scene about spectators responding to an action—that is, an action of conversion—is a structure that Hogarth developed in his first major painting, of Gay's *Beggar's Opera* (pl. 21). He shows the actors and actresses playing the roles of other characters who are themselves playing roles, and with the viewer of the picture in precisely the role of the audience of a play, with the same sense of removal from the action and knowledge of its levels of illusion playing against "nature." A single example from Shakespeare illustration will suffice to make my point. Francis Hayman's frontispiece to *Hamlet* and his Vauxhall Gardens painting of the same subject (1738-40) build upon Hogarth's Raphaelesque formulation, not on preceding Shakespeare illustration (pl. 34). Hayman chooses the play scene and focuses on Claudius' reaction to the dumb shew. In the frontispiece he has elaborated on the situation (and in another version of the Vauxhall picture in the Folger Library), adding Prince Hamlet whose response to Claudius' response finishes out the scene. Or rather there is the spectacle, Claudius' response to it, and then the responses of Polonius, Gertrude, and (looking out of it) Ophelia to Claudius' response, and Prince Hamlet's response to both the play and the response of Claudius and the others to Claudius'. Finally we, the viewers of Hayman's representation, enjoy this complex of responses and perhaps relate the theme of play-acting to our own lives.

The basic contrast between Michelangelo's and Raphael's narratives which I am exploring was already clear in the latter's paintings in the Vatican Stanze. These were painted on the four walls of rooms that did not permit the expansion upward and downward of superhuman sculptural forms.[5] The unit was human, not divine, and the story was of the group rather than the single human archetype. The four walls offered opportunities for direct contrast and comparison, for example, between the opposite walls of Theology and Philosophy (the *Disputa* and *School of Athens*), the Arts and Justice (*Parnassus* and the images of canon and civil law). In the Stanze there was, first, the spectator, immediately involved and himself an extension of the scene receding horizontally beyond the room as Michelangelo's rises above it. Second there were the portraits of historical figures with whom Raphael filled in his scenes. Philosophy, for example, was illustrated with "portraits" of Plato and Aristotle, Divinity with Dante, Augustine, Jerome, and others both ancient and modern. In the panel showing the historical foundations of civil and canon law Gregory IX, the giver of the Decretals, was given the face of Julius II. (Later in the Eliodoro *Stanza* the face of Gregory the Great turning back Atilla was given the face of Leo X, who by then had succeeded Julius.) Unlike the Michelangelo plan of isolated sculptural figures of ideal human form, these were virtually (to use the eighteenth-century term) conversation pictures on a large scale. Reynolds was only making an ultimate joke on this fact when he placed in the positions of Plato, Aristotle, and the others in *The School of Athens* caricatures of his own contemporary Englishmen visiting in Rome (Dublin, National Gallery). Hogarth had earlier, in the 1720s, used a parody of *The School of Athens* as model for his print *The Lottery*.

However much of an authority Raphael offered for joining portraiture and history painting, the tension is evident in the contradictory positions held by Jonathan Richardson and the Earl of Shaftesbury. Richardson argued that portraits were models of virtue and that portraiture is a liberal art, an essential part of history painting. Shaftesbury felt that portrait-painting was not a liberal art or to be esteemed so, because it is tied too closely to imitation, and so it is a contradiction in terms to paint a historical portrait. Imitation of a person (honest, literal transcription) is mere service compared to the imitation of a literary text or an idea, which offers the artist freedom of imagination.[6] For Raphael's art (with its portraits) functioned as the experience of this world, which partly perhaps explains why he was the hero of the English painters of the early eighteenth century.

A more technical aspect of the Cartoons needs to be mentioned. They were made as modelli for transfer into tapestries, and in that respect they resembled engravings—into which they were also of course made. This meant that they required a less personal style than ordinary paintings; they were meant to convey ideas that could be transmitted by a style "of approximately imitable generalizations"[7] which lends itself to translation into an assistant's painting, weaving, or engraving. For transfer into tapestries they also had to be reversible, functioning in much the same way as a design for an engraving. They were, therefore, seen both as cartoons and (reversed) as tapestries. They have, inevitably, a peculiarly ambiguous reading structure. Raphael's ultimate end was the tapestry, as Hogarth's was his engraving, which carries a strong sense of cartoon or design, implying idea rather than execution. Only when seen in their correct reversed state and correct sequence do they make complete sense as both narrative and aesthetic experience, with the proper temporal relation of cause and effect.

There is, of course, a relative difference between the axially-balanced scenes like *The Death of Ananias* and *Paul and the Proconsul* (pl. 32), where reversal is less important, and the more directional compositions in which a crowd at one side relates to a lone Christ or Paul at the other (*Paul Preaching at Athens,* pl. 33, *Feed My Sheep,* and *Draught of Fishes*). Looked at in one way, the composition leads the eye to the holy figure; in the other, the action and the figures of the followers emanate from the presence of Christ or Paul, a consequence of his being. The tapestry—or engraving—reads the first way, presumably the reading Raphael intended. As John White has argued, the eye was to move toward the climax of Christ's figure: "In both of the tapestries, the figures sweep from left to right and the observer's eye sweeps with them to its focus in the all-important figure on the extreme right. This same movement also stresses the natural left to right progress along the Chapel wall from one scene to the next."[8] The other reading remains, however, in the Cartoons themselves, and to some extent it survives in the Tapestries.

In other cases, there may be a different meaning in the different reading. *Paul and the Proconsul* establishes, in the Cartoon, a powerful relationship between St. Paul's gesture and its effect on Elymas. In the tapestry we move from the blind Elymas to the proconsul and then, finally, to Paul, the cause of the miracle. The tapestry is about the conversion of the proconsul in a way that the Cartoon is not.[9] And yet once we are aware of the reversal, we carry with us both readings, and when we look at other reversed pictures we may apply the ambiguous double reading to them as well. The psychological effect of such a "working counter-gestalt," says Freedberg,

> is to have introduced an element of opposition, and thus of tension, into the particular working out of form in the designs. Postures or gestures that might have a relative fluency in their original context of direction might, in their reversed sense, have assumed a quality of resistance or taken on an initially unintended degree of stress. Such tensions may have served to intensify, to a sensible degree, the temper of dramatic content in some of the Cartoons.[10]

Hogarth's paintings are invariably planned for reversal in precisely the same way as Raphael's Cartoons. But the designing for reversal itself makes the artist aware of the ambiguities in perceiving structures, and I have no doubt that Hogarth plays upon these in the parallel existence of painting and engraving, as well as in some engravings where he turns the structure back upon itself. To take only one example, in the first scene of *A Rake's Progress* (pl. 35), the engraved scene reads from left to right through the miser's death, his hoarded possessions, the son who has inherited and is now spending them, to the young woman he has made pregnant and is buying off, who appears the consequence of all of these things. The painting, however, has the pregnant woman in the left foreground, and she seems a sentimental figure whose tears inform the whole sad, hopeless scene of the Rake's wrong choice. The engraving—especially in the context of the other seven plates—retains more than a little of this sense of the pregnant woman as commentator on a poignant situation.

In short, a more elaborate series of relationships is established in the Cartoons than in the four walls of the Stanze. The long series of panels with parallel protagonists and stories, with primary and secondary gestalts ("each is a distinct and separable, but not intendedly a separate, integer"),[11] and with the soaring deities of Michelangelo above, offer a model of extreme complexity for a narrative artist, in particular one who wishes to make the contemporary world his subject.

Sir James Thornhill was the first to see the problem and solution of the Rubens-Raphael dichotomy, perhaps because he was himself part of the problem. His ceiling of the Great Hall of Greenwich Hospital (completed in 1717) was solidly in the old Rubens tradition, with rising apotheosis and spectators ringing the oval frame. Following the Greenwich decorations, however, he undertook the painting of St. Paul's cupola (completed 1720), and here his designs, compared with both Pellegrini's proposed modello for the cupola and his own paintings on the Greenwich ceilings, showed the way to an English compromise. He used the Raphael Cartoons as his model for the life of St. Paul, compartmentalizing, closing, and essentially rendering the story as a series of discrete panels that look rather like book illustrations. (From his other activities, we know that he was also aware that book illustrations were one way out of the problem of how to vend historical subjects in a society that had little use for such heroic gestures in painting or in opera.)

In the Upper Hall at Greenwich (completed 1724) Thornhill painted the royal family as a Verrio-type wall group with his self-portrait included. The monumental size and grouping keep it from being a conversation piece, but it looks ahead to English group portraits of the next few years and in particular to George Knapton's huge group of Prince Frederick's family in Marlborough House.

None of these leads were followed for a tradition of English history painting at this time. The issue was sealed in 1724 by the famous defeat suffered by Thornhill at the hands of William Kent over the decoration of the Cupola Room in Kensington Palace. This defeat not only closed off the court patronage Thornhill himself had enjoyed, but it demonstrated the important point—which Thornhill may have caught (Hogarth seems not to have)—that the badness of Kent's painting of history was irrelevant. The real point was that Kent was an interior decorator of genius whose work was ruling out the role of decorative history painting, removing the history from the setting, leaving only architecture and sculpture, subordinating history to part of a decorative scheme on the way to Robert Adam's complete relegation of it to innocuous decorative insets, subservient to his architectural scheme; or, in Kent's case, often to a setting for portraits or for old master paintings collected by the owner of the house.[12]

Thornhill ended his life with the symbolic gesture of producing paintings that were copies of the Raphael Cartoons—for the purpose of teaching artists but also presumably the viewing public. His idea was to educate both groups in ways of seeing, in the expectations they should have when confronting art in England.

What he saw, and Hogarth developed afterward in his own way, was the fact that the English painter, however native his source of inspiration, had to use graphic equivalents borrowed from the foreign (continental) tradition. He could not use only his native literary texts. Since the foreign images were baroque, he was inclined to use them in such a way as to emphasize the obvious discrepancy between the felt reality and the art forms in which it was expressed. Thus Hogarth used a Carracci *Procession of Bacchus and Ariadne* to depict Hudibras' contemporary adventures.

Hogarth's most fully-articulated statement of this position appears in his etching *The Battle of the Pictures* (1745, frontispiece), a ticket for an auction of his paintings. The relationship between modern English art and the old masters is one of agon, and moreover the old masters are the aggressors, invading Hogarth's peaceful studio. Two baroque religious subjects and one antique Roman painting (a *St. Francis,* a *Penitent Magdalen,* and the *Aldobrandini Marriage)* are penetrating modern canvases by Hogarth, and only two of his paintings are besting the old masters. Moreover, innumerable old master reserves are advancing on Hogarth's studio from the direction of Cock's auction house: for these are merely copies of old masters, and so infiniely multipliable. Despite the tone of beleagueredness, however, Hogarth's real point is that this agon of the old and new art is defined in terms of matching pairs: the Magdalen is in combat with Hogarth's Harlot, the Aldobrandini group with the young married couple in *Marriage à la Mode.* Modern English art can only be defined in relation to past art, even if in reaction against it. A London prostitute is a Magdalen-of-today, reduced to a smaller figure, one among others in a closed and detailed setting. The baroque sentiments and forms, Hogarth is telling his audience, are part of the negative context of his paintings: the *Harlot's Progress* only signifies as part of this agon.

On the other hand, for normative images Thornhill and Hogarth turned to the Raphael Cartoons, the originals of which were physically present in England. The Cartoons were in form and content the least baroque, the least discrepant, the least remote from everyday experience. They depicted plain people in plain, unadorned, unexaggerated but clearly-articulated, indeed monumental forms.

In *Hudibras, A Harlot's Progress,* and his other series Hogarth represented the English eighteenth-century version of the Raphaelesque High Renaissance principles of pictorial composition: the division into separable units and the clarity of each, the planar structure, the density of masses, the emphatic gestures of the figures, the simple almost popular imagery, and the ordinary humans turned into symbols of universal applicability. The subject matter was similarly low—if not fishermen and tax-collectors (as well as a Roman proconsul), then doctors, clergymen, and prostitutes (as well as magistrates), but not kings and gods. The pictorial structure was based on the presence not only of protagonists but (in terms of conversion) witnesses and (in aesthetic terms) spectators.

Nevertheless, there was a fundamental difference: details in Hogarth always seem additive rather than conforming to the High Renaissance principle of simplicity. Unlike the Cartoons, in each of which, "regardless of the quantity of forms, each design seems, in its entirely, simpler," Hogarth's quantity of forms complicates.[13] The principle of discrepancy and contrast is far stronger than unity in Hogarth's designs. There is a sense in which he was regressing to the quattrocento copia from which the Raphael Cartoons had completely diverged. He retained the demand on his viewer to read the parts before the whole comes clear; though he sometimes played with the first general impression of the whole in order to contradict it by a reading of the parts, thus producing a new whole. He was not trying to reproduce a High Renaissance work that "comes into the mind and eye of the beholder at once and all at once, in an instant unity." As Reynolds put it: "What is done by Painting, must be done at one blow."[14] Hogarth was producing a peculiarly English answer to the problem of painting history.

Hogarth's Bible: "Suffer the little Children . . ."

Because he was a painter, an English painter who wished to achieve greatness in history painting in a country where churches avoided religious images, Hogarth's chief literary model—as an artist, and at the outset at any rate—was the New Testament. The Raphael Cartoons were relevant for an English artist like Hogarth because they represented the New Testament, but also because they dealt with conversion among the low as well as the high and could be fitted into a sensibility that included such literary works as Bunyan's *Grace Abounding* and Defoe's *Robinson Crusoe*.

To Hogarth they were of particular interest because the plot of personal identity involving conversion pits the apostle against mobs of heathens; because Raphael gives us a complex interplay of comparisons and contrasts between the two parallel series on opposite walls, the careers of Sts. Peter and Paul, balancing one against the other, based on the schemata of preaching and healing, words and deeds, faith and charity, which Hogarth in various ways had in mind when he painted his progresses of a Harlot and a Rake—both as parody series (lives, careers, progresses) and as parallel lives like those of Peter and Paul, two apostles who go out to spread the word of Christianity and either

convert or are swept away (ironically themselves worshipped) by idolators and the avaricious.

With these generalizations in mind, we see that the Raphael Cartoons
begin with the act of conversion. In one case conversion comes through
contact with Christ, in the other it takes the form of a seizure; one
convert is raised from the life of a humble fisherman, the other is struck
down from the life of a persecutor, the killer of Stephen (in the tapestry
that hung as pendant to *The Draught of Fishes*).

Both apostles then face these others, in the case of Paul the idolatrous
gentiles and in the case of Peter the obstinate, disobedient, and avaricious Jews. Paul and Barnabas arc themselves taken for gods in Lystra,
and Peter strikes dead the avaricious Ananias and his wife. The Old
Testament sense of "Harlot," we should recall, was one who forsakes
the true god to follow idols and false gods: "How is the faithful city
become an harlot?" (Isaiah 1.21); and idolatry is a version of what
Hogarth comes to deal with in *A Harlot's Progress* and his other
progresses as "fashion," the will-o'-the-wisp that the Harlot follows to
her doom. The people around her either share her "idolatry" (her
Jewish merchant keeper) or seek mere personal profit (the clergymen,
physicians, and bawds).

In Paul's case there is also imprisonment (and escape), and in the
extra and final cartoon he is preaching in Athens to the heathen against
their idolatry and for the "god unknown." It is possible to imagine a
projection beyond the last of the Cartoons to the double martyrdom of
Peter and Paul; or to regard ironically their victories as, in the present of
the 1730s in England, defeats. Hogarth was thus to place Hercules, the
emblem of Heroic Virtue, in the position of a poor deserted girl in
London in *Harlot* 1 (pl. 36). Either as an extension to its obvious
conclusion, or as an ironic inversion, we can see the Cartoons of the
Acts of the Apostles as graphic material out of which Hogarth constructed his first progresses.

We might even find it useful to suggest that in a sense Hogarth took
what he needed from the Raphael story for the actions of his contemporary protagonists and then took from Michelangelo the transformational mode of the Sistine ceiling (Eve-Judith-Esther-Mary), adapting it
to his Harlot who appears in the pose of Mary the Mother, Mary
Magdalen, or Eve, and his Rake who appears in the pose of Christ. I do
not want to suggest a direct parallel to the structure of the Sistine
Chapel, but in general the matter of the Michelangelo Old Testament
appears above Hogarth's character, on the walls, in framed paintings,
and the matter of the Raphael New Testament appears below, in what
to Hogarth is a privileged position. There is always an impingement by

the higher on the lower, as there is (he repeatedly shows) by high art on the popular forms of English life and literature.

I am suggesting that in his early engraved series Hogarth was imitating the engraved Lives of the Apostles, of the Virgin also, and of Hercules, in order to show how the highest reach of Renaissance history painting will *now* look and serve an artist. He does this by mixing high and low materials in the manner of *Don Quixote,* or more specifically of his own large *Hudibras* plates of 1726. The highest (even sacred) art-literature is juxtaposed with the lowest, as Old Testament appears on the walls and New in the actions of the characters. The basic model, based on Raphael's Cartoons, is conversion: X (Paul, Harlot, Rake) is in some sense converted, and then tries to carry out acts following from his conversion (i.e. healing or ministering to others), is surrounded by evil idolatrous heathens and avaricious Jews and wins out in various persuasive or extra-legal (or extra-human) ways—or, alternatively, loses out.

The *Harlot's Progress* is, in an important sense, about such a conversion. One can almost hear "Mother" Elizabeth Needham in the first plate say to the young girl from the country, M[ary] Hackabout: "Feed my sheep" or "Here are the keys of the kingdom" or "You are the rock on which I will found. . . ." Hogarth's progress is conceived in the Puritan tradition concerned with such a search for identity or selfhood, with the need to find a new and better self. He inherited these assumptions through his dissenter background; he read Bunyan and Defoe, and would merely have found confirmation in the Raphael Cartoons. Or rather, he would automatically have seen them in these strongly Protestant terms.

But two other consequences follow for his Harlot. She becomes a convert as an attempt at assimilation, in order to "whore after" false gods. Assured in her new self, which is a false self, she wipes out the true image of Christ in her. Conversion is no longer an appropriate transaction; it can be disastrously inappropriate. And then, having been thus converted, she in fact falls among the heathens, the avaricious and idolatrous, and far from trying to win them over as Paul did at Athens, she is herself made a false god in the metaphorical sense that the Jewish merchant (and her other clients) make her one. Being a contemporary Paul or Peter, as also the Hercules from secular myth, she can only be overwhelmed by the people around her who (as in fact happened to poor Mother Needham in the pillory) both worship and destroy her. She is, like Paul, confined in prison, and dies of the disease imparted by one of her worshippers while the heathens go on as if she had never existed. The actual projected end of Peter and Paul is ironically materialized in the final plates of the *Harlot's Progress.*

The Harlot has a child, a little boy who crops up in Plate 5 when she is dying and appears at her wake in Plate 6. In 5 he is taking a chop off the blazing fire while a pot boils over, picking a louse out of his hair while his mother dies, and in 6 he is preoccupied with something in his hands in the midst of the wake for his dead mother. In the first he is simply an emblem and an imitation of the doctors who argue over their respective cures while their patient dies, and in the second a parody of the false mourning that is going on for his mother. He is carrying on independently of the adults but makes a comment on their actions.

At this point I want to suggest that large Biblical concepts and assumptions may have helped to structure Hogarth's work, in precisely the way they did Milton's redaction of Genesis, *Paradise Lost* (see below, p. 101). Milton's plot, from its largest action down to its smallest image, is based on imagery of rise and fall, height and depth, based on the Biblical paradox of rising-falling, the abasement that exalts and the pride that abases: "Whoever shall exalt himself shall be debased; and he that shall humble himself shall be exalted" (Matt. 23.12). In the same way Biblical paradoxes served Hogarth as structures with which to express feelings of his own. Against the Old Testament sense of harlot as one who forsakes the true God to follow idols and false gods, we can set the New Testament sense associated with Christ, who says: "Verily I say unto you, That the publicans and the harlots go into the kingdom of God before you." "For," he adds,

> John came unto you in the way of righteousness, and ye believed him not;
> but the publicans and the harlots believed him: . . .

Similarly with children: the Old Testament children are Isaac, Moses, Ishmael, Joseph, and the first-born of the Egyptians; whereas the protagonist of the New Testament is himself the most put-upon of sons. When his disciples asked him "Who is the greatest in the kingdom of heaven?" he "called a little child unto him" and said, "Verily I say unto you, Except ye be converted, and become as little children, ye shall not enter into the kingdom of heaven." We associate children in the New Testament with Christ's words in Matthew (10.14-16):

> Suffer the little children to come unto me, and forbid them not; for of such
> is the kingdom of God. Verily I say unto you, Whosoever shall not receive
> the kingdom of God as a little child, he shall not enter therein.

Or the version in Luke (9.48):

> Whosoever shall receive this child in my name receiveth me; and who-
> soever shall receive me, receiveth him that sent me; for he that is least
> among you all, the same shall be great.

If the Old Testament is seen from the point of view of Solomon, the New is seen from the point of view of the baby who is brought to him and condemned to the possibility of being cut in two.

For Blake, at the end of the century, the verse is Isaiah 11.6: "The wolf also shall dwell with the lamb, and the leopard lie down with the kid"—which ends, "and a little child shall lead them": the prediction of the Messiah. Hogarth sets the stage for the Blakean child of *Innocence,* as well as the fiery Orc of *America,* in the context of the Biblical paradigms of adult-child relations. The same emphasis could be traced to the great Shakespearean plays in which the children tend to be wise and vulnerable, going to their deaths spiritedly.

In Hogarth's work the harlot, child, and black slave are three of the categories of outcast, of which the Good Samaritan is the most promin-ent New Testament example, himself a type of Sts. Peter and Paul. If "the least of these" is the Biblical category that covers these figures who play such a large part in Hogarth's work, then "provincial" is the immediate, contemporary, sociological denomination: someone from the provinces who has come to the capital London. This provincial is first a fictional character, a figure in an urban landscape, and second a point of view, an aesthetic and also moral perspective adopted by an artist. My example is Hogarth's Harlot who is literally a provincial, whom we first see arriving in the York Wagon from the north of England (pl. 36). She is set off by the even more provincial black boy who is dressed in western clothes and who is a servant in the house of the Jewish merchant, the Harlot's keeper (pl. 37). All three of these figures are, in one sense or another, provincials, outsiders in London society, but they also have in common the (presumably modern) desire to be assimilated, i.e. in the sense of "harlot" as one who follows false gods. The black boy and the Jewish merchant function as different aspects of the Harlot's assimilative desire: one has been forcibly assimilated, the other is trying—by becoming rich, collecting art, and now taking a young gentile woman—to assimilate himself. The Harlot carries aspects of both: she has come to London to be assimilated, but her assimilation is almost from the start beyond her control, as she is picked up by a bawd and sold to a rich keeper, then is exploited by lechers, magistrates, prison warders, physicians, and others, all denizens of the capital city.

But the figures we are dealing with also represent for Hogarth-the-artist a distinctive point of view from which to look at London; or rather the prostitute and the black child do—for the Jewish merchant, perhaps because Hogarth feels he *is* assimilated, has succeeded where these others fail, has become one of the exploiters and is no longer a provincial.[15]

I do not want to suggest that the Bible is Hogarth's source so much as his conditioning for a way of seeing the world around him, a conditioning that was assisted by the sentimental view of harlots and outsiders in *The Spectator*. The earliest versions of the figure I am now examining in Hogarth's work are his dogs, the very English dogs who appear in his early conversation pieces.[16] A typical dog in *The Wollaston Family* (1731, Leicester Art Gallery) is the one figure in an artfully-arranged party who is disrupting the order and—if you like—pomposity. He makes a wrinkle in the rug for one thing, and for another he is standing up with his front paws on a chair, looking like a parody of the dignified host his master. The innocent questioning of a dog confronting a world of imposed human order: this is the point of view assumed by Hogarth, whose own father (like the Harlot) came to London on the York Wagon and met with disasters hardly less melodramatic than hers. Hogarth was, of course, proud of his provincial Englishness, and the quality of provincialism in general seems summed up early on in his association with pugs. A pug appears in his self-portrait, alongside his own face, whose face the dog resembles (1745, London, Tate Gallery). He compares himself physically and iconographically with his dog, as if to say that he and his art are the necessary doggish element in an over-refined society. In *The Strode Family* (Tate) this same pug appears, in the exact pose of the dog in the self-portrait, and he is growling opposite the dog that belongs to the family Hogarth is painting—who by contrast has a bone on his prosperous plate.

The dog is one way Hogarth injects liveliness, comedy, the natural, the instinctual—or himself—into a formally-posed portrait group. The child is another.[17] In *The Cholmondeley Family* (1732, pl. 42) the adults sit or stand around a table looking very formal; but in the next room, cut off from the adults, the two boys are creating havoc, knocking over piles of those precious status-symbols books. In this case the family dog is unnecessary and so is sound asleep. In the drinking-carousing scenes Hogarth also began to paint at this time it is the adults themselves (who apparently commissioned him to paint them this way) who are falling down and knocking over furniture. The child is no longer needed to draw attention and the dog is asleep. This is, of course, because the adults are not now pretending to be other than animals.

The other kind of picture Hogarth was painting in the early 1730s, as he launched his career as a painter, was a group portrait that included well-known public figures and a comic action with a moral twist. In *The Denunciation* (pl. 27) a young woman is swearing that the father of her baby is the respectable citizen opposite (whose jealous wife is berating him). The magistrate and the respectable citizen are recognizable portraits, or at least recognizable types—we might say adult, governing (or ruling-class) types. But what one notices, off to the side, is the pairing of a child and a dog who act as a commentary on the masquerade that is going on between the prospective mother and her lover. The child and dog are not disordering the scene so much as parodying the adult masquerade, revealing something *about* adulthood without losing the animal, natural, instinctual truth they bring to it. They are essentially emblematic, expressing one of Hogarth's basic insights into his own society. They lead up to the courting dogs in *A Rake's Progress* who underline the animal basis of the wedding between the penniless rake and the rich old one-eyed woman, and to the manacled dogs in *Marriage à la Mode* (pl. 44) who show us the true plight of the young couple that is being joined in this contracted marriage by their fathers, the older generation, respectively a merchant and an earl.

But we must return to the sheer disturbance. In *The Christening* (pl. 28) a little girl spills the baptismal water. She does this in a scene of as many adult disruptions as that first scene of *Marriage à la Mode*: the "father"-husband is primping before a mirror while in the rear the mother is being consoled by another man, presumably the infant's real father (as the young husband, the earl's son, in *Marriage à la Mode* is absorbed in a mirror while his bride is being consoled by the family lawyer). Moreover, in *The Christening* the officiating clergyman—acknowledged by contemporaries to be a portrait of the notorious Orator Henley—lets his eyes wander away from his service to the low-cut dress next to him. In this context the child who tips the font is partly the older sibling looking for attention, but she is also drawing our attention to the mess at the bottom of all the hypocrisy and pretense of this "sacrament" of baptism. She is saying by her gesture: Enough of this pretense! and at the same time saying: Look, I can do the same thing you adults are doing. These are the two roles children play for Hogarth, roughly corresponding to the two Biblical senses of harlot.

The conversation picture that sums up what Hogarth has to say shows children performing before their parents in Dryden's play *The Conquest of Mexico* (pl. 43). The children in the audience are watching other children acting the adult roles of Cortez in prison being fought over by the two princesses, both of whom are in love with him: the same disruption of social structures we saw in the earlier pictures. The fathers in the audience are talking soberly among themselves, paying little attention to the performance; the mothers and nurses are addressing themselves to the play, except for the one who is ordering her small charge to pick up the fan she has dropped or knocked on the floor. The small spot of disorder in the audience (now accidental) corresponds to the very large one in the moment of maximum tension that is taking place on the stage between Cortez and the two princesses.

Up on the walls are portraits of the host and hostess of the house, and on the fireplace mantle is a bust of Sir Isaac Newton. Newton had been a kind of patron to the Conduitt family, who are giving the party in their London town house, and the bust is commemorative—it probably actually sat on the mantle in this way. But he is of course more generally the Sir Isaac Newton who formulated all the Laws of Nature, such as the Law of Gravity that has been demonstrated in a small way by the fallen fan the little girl is being commanded by her mother to pick up, and in a more general (a more figurative) way by the natural passion being dramatized on the stage. Whenever a child does something—or a dog—it is associated with a law of nature such as that of Gravity, and there is an attempt to countermand it by an adult presence, a parent. (In the first scene of *Marriage à la Mode* the fathers' attempt to enforce the marriage of their children is compared—in the painting incongruously stretched across the ceiling—to Pharaoh trying to ride in his chariot through the parted waters of the Red Sea.)

There is a spectrum of liveliness running from the dead pictures and bust on the wall down to the detached gloomy fathers, from the maternal and watchful mothers to the children—who are either being natural and instinctual or (in varying degrees) acting out the roles of their parents the adults. In this particular case they are acting the roles of adults whose words and actions are very formalized and ordered indeed, in Dryden's heroic couplets and in the elaborate etiquette of love and honor.

Like the dog, the child also served as a spokesman for Hogarth the artist, representing a fresh, unsophisticated, unjaded view of the world, which was essentially the New Testament's view of the Old, or Christ's of the Pharisees and Levites. These children set the stage for those violent children in Blake's *Songs of Experience*: the baby in "infant Joy" who leaps into the world: "Helpless, naked, piping loud: Like a fiend hid in a cloud. / Struggling in my fathers hands: / Striving against my swadling bands. . . . " Or the little boy who tells his mother he prefers an ale house (so "healthy & pleasant & warm") to the cold, dark church. Except that in Blake's world the child of Experience either subsides to sulk on his mother's breast or, if he rebels up to a certain point, is taken away by the priests and parents and burnt at the stake. A little older, he is the "fiery Orc" who sets off the American and French Revolutions before subsiding into a role as repressive as the one he has overthrown.

This is a later, more purely Biblical, more Romantic version of what Hogarth is doing. Hogarth's models were perhaps more directly the Augustan satirists, but their peripheral figures spoke for precisely the order that Hogarth is criticizing; Hogarth's emphasis comes from a strongly Protestant reading of the Bible, specifically a Latitudinarian one that can be associated with his friends the Hoadlys (as well as their mutual friend Henry Fielding) but which predates these relationships. We do not know his father's religion, except that he was apparently a dissenter. But Hogarth seems to have imbibed an English distrust of the Old Testament Law, which could reach all the way to the Antinomian belief that Christ's crucifixion abolished the Mosaic Law once and for all. One could read in Paul's Epistle to the Galatians that "Christ hath redeemed us from the curse of the law" (3:13) or in Romans, "For Christ is the end of the law for righteousness to every one that believeth" (4:10). Paul even asserts in Galatians (3:19) that it was not God himself but Moses, the mediator, who was responsible for the Law on Sinai. For orthodox believers in the mid-eighteenth century the result was a conviction that mercy was more important than justice, and this seems to have been as far as Hogarth cared to go.

There is another fact, however, that has to be accounted for. Hogarth's disruptive children grow up to become the Harlot and the Rake, who no longer say: Enough of this pretense! but only: Look, I can do the same thing you adults are doing. And so they retain a certain childlike innocence amid the experienced figures of society around them, whom they parody and who exploit and destroy them—literally kill them: figures representing both the obvious evils of society (the bawds and dissolute men of wealth) *and* the so-called pillars of society (the clergymen who ought to be taking care of these young girls from the country, and the magistrates who ought to show a little mercy in their dealings with them).

It is significant that the children are shown acting in a play, on a stage set off from the adult spectators, and that the scene chosen from the play is, precisely as it was in Hogarth's earliest painting of *The Beggar's Opera,* a prison. The children of the Cholmondeley Family were also set off *as if* on a stage, though the "audience" was as oblivious as the fathers in the *Conquest of Mexico* performance. But in one way or another the children are always cut off from the rest of the family, and Hogarth likes to show this by bringing together a stuffy audience, a theatrical presentation, and a prison cell: adult reality looking on (or carrying on in its own adult way) while children act out their version of what the adults are doing in the context of a kind of imprisonment, or—as sometimes happens—try to break out of the prison, as seems to be the case with the Cholmondeley boys.

It is well to remember that in *The Beggar's Opera* the costumed actors were performing a play that incriminated and ridiculed the audience that was watching it. Captain Macheath the highwayman was made (in both the play and in Hogarth's painting) to look and act like the prime minister Sir Robert Walpole, and the prostitutes and thieves inside the play were mimicking as well as playing to an audience identified as other, more respectable and successful thieves and prostitutes. This is emphasized by the inscription on the curtain, roughly translated, "You are looking in a mirror." In Hogarth's final version of the picture this relationship—which is the key one in all of these pictures of families and children and audiences and actors—is pointed up by his having Lavinia Fenton, who is playing the role of Polly Peachum, begging her father to spare her stage-lover Macheath, actually meet the eyes of her real, off-stage lover the Duke of Bolton, who is part of the audience (the attentive part, versus the bored, gossiping ladies on the other side of the stage).

So when Hogarth goes on a year or so later to engrave his first immensely popular series he called *A Harlot's Progress,* he uses the same structure: a young girl from the country arrives in London and immediately is involved in a small scenario with a procuress who is posing as a gentlewoman looking for a housemaid (in precisely the pose of the host in *The Wollaston Family* and other conversation pieces), while the audience consists of very attentive spectators on the right (the bawd's employers, waiting to get their hands on the girl) and a very uninterested spectator on the left (a clergyman reading the address of the Bishop of London, Walpole's agent for ecclesiastical preferment, to whom he will go for professional advancement), very much like the women at *The Beggar's Opera* who pay no attention to the perform-ance, and the fathers who turn away from their children playing *The Conquest of Mexico.* Whether this is an extension of the *Beggar's Opera* structure of a mocking parody of Raphael's St. Paul entering Lystra to be treated as a god is a moot point; the Harlot's arrival in London is, in every sense, over-determined. We are both witnesses in the Raphael sense and spectators in the theatrical sence of *The Beggar's Opera:* the precedents are both Biblical and Shakespearean.

There is no longer any child in this adult performance, but the girl from the country retains the child's innocence as she tries to act out the adult role in which she finds herself. The animal comment is here, however, in the dead goose (Winchester Goose = whore) hanging out of her basket, prefiguring the fate of the girl, and in the next scene (pl. 37) there is a monkey who is drawing attention to what is really happening. Notice it is the Harlot who is creating the disruption or diversion, but she is doing so in order to draw attention away from her larger disruption, her affair with the young man who is slipping out the door. The situation of order she is disrupting is that of her being kept by the Jewish merchant. The monkey, dressed up and in front of the mirror, is a comic, animal comment on both her and her keeper, both of them acting up to roles that are formulated for them by the models of the Old Testament pictures on the wall. The merchant has bought such pictures, and the Harlot imitates him, because London society tells them this is the thing to do if one is to become a London gentleman or lady of fashion. Her performance mocks his as the monkey's mocks them both (like the grim portrait faces and the Sir Isaac Newton bust on the wall of the *Conquest of Mexico* conversation).

The young lover escaping out the door is the only exit offered in the *Harlot's Progress,* where her own living space dwindles to a prison, a shabby garret in which she is wrapped in flannels—the sweating cure for the syphilis she has by now contracted—and ultimately a narrow coffin. Hogarth sees no exit for this child who failed to grow up, to make the adjustment passing from Innocence (associated in her case with the country) into Experience.

It is no accident that Hogarth chose to paint the children performing in the prison scene of Dryden's *Conquest of Mexico,* as he had earlier chosen the prison scene of *The Beggar's Opera.* His children, like Blake's, are locked up in closed rooms and seldom see the light of day; and when they are out-of-doors they are metaphorically imprisoned in the roles of their parents—of lovers, fashionable ladies, soldiers, lawyers, and so on.

I have already mentioned the fact that Hogarth himself as a boy of eleven found himself in the Fleet Prison where his father was confined. This experience is probably reflected in the obsession at the beginning of his career with punishment, prison exteriors, and then with interiors. The interiors begin as a stage set, for the fascination in *The Beggar's Opera* paintings is probably at least partly in the idea of a prison which is not a prison, and the conjunction of imprisonment with playing the roles of people much worse than yourself, who may turn out to be your magistrates and warders (as in the *Beggar's Opera* situation again, with Peachum and Lockit).

The central picture in this regard was *The Committee of the House of*

Commons of 1729 (pl. 26) with the warden who is guiltier than his prisoners. Throughout his career Hogarth's basic assumption seems to have been that society should be seen from the point of view of the prisoners rather than their judges and warders. The comic or sublime histories of his maturity simply allow Hogarth to develop more explicitly what underlies the conversation pictures. They are anti-heroic, sharply critical, with the "truth" expressed by animals of various sorts, instinctual forces that contrast markedly with the authority figures in the old master paintings (usually Old Testament subjects) on the walls who appear to punish or exploit the "children" in the scenes below. It is a world seen still from the point of view of the child, and of the child locked up in prison with his parents. The child itself who survives in the world of the Harlot is the self-contained urchin who ignores his mother's death-throes in order to pick lice out of his hair and a chop off the fire, but appears at her wake, among her other pseudo-mourners, wearing a parody of mourning attire.

In the most explicit of Hogarth's series, *Marriage à la Mode,* the children do not even get the chance to survive their youth. They have become the poor child prostitute dabbing at the syphilitic sore on her mouth and the last heir of the earls of Squanderfield, a girl who carries the signs of her father's disease, and who is significantly brought back together here with the dog—both dog and child now stunted and starved in a world of adulthood (pl. 47). But the child's parents themselves have been presented as other children who were destroyed by their callous parents who arranged and imposed their marriage on them, in a room full of paintings of martyrdoms and murders.

From the late 1730s onward Hogarth's center of interest can be said to shift from the prison to the hospital, first to the charity hospital, St. Bartholomew's where he painted the *Parable of the Good Samaritan* and *Christ at the Pool of Bethesda,* and then to the Foundling Hospital, on both of whose boards of governors he served. Seen from the point of view of these two charity hospitals, the comic-history paintings become in retrospect the stories of castaways, the poor without powerful friends, children without parents—and these become essentially the grown-up protagonists of the earlier paintings, the harlots and rakes who have been turned loose, the man fallen among thieves and ignored by the Levites and Pharisees who is succored by the outcast Good Samaritan only.

In this phase Hogarth painted his most ambitious works for the Foundling Hospital. *The March to Finchley* (1750, Foundling Hospital) is a contemporary history painting showing the English troops who have just—in 1745, five years before he painted them—been ordered to march north to meet the army of the Young Pretender, Charles Edward, on the orders of the Hanoverian king, George II. The poor, confused, chaotic soldiers are framed between signs of their ultimate parents Adam and Eve, and that earlier roistering father of his people, Charles II, whose head is the sign for a bawdy-house. They are torn between the duty to king-country-parents and the free and easy life of the loose attachments symbolized by the brothel. The subject of the picture is homelessness, every soldier a lost foundling, starting with the baby chicks who have lost their hen and the sad parody of a Good Samaritan group. This, I suspect, is Hogarth's definitive image of the role of the innocent in English society of the mid-eighteenth century.

I must also say a few words about another sort of child, less prominent in Hogarth's pictures but no less interesting in his way. This is the black boy—a negro servant or, as must often have been the case, a slave (another figure explored by Blake in *Innocence and Experience*). Every time a black boy appears he is both peripheral and subversive, a sharp comment on the grown-up English whites. He was standing in the background of *The Wollaston Family*, one of the possessions the host was shown among, but with a sharp twinkle in his eyes; and in the penultimate version of *The Beggar's Opera* (Mellon Collection, National Gallery, Washington) he was the one figure intently watching the play, or rather Lavinia Fenton playing Polly Peachum. In *Captain Graham in his Cabin* (National Maritime Museum, Greenwich) the black cabin boy is placed parallel to the Hogarth pug, who is trying on one of the men's wigs.

In the second plate of *A Harlot's Progress* then, the parallel between the Harlot and the black servant and the monkey, both dressed up by others, emphasized the aspect of determinism—that she really had no choice in that inn yard, alone against the forces of active evil and of indifference. She is as passive a victim as the black from Africa who has been forced into this role through no will of his own.

In Plate 4 (pl. 39 in this book) the black woman shown beating hemp alongside the harlot in Bridewell Prison exposes the reality under the costumes, the affectations, and the social-climbing. The Harlot is now in the hands of society, of her governors, and so is for the first and only time doing (made to do) useful and productive work—in fact she is forced to produce rope that will be used either by English trading ships or by the hangman. "Productive" is made metaphoric by the fact that she is now pregnant, literally about to produce something. The negress (who may also be pregnant) is there to indicate the reality of the Harlot's situation as now simply another form of property of the sort she became in Plate 2.

Two blacks appear in *Marriage à la Mode* 4 (pl. 45), one actively satirizing the married couple, or rather the husband Lord Squanderfield who has by this time been cuckolded by the lawyer who is enjoying the countess' company at her levée. The second black is in the same conventional pose as the boy in *A Harlot's Progress*: he is serving coffee, but he is also looking and laughing at the ultimate in civilized Europeans, the castrato soprano, who is a portrait of one of the famous castrati of the day over whom society women swooned and impresarios fought.[18] The black face and the sharp eyes and smile directed at the castrato sum up the theme of savagery and civilization, which is at the bottom of the story of parents who destroy their children in order to control their estates. It is hard to think of a better example (at least from the English/Hogarthian perspective) of apparent civilization concealing savagery than the child who is emasculated in order to perfect his singing voice for the delectation of his elders, and this is set off by the *supposed* savage, the African black who serves these civilized people in a context of art-collecting, marriage contracts, and coronets, the forms which conceal the savagery of the private lives of earl and countess, of parents and children, which will erupt in murder, execution by hanging, suicide, and extinction of the family line.

In both *A Harlot's Progress* and *Marriage à la Mode*, the black becomes, in the context of the series and the stories of the white people, an emblem of someone else's personal property—the Harlot of her keeper, later of any man who can pay her fee (her name is Hackabout) and of the law that tries to make her into a productive citizen; and of the children who are the chattels of their respective parents. I suspect that all of these find their associations with Hogarth himself as someone who does not enjoy "the fruits of his own labor" (the phrase used about blacks in eighteenth-century anti-slave trade writings), which of course also sums up Hogarth's sentiments about the artist's (and his own) exploitation by print-dealers, connoisseurs, and collectors.

In an oil sketch in the Ashmolean Museum that is related both to the second of the *Rake's Progress* pictures and to the fourth of *Marriage à la Mode,* there is a black boy holding up for display a painting of Jupiter's eagle carrying away Ganymede (as the mocking boy points to Actaeon's horns in the collection of art objects the countess and her lover have brought back from an auction—and the castrato soprano sits beneath the same painting of Jupiter and Ganymede). There is probably a pun intended in the juxtaposition of the black boy and the "dark master" painting (so-called) of the sort Hogarth ridiculed, but the main point of the tableau is the contrast of art (or high culture) and savagery (or nature), the dangerously close relationship between the two in the world of London, and the idea that art itself is merely a commodity like the black boy who holds it up.

The black boy then is a metaphor, an emphasizing of a quality less apparent in the white protagonist, and he is also an indication of the natural that is being suppressed or repressed by the sophisticated whites. In *Noon,* the second of the *Four Times of the Day* (1738), there is a black man, in the role of Mars to a young white Venus, representing masculinity and sexual vigor, one of the most common attributes of the black in the eighteenth century, being contrasted with the effeminate Frenchmen who are standing on the other side of the pavement—in effect an image of strong disorder opposed to effete order—related to the effect of the black looking across the room at the castrato soprano or the black holding a painting of Ganymede.

These children or dogs or black slaves (or apprentices or harlots) are safe, relatively harmless (because xenophobic English) images with which to express a critique of society in the mid-eighteenth century. They also support, however, the assumption of a Hogarthian "English" art as a virile, energetic outsider commenting on effete continental art and culture. Every story Hogarth tells, every parable of art he unfolds, is seen from the point of view of the *other* person in the story—the outsider, the peripheral, sub-culture figure. Thus when he goes to the Bible for a text, he chooses the Parable of the Good Samaritan, and when he alludes in *Industry and Idleness* (1747) to the Parable of the Talents he takes the point of view not of the master but of the servant; in the Judgment of Solomon, not of Solomon the judge but of the child who is allowed to be cut in half by his callous elders—for in Hogarth's sobering version the true mother never steps forward to save her child. In *his* version of myth or history or the Bible, this is always what happens, as in his rendering of *Moses brought to Pharaoh's Daughter* (pl. 48), another of the paintings made for the Foundling Hospital. It is a black woman there who is whispering the truth about the relationship of Moses to his two "mothers" at one edge of the scene.

Before turning to those biblical paintings, we should draw some conclusions from the material of this chapter. For one thing, it seems pretty clear that in the first plate of *A Harlot's Progress* Hogarth is emphasizing the Harlot's lack of choice (in the face of urgings from the evil and abandonment by "friends"), and that the real progression in Hogarth's work is from the parody of a Choice of Hercules to that of a Judgment of Solomon, in which the emphasis has decidedly shifted to the two parents and the judgment of an external society that condemns the child to dismemberment because there is no merciful parent to interfere. But I shall return to that important transition in the next section.

Looking back at the Harlot as she assumes the gestures of—or finds herself in a reenactment of—the Virgin Mary in the Visitation and the Annunciation (as Hudibras sees himself in the midst of a Carracci *Procession of Bacchus and Ariadne),* we may wish to conclude that the juxtaposition tells us that the Harlot is only a vessel, a passive instrument of some superior will—a "convert" in the sense of Saul-Paul, struck down on the road to Damascus. Mary is sent to Elizabeth to find out about God's will and she is told by the angel that she is pregnant (as indeed the Harlot proves to be also). But the angel is of course turned into a constable come to arrest the Harlot, and in the final plate she has become little more than a table for the twelve, quite passive in this scene which shows better than any other how Hogarthian satire operates: the dead body of the child-innocent is surrounded by the conversation picture of the social types who have used her and put her there.

I used to think that Hogarth contrasted the Old Testament with its harsh patriarchal judgments, its bloody punishments, its total commitment to Law, summed up in Plate 3 (pl. 38) in the sacrifice of Isaac by his father Abraham, with New Testament mercy. But now I wonder whether the New Testament is not also subverted, though less directly, as it is enacted in the scene itself instead of in the artists' representations of Biblical—Old Testament—scenes hanging above on the walls.

In Plate 2 (pl. 37) there was a direct relationship between the pictures on the wall and the actions of the people beneath them—almost as if the Harlot, her keeper, and her new lover had stepped out of the painting of Uzzah, the Ark of the Covenant, and the Levite Hogarth shows stabbing Uzzah in the back for his temerity in trying to steady the Ark, the sacred object (as her Jewish keeper violates the Law by touching her, a gentile girl). The paintings are reified in—are imposed upon, as formal structures—the figures in the room below. They are essentially self-imposed. But the third scene (pl. 38) becomes a further stage in which *Abraham sacrificing Isaac,* the Old Testament picture on the wall—now part of the Harlot's own collection in the shabby circumstances to which she has been reduced by her jealous keeper, who Shylock-like following the letter of the Law has cast her into outer darkness—is realized beneath it in a *New* Testament scene, a reverse Annunciation. To our horror we may begin to suspect that the same God who instructed Abraham to sacrifice Isaac also gave Mary her child and ordered the bloody consequences of that pregnancy. Or that mercy is as much a self-induced illusion as its opposite, Old Testament eye-for-an-eye justice.

In fact, if we visualize the six plates of *A Harlot's Progress* (pls.

36-41), hung on a wall as I presume they were in the eighteenth century (given the cramped wall space of the people most likely to own the prints and the habit of hanging pictures two or three deep) we will see the first three along one row and the last three below them in a second row. This is the way *Marriage à la Mode* has been hung in the National Gallery as far back as I can remember, and still was in 1980. We will then notice that there are visual-spatial relations set up between 1 and 4 and between 3 and 6, as well as between 1 and 3 and 4 and 6. These are the structuring pictures in terms of the hanging I am envisioning. Thus we have two New Testament scenes involving Mary related to two in which Mary is enacting or involved in the story of Christ's Passion. In 4, we now notice, she is in a pose that has nothing to do with her own story, at least as reproduced in Lives of the Virgin. Rather she is in the composition of a Mocking of Christ, with her suffering head flanked by the figures of a mocking woman (mocking her fashionable clothes, still worn in prison) and a warder who is threatening to flagellate her. In the sixth plate, as I have said, she is the passive element in a Last Supper. Plate 2 then introduces the Old Testament on its walls, and 3 joins the Old Testament picture on the wall with the New Testament scene taking place beneath.

Hogarth has set no order in the sequence of echoes; in fact each pair is reversed temporally. I presume this is because he does not want to suggest sequence so much as a set of analogies in which the Harlot is related to Mary as passive, chosen vessel and to the Christ of the Passion as God's chosen vessel for man's redemption. (What this does to Plate 5 I am not sure, unless there is a suggestion of the dividing of Christ's garments in the woman rifling the Harlot's trunk, and the two physicians are gambling at the foot of the cross.)

We should not forget the subscription ticket (pl. 52), that piece of evidence for all the analogies I am suggesting—the document which makes clear Hogarth's programmatic intention in the series as a whole. For here we see the same relationship, specified in Plates 5 and 6, between mother and child, and between both of these and the censor's arm. The latter appears in the putto who restrains the faun, who is presumably following Venus' injunction to Aeneas quoted on the wall ("Search out your ancient mother"), and in the other putti who are bowdlerizing Nature. In this sense the ticket is about the straightjacketing of nature, the transforming of it according to higher Rules of Order, and how this is visited on the child as well as on the mother. The ticket may help to explain why the Harlot is by analogy both mother and son, vessel and victim, as well as why (by an ironic inversion) the solemn clergyman in Plate 6 is the one who actually gets his hand under Nature's dress.

Hogarth is expressing a very basic Christian way of reading and interpreting, learned perhaps from a careful scrutiny of Biblical illustrations (such as the Sistine ceiling). There he would have seen identity as a transformational structure: the sinless Virgin, the mother of God, related not ony to the other Mary, Mary Magdalen, but to the sinful Eve, daughter of God (and of the virgin as mediator). The ordinary reference "Mary second Eve" (as in *Paradise Lost,* X, 183) makes it reasonable that he would have presented the girl from the country faced by temptation in the first plate of *A Harlot's Progress* as faced by the choice connected with Eve and in the pose of Mary.

While it is possible, in the light of Shaftesbury's advice to the painter, to see Plate 1 of *A Harlot's Progress* as a Choice of Hercules parodied— and such a parody as Milton's infernal parody of the Holy Trinity in Satan, Sin, and Death—it is also possible to imagine Hogarth going to Book IX of *Paradise Lost* with his classical paradigm of Hercules at the Crossroads. If he did so, he would have noticed the difference. The central temptation is of a woman, not a man, and her temptation is by a fair-seeming serpent who employs the "persuasive words, impregn'd with Reason" that Shaftesbury tells us Virtue uses to persuade Hercules of the correct choice. Vice lies on the ground languorous and passive, a sensuous alternative of lazy delights. Milton, as critics before Blake and down to William Empson in our own time have noticed, affords Eve no alternative voice, only the persuasive words of Satan. God is elsewhere, indeed having already (arguably) made the choice for her, and the angel seems to have turned his back much as the clergyman does in the first plate of *A Harlot's Progress.*

Eve is the prototype of Hogarth's Harlot, except that Hogarth has first given her the initiative—to leave home and travel to London—and then taken it away from her. God has disappeared. Not only the absence of the clergyman and the "loving cousin in Thames Street" (who has not met her) but any form of divine protection is notably absent from all of Hogarth's plates. In Hogarth's own terms, the Harlot is once again the Solomonic baby whose real mother is uninterested and absent and whose false one ("Mother Needham") is urging her to be her "daughter." The effect is the same: whether a Solomon's judgment or a Milton temptation of Eve, the sexually-tempted human is condemned to fall and die. Then when it is time for Adam's choice, he has only the sensual appeal of Vice and the shadow of the angel who does not argue or intervene: "Against his better knowledge, not deceiv'd, / But fondly overcome with Female charm," he falls, and this is followd by: "Carnal desire inflaming, hee on Eve / Began to cast lascivious Eyes," and the fall is followed by sexual indulgence of a fallen sort. Hogarth's Rake stands between a frail, impregnated version of Eve whom he is paying off and the stern image of his father the miser (pl. 35). As the subsequent plates show, he chooses for Eve and appetite—"an eager appetite, rais'd by the smell / So savoury of that Fruit" (740-41).

From the Bible, seen through sermons, Hogarth took the conceptual pattern of Charity, which included Pharisees and Levites as well as a man fallen among thieves and a Good Samaritan. It was a pattern that contained its own possibility of subversion or shifting emphasis from charity to respectability in a rigidly-interpreted Law. The great conceptual pattern to be found in *Paradise Lost* was choice—a situation which requires alternatives, parallel and antithesis, and a right answer. But what must have been apparent to someone approaching *Paradise Lost* from Prodicus and Shaftesbury was that the chooser really has no choice; choice is made the great moral value of the Fortunate Fall, and yet choice was removed from the Fall itself. The direction is open to Blake's "Poison Tree" where the tempter and the guardian—the serpent Satan and God—have become one. God is not simply absent but has become the tempter himself.

It must have been obvious to a Hogarth or a Blake how these structures could be used to support official ideology and also how to undermine it—by selecting those structures which were part of the ideology and those which were counter to it.

I realize that I am now summoning up a Hogarth who sounds suspiciously like William Blake. I am suggesting that the New Testament scenes may be typologically the fulfilment of the Old Testament pictures on the walls, related as they were on medieval altarpieces, and that Hogarth's conclusion is the Blakean one that the ruling class—the paternal figure—in both cases is equally unmerciful. This may be only another irony, an under-text that Hogarth floats and does not altogether repudiate. But the longer I look at Hogarth's prints and paintings the more I see of such subversive analogizing—a movement away from Augustan distinctions toward undifferentiation, from either-or contrasts to both-and equations. And in this respect I find him expressing what I have called the Shakespearean quality of English literature and the imagination.

We have seen an attitude toward high culture—high art and high literature—that covers much and leaves little for an artist himself to build upon. What is left are Shakespeare, the English artist of "nature," and the New Testament—which themselves, one suspects, taper off for

Hogarth into popular and sub-culture art forms. The Old Testament and other forms of high art—which would include the French classics—are used by Hogarth to make a statement about "the least of these." And by doing so, I rather suspect he was thinking along the line of his subscription ticket for *A Harlot's Progress,* where he says we must go back to our "ancient mother," represent the story of a harlot not a king or queen, and recover a lost purity. He was suggesting that the function of Christian art, lost (he may have believed) in the papal hegemony that was eventually challenged by Protestantism, had been to celebrate "the least of these," the harlots, children, and publicans. This function, concealed under the function of art to celebrate in baroque images of power the kings and generals and respectable people, he was hoping to recover.

High art or culture in this context means what is sometimes called ideology or superstructure. Hogarth will have none of this and seeks to paint from the outsider's point of view—that of the non-patron, the popular or provincial or child. In the next section I shall show how he functions in a reading of a high culture art form, history painting, which was painted for a ruling class bastion of ideology, Lincoln's Inn, of a sublime document, the New Testament.

Paul before Felix: Artist and Patron

Because we have begun chronologically, we have so far only dealt with the effect of Bible illustration on Hogarth's original work. We turn now to his own illustration of the Bible, which for him could not be undertaken until he had established his reputation as a "comic-history painter." His first attempt immediately followed the success of his second "comic history," *A Rake's Progress.* In the late 1730s, about the time he was also painting *The Tempest,* he painted two huge panels for the staircase at St. Bartholomew's Hospital of *The Good Samaritan* and *The Pool of Bethesda,* the secular and divine versions of Charity in action. These were, predictably, New Testament subjects illustrating contemporary paradigms, in particular that of Charity—appropriate to a charity hospital such as St. Bartholomew's. I have already written in detail on these paintings,[19] and it is sufficient to mention that the positive subject of the Good Samaritan's charity invokes also the negative subject of the Pharisees' pursuance of the letter of the Law rather than the spirit; so that a negative evocation of the Old Testament remains implicit in these paintings, connecting the subject of religion with Hogarth's other subject of aesthetics, in which the Law equalled the Rules imposed by art critics.

A decade later, at a time when he was turning from paintings in oil to pure engravings (with preparatory sketches) aimed at a popular audience, and in a remarkable way seeing from the popular point of view,[20] Hogarth executed two Biblical subjects, one Old Testament and one New, which summed up the direction his interpretation of the Bible was taking. One was a volunteered commission, for the Foundling Hospital, a children's equivalent of the charity hospital where he had painted the Good Samaritan, and so calling for the same sort of painting; the other was a commission by the Benchers of Lincoln's Inn to paint a large history either for the chapel or the Great Hall, to be seen by the lawyers and judges who worshipped or ate there.

For the Foundling Hospital he painted in 1746 *Moses brought to Pharaoh's Daughter* (pl. 48), the story of a foundling who is caught between his two mothers—a child flanked by two women. The inscription on the engraving reads: "And the child grew, and she brought him unto Pharaoh's daughter, and he became her son. And she called his name Moses" (Exodus 2.10). The moment of adoption is depicted: Moses is now beyond the stage of nursing, his true mother is being paid off, and he is being named and claimed by the princess as *her* son. But Hogarth represents it in terms of two conflicting loyalties, a child trying to make a choice, and a spatial separation between him and the new mother. But we, the viewers, know this is not a Choice of Hercules; it is presented as a Judgment of Solomon, with the confused child between the two mothers and the harsh Old Testament God presiding instead of the wise Solomon. The child is not choosing between two women—choice takes place only in the most profoundly ironic sense; rather two women are fighting for the child, pulling him apart in a literal way that is reflected in his pained expression.

It is a striking and characteristic picture given its juxtaposition in the board room of the Foundling Hospital with Hayman's unproblematic, happy group next to it of Moses found in the bullrushes by Pharaoh's daughter. (Both paintings, with two others by Joseph Highmore and James Wills, were donated in a package proposed and promoted by Hogarth.) Both Pharaoh's daughter and Moses' real mother, in Hayman's painting, are happy-looking, as is baby Moses. Whereas Hogarth has chosen the moment when the child, being brought up by his real mother, is turned over to his adoptive mother, Pharaoh's daughter, as money is passed to his mother and servants gossip behind the princess' back. The gap between Moses and Pharaoh's daughter is an insurmountable and formally significant cleavage, as contrasted with the meaningless gap of vague wilderness between Hagar and the angel and Ishmael in Highmore's contribution across the council chamber.

Hogarth's picture poses problems and vexes the viewer; perhaps makes him feel sympathy for the child, who is being oppressed by the adult world in a way reminiscent of the younger generation in *Marriage à la Mode* of the year before.

Moses brought to Pharaoh's Daughter connects, as did *The Good Samaritan* and *A Rake's Progress,* with the "comic history" Hogarth had just completed. The fifth plate of *Marriage à la Mode* (pl. 46) is, for one thing, the most clearly theatrical of the series, the flattest and most stagelike, and brings together the three protagonists in deadly combat. The adulterous countess has been caught with her lover, and her husband the earl has fought a duel with him and been stabbed. I have elsewhere discussed this scene as a mock Deposition, with the countess in the position of Mary Magdalen and her husband, propped so curiously and sagging unrealistically, of a Christ being lowered from the cross.[21] But the element of the painting that serves, I believe, as emblem or paradigm for the whole five plates is the tapestry on the back wall—once again, an Old Testament subject (pl. 46a).

It is appropriate that this scene should carry the emblematic center of the series, for it also exposes the truth that has been hitherto in various ways plastered over by the protagonists and their friends and relatives. Here the master of the bagnio literally throws open the door and casts light on the scene. In this context of dramatic disclosure, the tapestry shows Solomon ordering that the baby claimed by the two mothers be cut in half. Lawrence Gowing has written: "the comically crude tapestry illustrates The Judgment of Solomon, as if to confirm the ludicrous fact that the imminence of death is needed to expose the truer love."[22] That any true love exists among the characters of *Marriage à la Mode,* not to mention two cases of it, would require a great leap of the imagination. The Solomon tapestry depicts the painting's ideal metaphor: only when Solomon makes the theatrical gesture of calling for the baby to be divided is true emotion to be distinguished from hypocrisy.

The marriage, however, is cloven even if the baby was not. In short, there is no Solomon present. The bloodied sword in the foreground divides the wishbone-shaped shadow of the fire tongs, standing for the marriage. In the last scene the child is materialized, sickly and claimed by neither parent nor relative: her mother is dead, self-poisoned, and the remaining parent figure chooses instead a ring from his daughter's finger.

This judgment is a magistrate's "choice," between a true and a false mother, as Hercules' choice was between Virtue and Vice. But it is a judgment rather than a choice which affects the chooser-judge. And if one sees it from the point of view of the central figure—the child—then it becomes a passive situation, a non-choice of the sort Hogarth was getting into in the late 1740s, as in *Moses* he sees the story askew from the point of view of the child who is going to be pulled apart by his two competing mothers.

The tapestry in *Marriage à la Mode* 5 is thus an emblem for the whole series in that two competing parents are destroying a child: the choice is on the part of the parent (the mother in the story), the one who will give up the child rather than see it halved, and is therefore the true mother. But Hogarth's series is about two false parents who are willing to halve the child, as the girl's father is still doing in the last scene. In 5 then the emblem applies not only in a general way to the fathers but more directly to the countess' Solomonic judgment that kills both of the men. Although in appearance one is alive, one dead, in fact both are doomed and by the next plate dead. The countess is shown with the dead one, thinking she has the live one safe, which in fact Justice (Solomon, or the Law) is going to cut off as well: the message—consonant with the emblem of the Judgment of Solomon as appropriate for the whole series—is that authority, justly or unjustly, will destroy those under its power. Solomon is interpreted as the Old Testament judge, not as Wisdom; he is another version of, and parallel to, the murderous images of the paintings in the first scene of *Marriage à la Mode*.

The Judgment of Solomon, we have seen, is a motif which dominates the greatest of all English decorative schemes, Ruben's ceiling of the Banqueting House. Rubens' version offers, among other things, an authority for omitting the body of the other, the dead child (cf. Poussin's and Raphael's versions). When Hogarth uses the Judgment of Solomon, consciously replacing the Judgment of Hercules with its overtones of active choice, it is the harsh Old Testament judgment that he invokes, not the wisdom. Hogarth does not elide the fact that the two women who appear before Solomon were prostitutes. He uses the Judgment of Solomon as a tapestry decorating the wall of a bagnio-brothel, and again he shows Moses' true mother taking money. We realize we are witnessing another version of the girl from the country, the Harlot, caught between the venal clergyman and the false allure (the beauty patches—too many of them, concealing venereal sores) of the bawd and her employers. We are seeing the structure Hogarth uses overtly in his satires and covertly in his conversation pictures and history paintings. It is, in other words, a satiric structure and also a structure with which Hogarth personally orders experience for himself.

When he set to work on the painting for Lincoln's Inn, Hogarth chose another biblical scene, as appropriate to the lawyers as *Moses* was to the occupants of the Foundling Hospital. He chose to illustrate the story of St. Paul pleading his case before the Roman governor Felix in Acts 24 (pl. 49). I am sure that one reason he chose this text was that it allowed him to paint a subject which was an extension beyond the range (beyond the last episode) of the sequence of Raphael's Cartoons. It was as if he were adding a cartoon to Raphael's series. To do this he based his composition on *Paul and the Proconsul* (pl. 32), with Paul himself taken from *Paul preaching at Athens* (pl. 33). It was a subject about the conversion of a Roman governor who was to judge between Paul and Elymas the magician. Paul proved himself by blinding Elymas, by this miracle converting both Elymas and the proconsul.

The story Hogarth chose shared certain elements with the stories he had chosen in the late 1730s when he painted his first biblical subjects in St. Bartholomew's Hospital. One panel told the story of the Samaritan who succored the wounded man ignored by the priests for whom he was, by the Law, unclean. Just outside the frame of the other panel were the priests and Pharisees closing in on the lame man Jesus has cured and accusing him of carrying his mat on the Sabbath and then accusing Jesus himself of having performed a miracle on the Sabbath—a violation of the letter of the Law on which Hogarth was indirectly commenting.

The story in Acts begins when Paul is mobbed by the Jews for ignoring their laws and saved by the Roman soldiers who, learning that he is a Roman citizen, send him to Caesarea to be judged by the governor Felix. There he is proscribed by "an advocate named Tertullus," representing the High Priest and the Jewish elders, who says, "For we have found this man a pestilent fellow, and a mover of sedition among all the Jews throughout the world, and a ringleader of the sect of the Nazarenes: Who also hath gone about to profane the temple: whom we took, and would have judged according to our law" (24.5-6). Paul responds with a brief of his own, sober and reasonable, and Felix puts off a decision until the commanding officer from Jerusalem can report to him.

At this point we reach the scene Hogarth has actually illustrated, which he cites in the epigraph he attached to the engraving he published of his painting:

> And after certain days, when Felix came with his wife Drusilla, which was a Jewess, he sent for Paul, and heard him concerning the faith in Christ. *And as he reasoned of righteousness, temperance, and judgment to come, Felix trembled,* and answered, Go thy way for this time; when I have a convenient season, I will call for thee. [24.24-26; the passage quoted by Hogarth is italicized]

The first liberty that Hogarth has taken with his text is to introduce into this private meeting of Paul, Felix, and Drusilla the figure of Tertullus and the trappings of the courtroom. In this way he makes a picture that, rather than illustrating the Biblical text, is about a bad lawyer, Tertullus, and a bad judge, Felix, who can only be moved—terrified, made to "tremble"—by extra-legal force, by so to speak the name of Paul's God.

Let us begin with the appropriateness of Hogarth's graphic model, Raphael's Cartoon, *Paul and the Proconsul*, which also shows a person with his own spiritual authority facing a Caesar—a person of official, conventional authority—and turning the tables on him. Hogarth's use of this model certainly showed the way, through his engravings of the painting (though the painting itself was on public view), for the artists who worked for Boydell. He offers a structure that reappears in Benjamin West's *Ophelia before Claudius and Gertrude* and an illustration for *Measure for Measure* in which Angelo, the official but false judge is on the dais, and he is the guilty party vis-à-vis Claudio and Isabella the accused but innocent parties, as well as vis-à-vis the Duke who is in reality judging *him*.

But we should recall that Poussin's version of Raphael's *Paul and the Proconsul* cartoon was in fact a Judgment of Solomon (Louvre), with the two children, the one live and the other dead, flanking Solomon as Tertullus and Paul flank Felix. Hogarth's painting is also a parody Judgment of Solomon, very unlike the Rubensian iconography of the Banqueting Hall. *Paul before Felix* is another subject that should be a Choice of Hercules but is in fact a Judgment of Solomon, or a magistrate's judgment with wise Solomon absent.

Bishop Hoadly's sermon, "St. Paul's Discourse to Felix, preached before the King, February 15, 1729/30," is a second text Hogarth can be said to have illustrated in his painting. The sermon is about a law that is beyond the law: "[This scene] gives a very uncommon Appearance; the *Prisoner*, undaunted and unconcerned at his own Danger; the *Governour*, terrified and *trembling*, as is his *Prisoner* had been his *Judge*; and were now pronouncing a Sentence of Condemnation upon him."[23] Though Hoadly and Hogarth were good friends, it is not necessary that Hogarth recollected the sermon, for in 1741 Samuel Richardson (who had already urged Hogarth to do a series on apprentices and to illustrate *Pamela*) published his sequel to *Pamela*, *Pamela in High Life*, in which he introduced a scene modeled on Hoadly's interpretation of Paul and Felix. Pamela learns that Mr. B., now her husband, has begun to show interest in a countess, with whom he has taken to talking about the virtues of polygamy. Her suspicions thoroughly aroused, she invites him into her closet, where she has arranged chairs as in a courtroom, and sets herself up as the accused and him as the judge and accuser, saying:

> methinks I stand here as Paul did before Felix; and, like that poor prisoner, if I, sir, reason of *righteousness, temperance,* and *judgment to come,* even to make you, as the great Felix did, tremble, don't put me off *to another day, to a more convenient season,* as that governor did Paul; for you must bear patiently with all I have to say.[24]

Pamela's innocence and Mr. B.'s guilt turn the tables between judge and accused in precisely the way Hoadly interpreted the text. This turning of the tables, the delay in judgment by Felix, and the general theme of judgment, magistrate's court, and lawyers as corrupt were embodied in Hogarth's version of the story. But the passage and the painting illustrating it were a little more subversive than we have so far suggested, as we can see by returning to the context of Richardson's passage—Mr. B.'s adultery—and looking ahead to Laurence Sterne's sermon "Felix's Behaviour towards Paul Examined" (published in 1766), which could have been written with Hogarth's picture in mind— or, for that matter, by Hogarth himself.

Sterne zeroes in first on verse 26, the verse following the one Hogarth quotes: "He hoped also that money should have been given him of Paul, that he might loose him" (or, in the words of the New English Bible, "At the same time he had hopes of a bribe from Paul; and for this reason he sent for him very often and talked with him").[25] As Sterne notes, " 'tis AVARICE, and that too, in the most fatal place for the prisoner it could have taken possession of,—'tis in the heart of the man who judges him." It is not, judging by Hogarth's practice elsewhere, odd that he prints as epigraph a text that is in itself innocent, saying only that Paul's talk of God terrified Felix, but is immediately followed by a verse about the judge and lawyer's traditional love of money, their judicial corruption.

The epigraph is preceded, however, by an even more interesting verse, the one about Felix's "wife Drusilla, who was a Jewess." Sterne, with the same information Hogarth would have had—and Richardson obviously had when he composed his scene in *Pamela in High Life*— draws attention to what *else* we know about Drusilla:

> for as Josephus tells us, she had left the Jew her husband, and without any pretence in their law to justify a divorce, had given herself up without ceremony to Felix; for which course, tho' she is here called his wife, she was in reason and justice the wife of another man,—and consequently lived in an open state of adultery.[p. 107]

93

When in this light we read the verse Hogarth quotes, we see that it is not Paul's invocation of the deity but specifically his turning "to questions of morals, self-control, and the coming judgment" that causes Felix to become alarmed and exclaim, "That will do for the present; when I find it convenient I will send for you again." In other words, Paul is accusing the judge himself, turning the tables on him in precisely the way Pamela does with Mr. B., by saying in effect: Who are *you* an adulterer to accuse me?

This may also explain the last verse (27) in which we are told that Felix left Paul in custody "willing to show the Jews a pleasure" (or "wishing to curry favour with the Jews")—bad enough for a person sitting in judgment, but even worse when we realize it is to save the feelings of a particular Jew, his mistress Drusilla. Sterne goes on:

> it was scarce possible to frame his discourse so. . . . but that either her interest or her love must have taken offence: and tho' we do not read, like Felix, that she trembled at the account, 'tis yet natural to imagine she was affected with other passions, of which the apostle might feel the effects— and 'twas well he suffered no more, if two such violent enemies as lust and avarice were combined against him.

Let me note one other fact to which attention was drawn in the eighteenth century, though quite innocently, by John Ireland, the Hogarth annotator and collector. He claimed that the reason Hogarth dropped Drusilla from the final engraved version of the painting (by Luke Sullivan) was that it was "thought that *St. Paul's* hand was rather improperly placed" in relation to Drusilla's body.[26] Of course, Hogarth did this—and retained it in the painting—quite on purpose, letting Paul indicate by his hand (and a characteristically Hogarthian trick of perspective) where the source of Felix's sin in fact lay. Having fixed this detail in the painting, and in the first engraved version (engraved by himself), he could drop it in the second as another case of the chaste classicizing he was assuming as the direction in which such history painting should be taken. In the same way he also dropped the satyr who was lifting Nature's dress from the subscription ticket, which was again *Boys Peeping at Nature.* The burlesque ticket was a scatological version with Felix's fear, in this case leaving a physical manifestation (pls. 52, 53).

We know Hogarth made the painting so large that it would not fit in the chapel, where the benchers intended to hang it, and so it had to go in the Old Hall. The minutes of 12 December 1747 show that the Benchers resolved that it would "be placed against the wall at the west end of the Chapel, according to the subject proposed by Mr. Hogarth." But when the painting was finished a year later it was in fact hung, apparently because of its size, in the Hall above the dais. We do not know whether Hogarth purposely made it too large for the Chapel, but the result was that it did hang where it carried the maximum ironic impact.[27]

The Old Hall, completed the year Columbus discovered America, was the oldest by half a century of the surviving halls of the Inns of Court and Chancery. The dais at the end was originally high table, and the hall was a dining room. From 1737 on, however, it was used more or less continually for sittings of the Court of Chancery, and so the Lord Chancellor sat on the dais under Hogarth's picture. The hall was also still used for dinner by the benchers and students, who would have in the eighteenth century eaten at 4:30. According to the view drawn by Pugin and Rowlandson (published by Ackerman), the hall was divided in half with fixed tables for counsel in the upper half of the hall: Hogarth's picture can be glimpsed above the dais and the heads of the presiding magistrates. The Lord Chancellor was protected from seeing the painting by an awning-like projection over his head; but it was painfully visible to the audience of counsels and others.

Although the official explanation would have been that the picture placed the lawyers in a divine perspective, showing their subservience to a greater power of judgment, this is to ignore the details and the context; it is to see the picture from the point of view of Felix, or of the judges and lawyers, the benchers of Lincoln's Inn, the patrons who commissioned it. I am sure this was the selective vision employed by the legal profession. I have read no commentary on the painting that would suggest otherwise. In general this is the way commissioned history paintings operated. Rubens painted his ceiling of the Whitehall Banqueting House from the point of view of the king who sat at the head of the hall, and of the king his father who figured in a series of fiat lux and apotheosis gestures above him. Every detail here indicated the wise scholar king as Solomon, and when James is shown as Solomon offering his ironic judgment on the two women who both claim the same child, Rubens gives it to us straight: we dutifully suppress the detail that the two women (here England and Scotland) were prostitutes.

Hogarth has in fact painted his *Paul before Felix* from the point of view of the accused—in this case the condemned. We read the painting as Paul's story, with Felix in the Raphaelesque position of the converted proconsul and Tertullus of the defeated alternative Elymas. How did he get away with this strategy? Probably by invoking, as he did, the authority of the Raphael Cartoon, which subsumed any subversive trace that might have been detected. Moreover, the composition of the Raphael Cartoon-tapestry-engraving, with its reversals and backward-forward readings, conferred sufficient ambiguity on Hogarth's design that a viewer could have it either way, as about Paul or about Felix, as about a prisoner or a judge. It could also be argued that *Paul before Felix* is only a *memento mori*, an admonitory image for the judges to remind them that they are fallible humans.

The irony, however, is too complex. The model is Swiftean irony, not the medieval tradition of *vanitas* (compromised, for example, by the detail of Drusilla's hand). Or it is Shakespearean generosity, the inclusion of both contrasting points of view. It is all of these, depending on the direction from which we approach *Paul before Felix*: a work of literary complexity equal to the greatest contemporary works of Swift, Pope, or Fielding.

We should notice the fact that this painting was carried out at the same time Hogarth was engraving *Industry and Idleness* (1747) and gestating the six popular prints of 1751, which operate in a similar way.[28] It has to be seen in the context of *The Reward of Cruelty* (1751–52), which shows the "cruel" Tom Nero being himself dissected under the supervision of a surgeon posed as a magistrate in a courtroom. *Industry and Idleness*, for example, was bought by masters and hung on the walls of their shops to admonish apprentices, but when read by apprentices it said something quite different from what it said to masters.

What characterizes Hogarth's work as subversive—or proto-revolutionary—is his refusal to take such official statements at their face value or as official. *Paul before Felix*, the high art equivalent of *Industry and Idleness* and *The Reward of Cruelty*, is ostensibly addressed to the legal profession who commissioned it, but its true meaning addresses itself to defendants. While in situ the painting was seen only as *velute in speculum* by the lawyers themselves, in the engravings it reached an audience that could separate the judge and lawyer from the prisoner and see from the latter's point of view. But as the whole apparatus of the engraving tells us (the two versions, the burlesque, and the *Boys Peeping at Nature* subscription ticket—plus the engraving of *Moses brought to Pharaoh's Daughter* which was also included in the package), the protagonist—the prisoner—is implicitly William Hogarth the artist, who by this time seems to be regarding *himself*, or the English artist, as the Paul of English society, carrying his message of conversion, attacking idolators and the avaricious. The conversion has to do with the role of the artist and of English painting, summed up in Hogarth's signature "William Hogarth Anglus pinxit." The satire on avaricious idolators, the moral half, has now picked up an aesthetic significance: the judge is the connoisseur or critic of art to whom Hogarth was by this time addressing himself in *The Analysis of Beauty*

(1753), in the judge's funerary monument on the far right of Plate 1, and later in the judges of *The Bench* (1758). In the *Paul before Felix* series of engravings Hogarth was offering his subscribers a judgment—an easy one between his *Paul before Felix* and the Dutch "scratches" he parodied in his etched "Burlesque" of Rembrandt, and a more difficult one between his own engraving of *Paul before Felix* and the chaste, neoclassical version he had prepared and had engraved by Luke Sullivan, suppressing Drusilla (as the satyr is suppressed from the subscription ticket, *Boys Peeping*).

Paul is, of course, only the final summation of Hogarth the provincial, advocate of provincial (i.e. English) art and the image of the true English artist ("Anglus") as a dog, child, prisoner, or other outcast. At the very end of his life in *The Times*, Plate 2 (1763) his signature is a paint pot that could equally be a chamber pot.

What Hogarth's *Paul before Felix* shows in particular is an epitome of the decline and eclipse of patronage in the mid-eighteenth century. The artist can now address himself to a more general public reached by engravings, in which case the patron becomes either irrelevant or the censor whom the artist circumvents to address his audience; or the artist can accept the patron's commission (and Hogarth tries to have it both ways) but see from the point of view of someone other than the patron. *Paul before Felix* is really a flag of artistic independence, and as such it also shows that the artist now brings his own concerns to the literary text, not vice versa; though once he has done so he may be influenced, his expression or his development of the subject determined, by the model he has chosen: for example, Hogarth has brought his interest in judgment/mercy and guilty/innocent punishment, but then the formulations he adopts, even when he is inverting them, change his own formulation in subtle ways.

In Hogarth's case, he is illustrating the biblical text, but (1) he structures the painting on the visual images of Raphael—on conversion and persecution, with many opponents and one Samaritan-like hero—in the Raphael composition of one or two opposed picture planes. (2) But he also imposes on the story the literary impress of his time, and I suspect of Milton's *Paradise Lost*, with its structure of choice; and further (3) the literary impress of Shakespeare, which is the preference for psychological and moral complexity over formulation and unity of impression— which undercuts and complicates the pattern of moral choice, turning it from an either-or to a both-and (or in Hogarth's case, perhaps neither-nor) choice or into a Judgment of Solomon.

In relation to his audience the question is simply whether he identifies with the interests of his patrons or customers—and so of his literary text? With whom does he force *us* to identify? The originality of Hogarth as artist is partly at least in his tendency *not* to identify with the official—or what would be in the age of Verrio and Laguerre, let alone of Rubens and Van Dyck the official—point of view, but with that of the Other. This may be a deep-seated skepticism rather than what we would now call radicalism (a word Hogarth would not have known). But for a while at least it takes the form of identifying with the poor, even the criminal class, and much of the time with the minority or oppressed group—specifically with the prisoner rather than the judge.

We can see what this means in terms of the Shakespearean, the dramatic model. Moral subjects were painted and engraved to prove "that virtue in this world was rewarded by social and financial success. Thus those who could afford to buy these pictures—cheap as they were—had their own virtue confirmed." The procedure was ordinarily, as John Berger has put it, that the owners "identified themselves not with the *characters* painted but with the *moral* which the scene illustrated."[29] This I believe is where Hogarth parts company with the tradition of moral subjects. He forces us to identify with various characters, not with the *moral* promulgated, and the result is to question the *moral.* Seeing through the eyes of various characters is, I submit, the Shakespearean element. In Hogarth's case this means the point of view of both the master and the servant, of the patron and the painter, and includes the odd peripheral perspective given by a dog or child or black slave, or by the poor peripheral protagonist himself, the harlot or rake.

IV. THE MILTONIC SCRIPTURE

While the New Testament remained Raphael's, as the century progressed the Old Testament came to be Milton's. *Paradise Lost* was an "illustration" of Genesis, an interpretation or verbal commentary on that text. Its authority for English poets from shortly after its publication until well into the nineteenth century, from Dryden to Wordsworth, was overwhelming. The literary paradigms Milton constructed from Genesis and transmitted—as Michelangelo and Raphael did graphic ones—were few, simple, and easily grasped.

One was the Fortunate Fall itself, the Felix Culpa that tells the story of Adam, his fall, and his wandering. Defoe retells it in *Robinson Crusoe,* Fielding in *Tom Jones,* Johnson in *Rasselas,* Godwin in *Caleb Williams,* Wordsworth in *The Prelude,* and Mary Shelley in *Frankenstein.* As a model for narrative fiction it is the alternative to the story of Don Quixote's travels. While Quixote's journey begins with madness, Adam's begins with a fall which is a rebellion against a father, a past, and an identifiable self. But as the list of Adams unfolds from Crusoe to Frankenstein, we see an increasingly ironic attitude toward the original story, and we follow a shift from the point of view of the putative author (Moses or God the Father) or the Creator to that of the creature. In Blake's poems of the 1790s the story has been turned on its head. From a normative paradigm it has become a restrictive Law; God's perfect plan has become a betrayal, and his covenant has become a "charter" like those listed in his *Song of Experience* "London."

A second paradigm, a situation or dramatic scene rather than a narrative structure, was the Temptation of Eve by the serpent and, repeated, of Adam by Eve. Milton himself had a visual tradition to draw on for the compact, intense, and single-minded interrelation of two figures;[1] he also had the dramatic precedent of classical Greek tragedy, on which he knowingly drew in Book IX. Here was the opposite emphasis from the contemporary view of Shakespearean drama as sprawling and epic, as unfocused and dramatic in its conglomeration of different points of view. The Miltonic emphasis increasingly dominated Shakespearean criticism in the second half of the eighteenth century, when artists began to turn Shakespeare into a Miltonic poet of intense centripetal character relations rather than larger-than-life single characters whose actions radiate outward with centrifugal force on the crowds of characters around them.

Milton's version of the Temptation greatly expands the complex role of Satan, the antagonist, and literary imitations at first were more about Satan the tempter than about the temptation of Eve, let alone about the really problematic role (which Blake was to explore in great detail) of God the Father. The contemporary mode in the first half of the century was satiric; Satan embodied the false-seeming, the oxymoron of dangerous impotence, and the mock-heroic bombast of a satirist's object in the age of Charles II and the late Stuarts. Every political action could be read by the satirist as a temptation involving the satanic tempter and the gullible tempted (e.g. prime minister or favorite and king), a version of the knave-fool relationship explored in subtle ramifications by Dryden, Swift, and Pope.

Mingled, however, with Satan's temptation was the consequent choice of Eve (and then Adam). As I have suggested, this was a religious version of the classical Choice of Hercules, which Milton sacralized in the greatest of all *Paradise Lost*'s paradigms, that of human choice. Closely related to this image of Adam or Eve between the tempter and God or angel, visually at any rate, was the demonic interrelation of Satan, Sin, and Death, to which I shall return in more detail. But there was also the possibility of emphasizing the tempted and fallen woman, Eve, who became the heroine—as analogue or opposite—of a great many plays and novels with Miltonic overtones from Rowe's *Fair Penitent* to Richardson's *Clarissa*.

If Shakespeare offered a skeptical questioning of all organizing structures, the Miltonic Scripture—like the Biblical—offered a way to organize experience around certain simple paradigms. If Shakespeare stood for incident, invention, copiousness, and the infinite variety of human nature, Milton stood for the terrific conflict of opposing forces—good and evil, past and present, fall and redemption—embodied in a man and a woman or a tempter and a tempted. These dualities Milton shaped into a powerful aesthetic unity. The sense of the poet shaping and ordering intractable material, of the poet exerting complete authorial control with no detail that is outside his "plan" (in this sense an analogue to God the Creator in his epic), was very strong—so strong that the poet was himself in some ways the real protagnist of the epic. He was both justifying God's ways to man and holding out, the last of the Saints, against an England of Belials and cavaliers. His enterprise was, in fact, unashamedly an analogue to the story of the Son's incarnation-atonement-redemption of man's sin. Alexander Pope in one way, hardly less ironic, assumed the same role in *Dunciad* IV, Thomas Gray in another in *The Bard,* and the painters were not slow to apply the centrality of the poet to themselves, drawing attention to themselves, for example, with the mannerist exaggerations of their styles.

The Garden of Eden, and Milton's poetry describing it, became the refuge and the ideal state from which man is expelled and falls. As James Turner and others have shown, much of English landscape poetry, painting, and gardening in the eighteenth century drew upon Milton's garden.[2] Legitimated pastoral-georgic relationships, or choices of active life or retirement at their most complex and ambiguous, utilized the Biblical sense of a garden. The two kinds of landscape described in *Paradise Lost,* Eve's immersion in her own image in the pool and Adam's looking up and around him in order to catalogue flora and fauna, corresponded to the ways a landscape painter attemtped to order the wilderness that experience spread before him. Landscape painting tended to fall into one or the other of these categories, but it also tended to retain the Miltonic structure of moral choice.

From the graphic point of view, the primary paradigm of *Paradise Lost* was the contrast (which for Milton is always a choice) of light and dark, height and depth or rise and fall, set up in the invocation, to Book I:

> What in me is *dark*
> *Illumine,* what is *low raise* and support;
> That to the *highth* of this great Argument
> I may assert Eternal Providence,
> And justify the ways of God to men.   (I, 22-25; italics added)

The imagery of *Paradise Lost* bears upon these interlocking contrasts of high as both spiritual eminence or exaltation and also pride, and of low as both humility and also moral degradation and despair. They in turn play upon the biblical paradox of rising-falling, abasement and exaltation: "Every valley shall be exalted, and every mountain and hill shall be made low" (Isaiah 40.4).[3]

The paradigm of light-dark and heighth-depth leads most obviously to the subject painting of Fuseli, who, however, always renders his sublime images slightly askew by the exaggerated, caricatured expressions of his faces (and perhaps also his careless painting technique). Fuseli in fact derives—we might say—from the Miltonic *mock*-epic mode in which the conventional epic catalogue of heroes is turned (as in Book I) into a list of the fallen angels who later wandered the earth renamed Moloch, Belial, and even Saturn and Jove, false gods and heathen idols whom fallen men continue fallaciously to worship. The Miltonic catalogue mocks the old chivalric matter of Renaissance epics and the contemporary historical (Restoration) ideal of the "cavalier," of Charles II's favorites Buckingham and the "Sons of Belial" who "when Night / Darkens the Streets, then wander forth . . . flown with insolence and wine" (I, 500-502). There was, in short, a mock mode implicit, and sometimes utilized, in *Paradise Lost;* and if it was not picked up by artists from that source, it was available in a more accessible, but also less pure form, in Pope's *Rape of the Lock* and *Dunciad.* This was the Fuseli mode, taken I have no doubt from Milton rather than Pope.

But landscape was the solution to the problem of the powerful English burlesque tradition—the Hogarthian mode in which the Michelangelo or Old Master remains as a mock-heroic vestige rather than as a primary precursor of the graphic tradition. Fuselian figures in the landscape merely drew attention to, reinforced, or moralized the large natural contrasts of sunlight and shade or calm and storm. In fact, by the end of the century in the paintings of J.M.W. Turner and John Martin, the relationship of figure to landscape was as close as in the central books of *Paradise Lost.* First J.R. Cozens and then Turner developed the simple light-dark, high-low contrats of *Paradise Lost* in paintings of demonic landscapes (Lakes Albano, Nemi, and Avernus); then Turner retained the literary (Miltonic) fringe of the fallen human elements, where history is the mode of the fallen world and figures are slightly caricatured, creating a distinctly mock-heroic contrast with the sublime natural landscape.

We might even relate this landscape contrast to what Geoffrey Hartman has referred to as Milton's "counterplot," the assertion of divine imperturbability, order, and continuity in and around a momentary eruption of human intransigence, a tiny repetition of the Fall.[4] In Turner's landscapes this becomes the small gesture of hybris or (to use his own term) a "Fallacy of Hope" that is habitually carried on by fallen humans beneath an "imperturbable" landscape. The effect is related graphically to a painting like Peter Brueghel's *Fall of Icarus* (Royal Museum, Brussels) which shows Icarus a tiny falling speck, hardly noticed, in a landscape of ploughmen keeping at their work, crops growing, seasons changing, and God's natural order persisting. It is the effect Milton achieves through words when, for example, he has Satan "Hurl'd headlong flaming from th' Ethereal Sky / With hideous ruin and combustion down" (I,44-46): the violence of Satan's (like Icarus' or Phaeton's or Adam's) fall is contained by the "Ethereal Sky" through which he passes; as Mulciber's fall—

>   from Morn
> To Noon he fell, from Noon to dewy Eve,
> A Summer's day; and with the setting Sun
> Dropt from the Zenith . . .   (I, 742-44)

—is caught in the diurnal routine of the natural creation to which his aberrant human action is subordinated. The cycles are themselves, of course, fallen in the sense that there were no seasons before the Fall in Paradise (that pastoral world). But they remind the reader of the overarching divine plan into which Satan's momentary revolt fits.

I think this passage—this "counterplot"—describes quite accurately the function of Turner's landscape at its most literary; though it obviously oversimplifies Turner's landscape to call it imperturbable. But the Miltonic simile also opens the whole subject of representation through similitude in art. Fuseli, for example, illustrated Milton by rendering the similes as an area in which the artist's imagination was not fettered by the Miltonic action itself, the stark contrasts of choice, and which moreover offered him discrepant patterns of words that were similar to, or reminded him of, qualities he did not want to lose from Shakespeare's poetry.[5] He found it expedient to maintain the earlier sense of the epic simile as the poet's opportunity to soar, to lift his subject even higher, as well as the particularly Miltonic sense of catachresis.

Indeed, at this point Shakespeare and Milton momentarily make contact for the eighteenth century. In Milton, however, the catachresis is attached to a theological concept. Similes begin to appear whenever Satan is at hand and history impinges upon Eden; they project us into a post-Edenic fallen world that is often contemporary Rome or London, and they often take the specific form of comparisons to observers who are lost or have trouble seeing what they want to see. As Leslie Moore has demonstrated, a "belated Peasant," confused "pilot," lost "night-Wanderer" or "Mariner" tries to interpret an uncertain sign in the midst of a dark and dangerous landscape.[6] These "observer similes" embody the ambiguity of fallen life, the unbridgeable distance separating God and man. The disunity of this fallen world is reflected in a syntactical ambiguity of almost Shakespearean proportions at the heart of the similes.

On a theological level, the central issue of the epic, Incarnation, begins with the identity of God and Son, and proceeds to the similitude between God and his creature man (created in his own image) before the Fall. This similitude, which posits a likeness but not an equality between elements located at different degrees upon a scale, is denied first by Satan's pride and then by Eve's and Adam's refusal to abide within its "bounds". They attempt to narrow the gap or seek identity, and so fall, after which similitude is radically reduced to the loose catachrestic association of simile. The Shakespearean catachresis finds its way into the Miltonic epic in this way, and so—we may suspect—remains in the "sublime" art of Fuseli and Turner. One explanation for the sense of dissimilarity always at work in Hogarth and Blake as well as Fuseli and Turner can be related to Milton's representation of the fallen world. Pope's use of discrepant similes in *The Dunciad* works from the Miltonic premise: as a satirist, he is using simile to represent depraved, degenerate men and women.

The Miltnoic simile, therefore, while showing a settled georgic seasonal order in the world, does so at a distance that removes man from the imperturbability of that order and leaves him in a dark, confusing area that lacks the "divine effect" he needs to interpret or read signs. The simile shows him trying to connect two different things and calling them similitude when this is no longer possible. One interpretation of Turner's disjunctions between the landscape and the human elements in his paintings can be based on the Miltonic interpretation of experience.[7]

The Miltonic simile also reminds us that the way something looks is of crucial importance and that the observer's role in an action is central in the empirical tradition that runs from Bacon and Locke to Hume. Milton, of course, sees observation as having built-in limitations and concludes that insight is better than outlook. The conclusion is intensified in the figure of the blind bard himself. Blake and Turner, in their different ways, find this a useful model to follow for the stage beyond fallen simile which is prophetic unity.

Shakespeare and Cervantes, I have argued, were in large part liberating models, Milton and the Bible models of order and restriction. There was still a strong, even neurotic need for order felt by educated Englishmen, and this was filled by the binary structures of good and evil, God and Satan, right and wrong choice found in the Bible and dramatized in heroic verse in Milton's poetic version of the Old Testament. The New Testament offered more open structures, with a hero who could be interpreted to accord with one aspect of Don Quixote. The century ended with Blake rewriting Milton and setting the New Testament fiction against the Old, and even drawing subversive fictions from the Old. But behind these artists of the second half of the century the figure of Shakespeare will still loom, either because he is being turned into a Miltonic poet or because it was all too clear that his plays offer no paradigms or plots or forms that dominate the period but rather the model for the undermining of forms, the questioning of them or at least the recognition of their unresolvable complexity.

Satan, Sin, and Death

I have indicated the direction choice took in Hogarth's work, and I have

added Book IX of *Paradise Lost* as a possible explanation of another
sort for this direction. But there was a second paradigm in *Paradise
Lost,* closely related to the Temptation's serpent, Eve, and absent angel;
this was the meeting of Satan, Sin, and Death in Book II, which dominated the thinking of English artists in the second half of the century,
finding its apotheosis (or strongest interpretation) in Edmund Burke's
account of the sublime, thereafter informing the interpersonal relationships that shape the paintings of Fuseli and Blake.

The first graphic representation of the scene was the 1688 illustration
by Henry Aldrich, which placed Satan between Sin and Death, presumably based on Milton's description of the pair sitting on either side of
Hell Gate (pl. 54).[8] Aldrich conflates the moment of challenge—Death
in the distance alarmed by the presence of this intruder—and the
moment of Satan's departure toward Eden. (To do so he shows the gates
broken down, which were in fact opened with Sin's key.) Insofar as
Aldrich's illustration supports an interpretation of the trio, it is the one
developed by Milton's earliest admirers among the poets, Dryden,
Pope, and the Augustan satirists. Satan, Sin, and Death are an infernal
parody, an unholy Trinity, the Father flanked by the Son and Holy
Ghost who later set about their own parody-creation (imitating the
creation by the Trinity in Book V) in the construction of the bridge from
Hell to earth in Book X. Louis Cheron's headpiece to Book II (1720, pl.
55) balances the three as a hieratic trio, and underneath appear the lines
describing the Satanic imitation of God's enthronement which served
Dryden for his description of Flecknoe in *Macflecknoe and* Pope's of
Cibber (a few years after Cheron's design) in *Dunciad* III. Allusion and
parody, in short, are the first uses to be made of Milton's scene.
Hogarth's placement of his Harlot in a parody of the Life of the Virgin
functions in much the same way.

Addison opened the eighteenth-century attack on Sin and Death in
Spectator 273 by criticizing the improbability and indecorum of including such grotesque figures in an epic, but in No. 309 he admitted his
admiration for Milton's invention. He showed that the scene can be
interpreted (and so used) as an allegory of genealogy: "*Sin* is the
Daughter of *Satan,* and *Death* the Offspring of *Sin.*" And this leads him
to draw attention to the "Sublime Ideas" evoked by the confrontation
of Satan and Death: "The Figure of Death, the Regal Crown upon his
Head, his Menace of Satan, his advancing to the Combat . . . are Circumstances too noble to be past over in Silence, and extreamly suitable
to this *King of Terrors.*"

If the second of these insights was to serve Burke, the first was picked
up by the painter and enthusiastic Miltonist Jonathan Richardson in his

Explanatory Notes and Remarks on Milton's "Paradise Lost" (1734). The best thing in *Paradise Lost,* the epitome of the whole argument, Richardson argues, is the genealogical allegory of Satan-Sin-Death—"a kind of paraphrase on those words of St. James I.15. Then when Lust hath conceived it bringeth forth Sin, and Sin when it is finished bringeth forth death."[9]

Richardson's importance, however, lies in the fact that we know he drew Hogarth's attention to the episode of Satan, Sin, and Death (if the *Spectator* had not already done so), for he read passages from his book to the artists of the Slaughter's Coffee-house group, one of whom was Hogarth.[10] Within a year or so of the publication of the *Explanatory Notes and Remarks,* Hogarth had followed his recommendation of this subject for the aspiring English history painter, much as he had earlier followed Shaftesbury's advocacy of the Judgment of Hercules (pl. 56). Indeed Richardson was urging upon artists another such trio with tangled psychological relationships of a very similar sort, although this was not the aspect he recognized. His own interpretation he embodied not in an illustration of *Paradise Lost* but (since he was a professional portraitist) in a fascinating portrait group consisting of a self-portrait, his son Jonathan Jr., and—looking quite alive, though glancing away from the other two—John Milton. The image of poet, critic, and critic's son (who served as Richardson's scholarly eyes and ears) is his own allegory of genealogy and recalls his well-known reference to his relationship with his son as "the complicated Richardson."[11]

Perhaps the sexual-generational relationship implied by the allegory Richardson admired caught Hogarth's fancy because it echoed his own conversation pieces of the early 1730s. His composition reflects the basic arrangement of many of his conversation pictures in which a host or hostess employs a mediating gesture, drawing together guests or guests and family: in *The Western Family* (pl. 57) by just such a gesture as Sin employs between Satan and Death, but more usually by one like Polly Peachum's between her father and lover (pl. 21). Hogarth has domesticated the Miltonic story, making it a family romance which was understandable to himself, much as Jonathan Richardson had done by emphasizing the genealogy he felt in his own relationship to Milton on one side and to his son Jonathan Jr. on the other.

Looking back, at about the same time he was working on his *Tempest* illustration, Hogarth must have realized that the *Beggar's Opera* paintings could be interpreted in two aspects: Macheath is choosing between his two "wives" Polly and Lucy, as the words of the song he is singing suggest, and this is a Choice of Hercules between Virtue and Vice. But he wants both, and Polly and Lucy are to him six-of-one and half-adozen of the other. We might say that Hogarth subverts the topos by leaving the moral choice itself in doubt. The composition, however, has a second aspect, for it can also be read as a female mediating between two jealous males. Polly and Lucy are each the center of a grouping in which they try to reconcile a father and a lover. In *Satan, Sin, and Death* then Sin's face is turned toward her father and both arms are outstretched to hold apart the angry father-lover and son-lover. A gesture of reconciliation has hardened into one of separation, but the woman is now unambiguously the central figure. The context makes it clear that the father and lover/son are fighting for the daughter. They are not only held apart by her but are contending for her favors. *Satan, Sin, and Death* is the painting in which Hogarth exposes the deepest level of conflict in his *Beggar's Opera* and *Tempest* paintings.

By emphasing the triangular psychological relationship he has not only revealed something about his *Tempest* painting but has lifted the trapdoor on the conflicting instincts at work in Milton's scene, hitherto unnoticed by illustrators. His emphasis on the lover-daughter as mediator as well as sexual object also connects this painting with the ones in which a pretty female mediates between an artist (musician or poet in *The Enraged Musician* and *The Distrest Poet)* and the threat of external disorder directly aimed at him by the outside world. Whether the poet is the Superego/Father and the sub-culture types of the street are the interloper lover, or vice versa, is a question relating to a deeper level. On the surface the pictures are about the beautiful girl as one form of nature *(la belle nature)* bridging the gap between the artist and intractable things-as-they-are—between an over-formalizing poet or musician and the chaotic world of street noises and bill-collectors. Hogarth is even-handed in his emphasis, but the wife or milkmaid is the role in which he sees Sin, the mother/daughter, as she tries to relate Satan, the rebel/father/lover, to that unknowable shapeless chaos called Death, who is both son and lover as well as a father in his own right.

In *The Pool of Bethesda* and *The Good Samaritan,* which Hogarth painted on the staircase of St. Bartholomew's Hospital in the late 1730s—at about the same time—the central figure is in both cases a male, and plainly a mediator. In *this* context the musician's milkmaid and poet's wife are mediators. But in the context of *Satan, Sin, and Death* (or *The Tempest)* they are sexual objects as well, and they distinguish this aspect from the primary one of mediation in the St. Bartholomew's paintings. I have elsewhere noted connections between the mediating role of Christ in *The Pool of Bethesda* and the mediator/ sexual-object Sarah Young in *The Rake's Progress,* which immediately preceded the painting of these Biblical scenes.[12]

Drusilla in *Paul before Feix* is another of these female mediators, drawing more on Sin than is usual for Hogarth. In fact the ground base of his painting is the implied sexual relationship—the challenge Paul is making to Felix in terms of his mistress Drusilla. Paul's hand is placed in such a way as to suggest that this challenge is involved in Felix's judgment of him, but also to indicate the falsity of this Jewish woman who should be Paul's mediator but is in fact his judge's mistress. Her absence from the final engraving is not only an attempt to simplify and classicize the design (un-Rembrandt it), but also acknowledgment that there *is* no mediation in the figure of *this* woman. What she tells us about Hogarth's attitude toward the Charity he celebrated earlier (in Sarah Young, the Good Samaritan, and Christ) is that Charity has now become merely a part of ruling-class ideology—a buffer between rich and poor, magistrate and accused, Felix and Paul that serves the former.

Hogarth's painting sums up the period just before the publication of Burke's *Philosophical Enquiry into the Origin of our Ideas of the Sublime and Beautiful* (1757) but also carries within it the seed of the later period. Burke, who may have seen Hogarth's painting in his studio in the 1750s, begins his discussion of terror as obscurity by arguing for the superior sublimity of the poet's more suggestive (because vague) words over the painter's graphic image which unfortunately has to specify what the poet leaves to the imagination. Hogarth's painting, though unfinished and not very distinct, could nevertheless have elicited the sort of response Charles Lamb later made to illustrations of Shakespeare in Boydell's Gallery: "To be tied down to an authentic face of Juliet! To have Imogen's portrait! To confine th' illimitable."[13] There is no doubt that Hogarth's figures are slightly comic in their reach for the passions.

Burke also takes Hogarth's particular composition (for which, as I have shown, there was no graphic precedent among Militon illustrations) and simulates it on his page, shifting the emphasis from the woman to the confrontation of interchangeable fathers and sons (in Hogarth's own terms, poet or chaos, musician or sheer noise). The verbal example he adduces for obscurity is Milton's Death: formless, obscure, he cannot be grasped or comprehended. But Burke manufactures the confrontation of Satan and Death by introducing the image from Book I of Satan rising to address his legions and juxtaposing this with the image of Death threatening Satan with his fiery dart in Book II. Our response now derives from viewing not a static figure, however threatening or obscure, but a mutually aggressive action; not just Satan or Death but the two confronting each other; and not just a confrontation but consecutively Burke (seeing himself as) facing Death and then facing Satan confronting Death, so that we see him assuming the role of each in turn. Between Satan and Death in this scene (invisible—not mentioned by Burke) is of course the figure of Sin, the daughter-lover, mother-lover of the two contestants.

The interchangeability of challenger and challenged is what Burke stresses. Satan is both father and son, figure of authority and challenger of authority, of the crowned guard of the gate; the point being that it is a reciprocal relationship in which they are challenging each other and will continue to change places, the father with the son, the tyrant with the rebel.

I am sure Burke is recalling Addison's "Sublime Ideas" evoked by the "King of Terrors" menacing and advancing on Satan, and he may also be recalling another interpretation of Milton's scene, William Collins' "Ode to Fear" of 1746.[14] Collins' poem (with its "shadowy tribes of Mind" in a "world unknown," and "unreal scene") is closer to Burke's idea of "obscurity" than Milton's passage, and his plot picks up the story at the point where Satan is confronted by Sin—as the speaker, now the poet, is confronted by Fear, who is confronted by a fearful object: "What monsters in thy train appear" and the "ravening brood of fate / Who lap the blood of sorrow" suggest a memory of the monsters that have been engendered by Sin and Death and that eat at her bowels. The poem itself is an attempt to employ personification in the general manner of Milton's famous scene, but the reference is also to the creature Danger who pursues Fear (as Death did) to rape her, and now threatens through her the poet/Satan protagnoist. The personified Danger merges with Vengeance, a female figure who "Lifts her red arm"—a reference which in fact associates her with powerful male figures, God the Father and Jove.

I suspect that Burke had this poem somewhere in his mind when he constructed his example of "obscurity." It is also significant for Burke's interpretation that Collins' two illustrations from literature are political-patriotic and domestic-romantic: first, Aeschylus who as poet invoked Fear but at the battle of Marathon (a Greek victory over the tyrannic Persians, which meant Greek liberty) disdained her and "reached from Virtue's hand the patriot's steel," and, second, Sophocles who sought Fear in the incestuous relationship of Oedipus and Jocasta. The situation of Sophocles' Oedipus confronting Laius is the one Burke implies; and in the Collins context it becomes a gloss on the relation of Satan as the poet seeking his muse, Sin as the mother-lover Fear, and Death as the paternal Danger conflated with Vengeance. Collins, however, produces an image not quite consonant with Burke's:

he makes Hogarth's image of the pretty young mediator over into one of the poet trying to relate to the terrifying, inchoate world—formless and intractable—through the mediation of a female muse figure. What began as an Augustan conception of the parody of divine creation becomes a Romantic one of poetic creation, raising questions through the genealogical parody of Satan, Sin, and Death about the relationship between God and his creation, Satan and his parody creation, and the poet and *his* creation. And what had begun as a paradigm of choice or at least mediation has become one of irremediable and interchangeable confrontation between authority and rebel.

In Henry Fuseli's versions of the scene (beginning 1776) Death is even more the Other, inchoate matter contrasted with the Michelangelesque angel of light, Satan (pl. 58). The struggle makes a geometrical triangle with the emphasis on the powerful lines of force connecting the figures. Sin is drawn as both referee and connecting link. A single unbroken line runs from Satan through Death, as between antinomies of the sort that later came to be called Apollonian and Dionysian, between a Winckelmann Greek god and a strange, irrational, gothic shape, in one version with his head inclined so far back as to make him nearly headless (1799-1800, Los Angeles County Museum). Fuseli's Satan is the Greek/Enlightenment rebel trying to break out of the confines of Pandemonium by vanquishing the gatekeeper of Chaos. He is now developing graphically the paradigm of Satan as rebel against the forces of darkness embodied in king and church.

Another attraction of the Miltonic passage to painters was that Sin was bound to remind them of Horace's description in his *Ars Poetica* of a painting that "began as a lovely woman at the top / Tapered off into a slimy, discolored fish." This was one of the passages that connected painter and poet in the poem that was the crux of the *ut pictura poesis* ideal sought by so many English painters in the eighteenth century.[15]

Burke's invisible but implicit Sin also becomes the pale maiden pursued through the long shadowy corridors of castles by gloomy tyrants in the gothic novel. In Walpole's *Castle of Otranto* (1765) the terror (and the supernatural intervention) followed from a domestic perversion that recalls not only the gothic decorations superimposed on an ordinary house like Strawberry Hill but the Miltonic decoration Hogarth had added to a conversation piece in his version of *Satan, Sin, and Death*. Walpole's gothic novel is another story of the struggle for possession of a property, along the lines of *Tom Jones* or *Roderick Random,* with gothic trappings. But something of Burke's "obscurity" lies in the domestic perversion, which reaches from Manfred's defiance of the lawful inheritance manifested in the huge father image of Alphonso the

Good, to his implicit rivalry with his own son and his attempt to take his place, marry his intended, and propagate his own heirs ("instead of a sickly boy," he tells Matilda, "you shall have a husband in the prime of his age"). In short, Manfred is both rebellious son and tyrannic father.

With the shock of the French Revolution in 1789, Burke revived his aesthetic model to describe his own ambivalent confrontation with revolution. In his *Reflections on the Revolution in France* (1790), he described the Revolution as a false-sublime event, but one which had all the characteristics of the Satan-Sin-Death confrontation, with Sin now materialized in the figure of the queen Marie Antoinette. He builds his *Reflections* around the confrontation of the parricide revolutionaries and Louis XVI over the body of the queen-wife-mother (as son/father-mother/wife). The woman is now very visible, her beauty and grace described in full detail, and the sexual threat of the aggressive male mob spelled out. This sexual triangle remains the paradigm behind Burke's subsequent attacks on the revolutionaries, in which he brings out the cyclic implications of the Satan-Sin-Death relationship by flattening the allegory into a sequence. The repressive father and the energetic son keep changing places: first the son destroys the father and then of necessity internalizes him and becomes more repressive, more the tyrant than he was.

With Burke's *Reflections* the fictional situation intensifies into the confrontation of servant and master, Caleb Williams and Falkland, in Godwin's novel called *Things as they Are* (1794), over the trunk containing evidence that Falkland is a murderer: Death faces Satan over Sin, in a scene remarkable for its sexual overtones. Out of this scene grows the ambiguous pursuit in which Caleb and Falkland become both pursuer and pursued, virtually interchangeable figures by the time they reach the end, which is not an end but a cyclic exchange of roles: Caleb is now the murderer himself. A year after *Caleb Williams*, in 1795, M.G. Lewis' *The Monk* was published, and the alternation of attraction and repulsion we have noticed in Burke's account of the revolutionary experience appears as Ambrosio's revolt from the monastic life in which he has been confined from childhood into a sexual explosion, which leads to his own assumption of pious hypocrisy, compulsion, rape, incest, and murder. Ambrosio is rehearsing the stages of the cycle Burke saw in the French Revolution itself, expressed first by an explosion of liberation-energy-sexuality, and then by counter-revolution, in which the rebel Satan first attacks and then becomes himself the God-the-Father he rebelled against.

At bottom Burke is transforming life into art, creating a sublime art of Aristotelian tragedy in order to understand contemporary events that have gotten out of hand—which Blake and Paine would turn into something closer to a comedy. In the one case the son kills the father for the sake of the mother and expiates his crime through suffering and knowledge; in the other the irrepressible sexual energy simply bursts through the false barriers erected by society and the family, fulfilling itself in love. The revolution naturally appears to the poet in terms of a family, of father and rebellious son, and the dramatic form (Oedipus complex aside) is tragic: Aristotle explained that the material best calculated to produce the emotions of "pity and fear" is the family: "Whenever the tragic deed . . . is done within the family—when murder or the like is done or meditated by brother on brother, by son on father, by mother on son, or son on mother—these are the situations the poet should seek after."[16] What Aristotle's tragedy requires—the two terms, reversal (peripeteia) and recognition (anagnorisis)—Burke finds in the situation of the family and in the insight of the observer who is both a participant and not a participant. In other words, the overthrow, the *de casibus,* is followed by a recognition, but not by the figure in the fall but by the observer of it, who sees himself *becoming* the protagonist of the drama (as the revolution spreads from France to England): *he* sees a fall, a peripeteia, and then has an anagnorisis. The tragedy, the revolution, is a rewriting of Aristotelian tragedy in terms of Burke's Sublime, which requires his experiencing from a safe distance his own story, hating it as he relishes its thrills.

The connection between the family as the metaphor for revolution and Milton's *Paradise Lost* as a whole should be obvious enough, but it is also easy to see why Satan-Sin-Death remained the paradigm for most writers and painters rather than the less peripheral and less safe story of the Father and Son themselves in Book III. The appearance of Burke's *Reflections* only fixed the subversive meaning, while the visual interpretations continued to follow Hogarth's conversation piece model for the infernal triangle. (Hogarth's painting was by the sixties in Garrick's collection, available a little later in a print by Charles Townley, and in the eighties in one by Rowlandson.)

James Gillray's parody of 1792, *Sin, Death and the Devil* (pl. 59), reflects the Regency Crisis just past and the present struggle between Pitt and Thurlow, mediated by Queen Charlotte. The most noticeable absence is of the real father, King George III. Pitt is borrowing his crown and Thurloe has the role of the father-lover. With the Queen assuming the usual royal role of mediator between Prime Minister and Lord Chancellor, the myth is totally subverted. The sexual dimension is not absent: Queen Charlotte's right hand, serving as a fig leaf for Pitt/ Death, is derived from Paul's hand in relation to Drusilla in *Paul before*

Felix. The allusion is to innuendoes about the relationship between Charlotte and Pitt, more fully suggested in their dangling, touching figures in *The Hopes of the Party* (1791).

James Barry retains some sense of the political occasion in his illustration made in the 1790s (pl. 60).[17] A protégé of Burke, Barry replaces Hogarth's domestic interior with a neutral space virtually filled with figures from Michelangelo. Sublimity is the subject, embodied in the two powerful male contenders who frame and enclose (nearly eclipsing) Sin, who does not, like Hogarth's Sin, in the least resemble Polly Peachum. She is a more primitive creature, not found in English drawing rooms. The viewer is made to associate with Satan, and in a separate drawing/etching Barry also illustrated the scene of Satan rising to address his troops, which Burke had conflated with the image of Death-as-seen-by-Satan.

William Blake was no lover of Burke's theories, but he knew them: he was thinking of Burke when he annotated Reynolds' *Discourses* with the remark, "Obscurity is neither the Source of the Sublime nor of any thing Else." He read the *Philosophical Enquiry* "when very young" and hated it, but in his own version of *Satan, Sin, and Death* at the turn of the century (pl. 61) he made Satan the young Orc-like challenger and Death the old, bearded, crowned Urizen (obscure in the sense of transparent), and merely made explicit the oedipal relationship he had been dramatizing since *Songs of Innocence.* As Blake sees, the problem is that Satan is the father and Death the son, but Death wears the crown and insists that *he* is being challenged. Blake puts the beard as well as the crown on Death and makes Satan the rebel. As he shows, in a profound sense Satan is both father and son, figure of authority and challenger of authority—of Death, the guard of the gate. His point is the same as Burke's that the relationship is precisely reciprocal. They are challenging each other and will continue to change places, the father and the son, the tyrant and the rebel, as one phase of the revolution passes into the next.

Another implication, explored by Blake in his *Songs of Innocence and Experience,* is summed up by Paul Ricoeur: "The Oedipus drama implies that the child desires the unobtainable."[18] Revolution is a regression to childhood, from the revolutionary's point of view to a time before parental repression, and from the counter-revolutionary's point of view to a time of childish, irresponsible mischief-making. In Blake, as in Rousseau, children are represented as an outburst of repressed energy. Then in later stages they are seen, by Hogarth in one way, by Blake in another, as children who refuse to grow up, or who have to be *made* to mature; or who continue to regress beyond the

113

oedipal to earlier stages—the anal, oral, and narcissistic.[19] Thus one component of the oedipal situation adumbrated by Burke—and developed by Blake—is the childish and regressive character of the revolutionary protagonist (which could also be put into the context of Wordsworth's return to simple folk, children, and idiots at the time he was showing his own sympathies for the French Revolution).

We are observing a paradigm shift, as the situation of choice gives way to one of mediation and this to dilemma and conflict over the possession of the mediator: all implicit in Hogarth's original shifting triads of figures, either two women and a man or two men (father and lover) and a woman. The model of Hercules and his correct choice has become a grim Judgment of Solomon and then the murderous oedipal confrontation at the crossroads. The choice is now buried in the past, in the father's abandonment of the son (as in the story of the monk Ambrosio). The hero kills his father over the wrong woman, and the allegory depicts the act of rebellion (or its consequence) as a repeated act of incest.

All of this connects with the shift from centrality of the Parable of the Good Samaritan to the Parable of the Talents. At mid-century the popular image was of Charity, the primary virtue of ordinary English churchmen, embodied in the Good Samaritan—an image developed by Bishop Hoadly in his sermons, Fielding in his novels, and Hogarth in his paintings at St. Bartholomew's and the Foundling Hospital. The paradigm involves a representative of the Law, the official culture, a Pharisee-Levite who ignores the man fallen among thieves because he is unclean, wounded, and probably dead, and a Good Samaritan, an outcast who can succor the wounded man *because* he is outside, and therefore ignores, the Law. He is a representative of a sub-culture—a dissenter, a child, an apprentice, a black. Although the parable was used to suggest the basic importance of works over faith, it very easily narrowed to the conflict between the outsider of virtue and the legalistic insider representing the ruling-class assumptions.

This parable gives way—starting with Hogarth's *Industry and Idleness*—to an ambiguous reading of the Parable of the Talents, one that is demystified and seen from the point of view of the poor servant rather than the matter. But now the spectrum of responses to a helpless human being (as in the Raphael Cartoons, the one good response against many bad ones) narrows to a simple power relation between a servant and his master, a son and his father, Caleb Williams and Falkland.

In the background we must retain the two basic types of interpretation we have seen applied to the Satan-Sin-Death confrontation: one genealogical, the other agonistic. Something of the unholy parody probably always remains, and Fuseli and Blake suggest throughout their works that they are aware of the parody aspect of their own (or any) art—their own bridges between hell and the earth, constructed over the gulf of chaos, which parody the acts of divine creation. The confrontation itself only underlines the central question of who is father and who son, who king and who subject—in short, who is creator and who creature? Something also remains of the old domestic triangle of father-daughter-suitor from Hogarth's conversation picture model. Then certainly Hogarth's modification of the paradigm into the triangle of poet-muse-chaotic reality (which is both genealogical and agonistic) puts its emphasis on the woman as muse-mediator, and leads, with only the intervention of a sublime upheaval, into the oedipal conflict of two men over the invisible middle factor, the woman—which again could be treated either as sublime or as parody sublime in the actual French Revolution.

Blake's Bible

Milton's Bible, especially Book III, addressed the paradox of determinism and free will, of a vengeful and a loving god, in the issue of whether Christ's sacrifice is Atonement—mere satisfaction for a slight to the Father in Adam's disobedience—or Redemption, which includes the fuller experience that makes Christ's whole life a paradigm for man and a defeat for the forces of Satan. Recognizing this as the official "Justification of the ways of God to man" (which in Pope's *Essay on Man* had become "Vindication"), William Blake reread the Old Testament story from the point of view of the creature (the *un*official view) rather than the Creator.

It is difficult to say at this point what is Shakespearean and what Miltonic. Hogarth's adaptation of Shakespeare involved painting pictures that incorporated more than one point of view on a subject. We could contrast this with the Miltonic point of view as negative capability with the egotistical sublime. Although coined by Keats about Shakespeare and Wordsworth, the terms apply as well to the dramatic grouping of different voices, different perspectives in Shakespeare versus the authoritarian voice of Milton's epic poet. If not putting himself in an alien personality, Hogarth was at least showing an awareness of different and unauthoritarian (or 'privileged') points of view. But when Blake carries negative capability—the point of view of the Other in the story of the Fall—into a contrary egotistical sublime, we find ourselves with a series of artists (perhaps already begun by Hogarth in his later years) whose point of view, however contrary, is Miltonic.

Blake assumes the Other's point of view as exclusively as Milton does the deity's. This is in fact, in different circumstances, Milton's own role of the Old Testament prophet against the king. Blake has another model, however, in a paradox of the Bible itself: like Milton's text it was a high culture object of veneration, a center of ideology, but it also offered the sub-culture a vocabulary of subversion. What many Englishmen saw in the mid-seventeenth century and again toward the end of the eighteenth was that Christianity itself was the great underlying model (as the French sensed by their absorption of Christian imagery) of revolution.

This reading depended upon a major deconstruction of the Bible, a veering away from the official interpretation of the Church Fathers, the commentators, and the Anglican clergy; and its home was among the dissenters, for whom the basic idea was that one goes to the Bible and reads it for himself. One discovers what the Bible said before it fell into the hands of the Fathers. This tradition of dissenter interpretation helps to explain the readings Blake arrived at, but it also draws attention to the dissenters' reputed history of rebellion and regicide, subversion and innovation.

While establishment Christianity, founded on the Bible of the Church Fathers, was content with an ordered status quo in this life, revolutionary Christianity—which harked back to the "true" reading of the New Testament—called for change. "How long, O Lord, how long!" was their cry, and their expectation was the reign of Christ upon this earth in the near future. They stood for, or easily were made to stand for, the desire for an imminent and total overthrow of the existing order and the substitution of "a new heaven and a new earth" in which would dwell "righteousness." Sometimes, as with the sixteenth-century Thomas Münzer and the seventeenth-century radical protestants in England, the result had been directly political and bloody. More often it remained only religious and involved a patient waiting for divine intervention. But the desire was always discernible to such conservatives as Burke; and it was always lurking in the minds of such radicals as Blake—to be entertained or acted upon.

As Melvin J. Lasky has shown, much of the revolutionary imagery of earthquake, light and dark, and radical as opposed to organic change, insofar as it was not simply an obvious equivalent, was derived from the dissenters and their selective reading of the Bible, especially the books of Daniel and the Prophets and the New Testament Revelation.[20] In the light of these images they read the crucial Gospels and looked back on the Old Testament.

Blake's particular reading of the Bible, however, was obtained through a reading of *Paradise Lost.* Milton gave him the paradigms and their contraries for his Empsonian reading which condemns God the Father, exalts Christ the Son, and makes an ambiguous Orc-like figure of Satan. This is the myth of Creation, Fall, and Redemption retold from the point of view of Adam, the transgressor. The Bible gave Blake a progression, a series of contrasts (father vs. son, king vs. prophet), a poetic prose, an apocalypse, and a role for himself as prophet. He read and rewrote the Bible in the light of the sub-culture (or heretical) traditions, but also in the light of what was happening in the 1780s and 90s in America, France, and England itself—or, perhaps more accurately, he interpreted what was happening in America and France on the model of the Old and New Testaments as he understood them, producing what he called his "Bible of Hell."

Blake plays the canonical text of Genesis against Milton's epic version, returning the Miltonic to an original significance. But this original turns out to be a "contrary" sense, which he derives from Satan's remark:

> But ever to do ill [is] our sole delight,
> As being the contrary to his high will
> Whom we resist.   (I, 160–62)

Resistance and contrariety are Blake's principles of biblical reading. Thus Genesis' "subtile serpent," which becomes Milton's "infernal serpent" via the tradition of Christian iconography, is returned by Blake to its original sense of a vital force that offers man knowledge and is then condemned by a selfish, knowledge-hording deity. His Orc, the spirit of rebellion, derives from Milton's Orcus or Hell (II, 964) because Orc is essentially a Satanic "contrary." In the same way, Blake notes in Genesis 3 a text quite contrary to Milton's, one in which God the Father gives Adam a wife only to discover that "a man [shall] leave his father and his mother, and shall cleave unto his wife: and they shall be one flesh." It is husband and wife (in the Puritan sense) or man and woman in the more contemporary sexual sense *pitted against* the Father; a conjugal union, a conjugal loyalty (which causes Adam to follow Eve in her fall), undermines God's patriarchal family, and so has to be destroyed. At this point Adam and Eve are "both naked, the man and his wife, and were not ashamed." After their disobedience they are made by the Father to feel ashamed of their bodies, their sexuality; and they therefore become Blake's "contrary" to the paternal command.

Blake's procedure is less an art of parody than of revision: revision of the Old Testament story, the Genesis and *Paradise Lost* story, and of these seen through the revisions of Swedenborg and other writers. The text, in other words, is alluded to by Blake in order to be revised and corrected. In this sense he is an example of the great illustrator of the repressed text who brings out its latent meaning which has been covered over by pious and tendentious commentators. He does it, of course, in both words and images. The words carry the plausible appearance (divided into chapters and verses) and sound of the Biblical text. For his visual equivalents he relies on his audience's knowledge of the two graphic sources: the Michelangelo and the Raphael Bibles. (Blake's own engravings after the Loggia designs were included among others made for the *Royal Universal Protestant's Family Bible of 1780*.)

Blake chooses for his own graphic tradition the Michelangelo Bible rather than the Raphael Cartoons (or even, except for a figure here and there, the Loggia designs). His choice makes clear the polarity we have begun to sketch between the Hogarth tradition and the later tradition represented, in their different ways, by Fuseli, Turner, and above all Blake. Hogarth thought in terms of Raphael's stable, classical forms, framed and arranged as a stage-set, describing man in his own social environment. Blake wants the unfixed baroque effect that could be derived from ceiling paintings like Michelangelo's. Hogarth's was a world of horizontal, social relationships embodied in many discrete acts that can be related as a series but juxtaposed in various ways. Blake thinks always in terms of spaces unconfined by perspective systems, of vertical chains of being based on oneness divided, and therefore in a way on the great vertical complex of similarity and difference based on the Incarnation that runs across Michelangelo's ceiling and down his walls on either side, coming to rest in the great vertical rise and fall of the Last Judgment.

But equally important, while Hogarth settled for representations of the New Testament and consigned the Old Testament to the walls of the rooms in which New Testament morality is played out (itself not unrelated perhaps to Michelangelo's vertical chain of ancestors, prophets, popes, and so on), Blake went straight at these insets and made them his subject. Hogarth's procedure was to desacralize the human actors by removing the divine level, the promise of divine providence; Blake reversed Hogarth's procedure removing instead the human. He directly parodies and satirizes the Old Testament mythology in a way that perhaps is closer to Gillray than to Hogarth, but which relates directly to Michelangelo's Sistine ceiling.[21]

To begin, he takes the bearded God of both Michelangelo and Raphael and applies it to the demiurge Urizen. As a particular example, he takes Michelangelo's God separating light from darkness and echoes the image in his representation of Urizen floating up through the water to shape chaos (*Book of Urizen,* p. 12, pls. 62, 63). Or he takes Raphael's God separating light from darkness from the first vault of the Loggia and turns him into Urizen advancing through his dominions (p. 23). But the first is almost immobilized in the water, and the second has one arm weighted down by the lantern he carries, the "globe of fire lighting his journey," and his head is drooping. He is without the energy of Raphael's or Michelangelo's God. Raphael's God creating the sun and moon, echoed in Blake's imaged Urizen launching his new world (p. 27), serves the same function: Urizen is a compressed and ungenerous version, more closely related to the cramped, somnolent Ancestors of Christ in the lunettes than to the expansive figure of God the Father. (See pls. 64, 65.)

The energy has been transferred from God the Father to Blake's response to the Father, the youthful rebel Orc. In Plate 3 the upper part of Orc's body is taken from Raphael's God appearing to Isaac, or perhaps from his God creating the sun and moon. Orc's energy (pl. 69) reflects upon the deity's lassitude, but Orc's general shape and function derive directly (as opposed to parodically) from Michelangelo's Ignudi, the images of heroic pagan, classical knowledge. It is in this sense that Urizen is a parodic version of God the Father at his creation, as when he is seated, slumped and immobile (as he often is), he parodies the energetic Prophets. In both cases he derives from the Ancestors of Christ, the least energized of the groups in Michelangelo's ceiling, some of whom are actually asleep, others fearful, and all ignorant: another form of father for Blake. The title-page showing Urizen is a clear case of a parody of a Prophet, perhaps Zechariah, and a direct representation of a sleeping Ancestor (pls. 67, 68). In turn, Orc can become Urizenized, and when this happens, as in the frontispiece to *America,* he has settled into the shape of one of the Ancestors. (Fuseli, we shall see, makes this the characteristic shape of most of his male figures, compressed, truncated, and in his own terms castrated.)

Blake's works represent visually an interplay of the cast of characters Michelangelo offers on the Sistine ceiling—a spiritual hierarchy of the spandrel nudes, the Ignudi, the Innocenti, the Ancestors of Christ, and the Prophets. (1) The bronze-colored nudes, cramped and confined within the spandrels next to the Prophets' thrones—enclosed, prisoners, or caged beasts, ignorant of the process of Redemption going on around them—are turned into Urizen and his close associates, who ironically, however, sport the long beards of the Prophets and Jehovah. (2) The Ignudi (pl. 68) are, by contrast, sculptural figures who stand out from their surroundings. These representations of the classical or pagan world, beautiful human bodies, half-conscious of what is happening but untouched by Grace, become the energetic figures Blake adopts for his revolutionary Orc and his poetic maker Los. This figure simply breaks the bounds of lunettes and picture frames. He rears up over the horizon like the Ignudi, as in *America* 6—or out of flames, himself resembling tongues of fire, in *America* 10 (pl. 70). The image at its most essential shows him as the center of a sunburst (pl. 69), breaking the circle that circumscribes him, with the center of gravity his loins. Light, youth, and sexuality join in Blake's image of reaction against the Ten Commandments of the Old Testament God. But his art is also involved: rising out of enslavement is equated with the bursting of Scamozzi's textbook diagram of the proportions of the human body—breaking out in an expansive sunburst, his hair twisted into flamelike points. This figure, who is sheer fetter-breaking energy, is somewhere on the ladder of illumination though short of the redemptive knowledge of the Prophets.

(3) The putti, or Innocenti, are the children who in both Michelangelo and Blake represent the state of purity that precedes knowledge. It is a far better state than that of the cramped, dozing Urizen, but it is essentially a junior version of the sheer energy of the full-grown Ignudi. (4) The Ancestors or "Fathers" of Christ the Redeemer, are nevertheless ignorant, fearful, or dozing within their lunettes. They stand in Blake's terms between us and the Redemption, another version of the bronze-colored nudes but older and further removed from the Ignudi. In their enclosures they are completely cut off from illumination (pls. 66, 67). Finally (5) the Prophets (pl. 68), who are as energetic and freestanding as the Ignudi but with the wisdom to foretell the Redemption of Christ, have the beards and books of Urizen but rise off their chairs and look upward or outward toward the future. These figures are the equivalent—in words if not images—of Blake's bard, the poet, and himself.

If we prefer we can say that Blake is working from the bearded fatherly figure of God to the beardless Ignudo who becomes Christ in the Last Judgment. It is one of Michelangelo's angels in the Last Judgment who reaches down to assist the saved, who as Los in plate 15 of *Urizen* reaches down to add light to the darkness, turning chaos into art.

The basic element Blake takes from Michelangelo's visual constructs is the concern to show visually different stages of being—literally of Incarnation, between the human and divine, expressed as Michelangelo does in terms of antique sculpture. These are hardly even allegorical figures so much as psychic divisions. It is the sculptural bodies of the Ignudi and the Prophets, rather than the shape of a lunette or a rectangular perspective box or a book's page, that define space in Blake's books, as in Michelangelo's ceiling. Blake exploits Michelangelo's openness, his sculptural rather than pictorial unities, and his structure based on relations of identity and difference, or of division, only slightly checked by a cyclic narrative. Contrasted with this organic form and its openness are those figures who are self-enclosed in lunettes or spandrels, metaphorically in ignorance or self-satisfaction. The captives and ancestors in the lunettes are, of course, contrasted with the Ignudi and Prophets as contraction to expansion (those basic Blakean terms), which is ultimately reference outward and the breaking of conventional bonds.

This scheme should be distinguished from the strategy of a somewhat earlier work, Sterne's novel *Tristram Shandy* (1759–65), which maintains the sense of enclosed and horizontal narrative space in order to shatter it and rearrange its parts, and so is still (in my terms) Raphaelesque. For Blake's strategy is not so much satiric—as it was for Sterne, who derives in many ways from Hogarth—as visionary. Blake himself is one of Michelangelo's Prophets, just as the heroic Ignudi of Orc and Los are not finally more than stages on the way to the higher revelation represented by the prophetic imagination. As in Michelangelo's plan, the task of the visionary is to free man from the bondage of received ideas, to prepare him for the Incarnation and Redemption, which is in Blake's terms the historico-spiritual response to the bondage of God the Father. Blake exposes the errors of the actual verbal and visual text of the Bible while preserving their truths, which to him meant restoring ideas to their original imaginary sense—before they had been perverted by the Church Fathers.

A very simple example, which can stand for the elaborations of *The Book of Urizen, The Book of Ahania, The Book of Los,* and the rest, is the tiny revision of the story of the Fall called "The Poison Tree." The speaker plants his tree in the inevitable garden as a trap for his friend/foe:

And I waterd it in fears,
Night & Morning with my tears:
And I sunned it with smiles,
And with soft deceitful wiles.

And it grew both day and night,
Till it bore an apple bright.
And my foe beheld it shine,
And he knew that it was mine.

And into my garden stole,
When the night had veild the pole;
In the morning glad I see,
My foe outstretched beneath the tree.

121

Fallen man, who has brought death into the world, is in fact simply the product of God as tyrannical creator/destroyer. The speaker is Milton's Old Testament God of Book III, renamed by Blake Urizen, and the poison tree is his Tree of the Knowledge of Good and Evil. The text illustrated could be Satan's words to Eve on the subject of God's prohibition/temptation:

> What can your knowledge hurt him, or this Tree
> Impart against his will if all be his?
> Or is it envy, and can envy dwell
> In heav'nly breasts?   (Bk. IX, 11. 727-30)

Man is forced, or tempted, into the act of resistance which is the Fall, accompanied by death, but also by knowledge—and with it *double entendre,* ambiguity, and irony.

For Blake's reading of the Temptation in the Garden also extends the original Fall from sexuality (the revolt of repressed man) to language (the Tower of Babel), the second problematic of man in relation to the revisionary situation of his art. Both are Milton-derived, sexuality from the sequal to the Fall in Books IX and X, and the Tower of Babel from Michael's prophecy in Book XII. For even the English language, as Blake refers to it, is but a "rough basement," a floor Los or Jesus puts under the fall as a limit, a minimal end to falling. He refers in *Jerusalem* to "the stubborn structure of the Language, acting against / Albion's melancholy, who must else have been a Dumb despair" (36:58–60).

There is, of course, a sense in which Blake privileges the word—the Prophet's or Bard's voice. As he gives time priority over space, he prefers the ear to the eye unaided. This is because the ear is an internal source of reference, the eye subject to outward distractions. The Blakean dichotomy is therefore internal/external, not strictly verbal/visual. The eye is despotic to the extent that its viewing is determined by perceptual structures imposed by convention. The sense associated with Urizen is the eye because he measures space, lays out caves, rationalizes darkness, and writes books. Urizen is the "I" of the one-point perspective system. Insofar as the word too formulates and charters experience, as for example the Ten Commandments do, it is fallen, a hard materialization of the sound perceived by the ear.

Blake, after all, as an artist-engraver who lived by his eye, had to recognize a truth in the seen—whether seen by the ear or by the inner-eye. His designs are totalities that inhabit a visionary world meant to be perceived by all five senses. The word and the image interact in a multiple-sensory space. His designs are anything but perspectival; nor for that matter do they rely on chiaroscuro or certain kinds of illusionism such as the use of "paltry Blots" that suggest three-dimensional space. If chiaroscuro is the spatial dimension of painting, the outline (the "bounding line") is the mental, but still visual, dimension. It is the verbal aspect that contracts and compresses in perspective and chiaroscuro.

And yet one consideration remains beyond Blake's conscious intention, and that is what W.K. Wimsatt has referred to as his different degrees of artistic competence.[22] The *Songs of Innocence and Experience* in one way sum up the conflict between the verbal and graphic traditions in England. Critics as different as Wimsatt and Harold Bloom have argued that the word in Blake's hands is so powerful that it overwhelms (and among other things, may make us regret) the graphic decorations with which he surrounds them. This is true of the merely illustrative quality of the image that accompanies "The Poison Tree." Interesting and complementary as many of the visual images are, it is possible to feel that they simply derive from a lesser genius and a lesser tradition—from lesser personal and national authority—than the words. Hogarth's solution, which was the solution of one whose graphic competence exceeded his verbal, was to join his images to the verbal tradition. Blake attempted to yoke (not marry, the relationship was too ironic for that) the two traditions as equals, though he was fully aware of the differences. Although he did not allow us the opportunity, we can now (as in Geoffrey Keynes' facsimile of the *Songs*) see the words alone on one page and the illuminated words-and-images on the other. The words alone expand to fill the empty space with their energy (their double and triple meanings, their immense connotations, their verbal contexts, their ambiguities); on the illuminated page they seem cramped and crowded and one's attention has to be drawn to them forcibly away from the pictures.

Since the above was written, Harold Bloom has eloquently summed up this point of view in a review of the catalogue raisonné of *The Paintings and Drawings of William Blake*. If we read Blake alongside his literary precursors, Milton and Pope, "clearly he invites and survives a close comparison with both" poets. But if we do the same with his obvious graphic precursor, Michelangelo, the relationship, "however we interpret it, becomes an esthetic embarrassment when we stare at works of the two artists side by side."[23] In the context of Michelangelo, Bloom can only describe Blake's graphic work as a new "mode," "visionary caricature"—which links him rather with Hogarth in the past, Gillray and Rowlandson among contemporaries, and points to the fulfillment of the mode in an artist of Michelangelesque stature, Goya. Perhaps this is only to say that Blake remains fixed within the tradition of Hogarth, using Michelangelo in the same way that Hogarth used his "old masters," as critical comments on the present, or indeed as catachretic comparisons or Miltonic similes in the fallen world of England in the time of the American and French Revolutions.

There was no graphic presursor for Blake in England, and even Hogarth was to him a literary precursor, an artist who showed him how to deploy his graphic sources. Blake had only the foreign and remote Michelangelo and he used him not as Reynolds, let alone Pontormo or Van Dyck did, but as Shakespeare or Hogarth would have. This means that the graphic for Blake is almost always secondary to a text, and especially so in the illuminated books. We might almost say that the graphic image is, in fact, used as Hogarth used his "old master" images, but as illumination to word in a psendo-Bible rather than (in a realistic stage-like setting) pictures on the wall to the actions of human beings.

Zoffany and Fuseli: The Miltonic Shakespeare

For Hogarth and Fielding the Shakespearean existed as a copiousness of invention and a thematic (and structural) emphasis on nature over art, and it sometimes produced a corresponding weakness of design. This Shakespeare dramatized what Fielding called a "mixed character," a figure acknowledged in *Tom Jones* and silently conveyed by Hogarth in his replacement of either-or choices with the irrationality of both-and inclusiveness. For both artists Shakespeare offered a dramatic precedent for a "novel" form (whether called comic epic in prose or comic history painting or modern moral subject) opposed to the epic and other classical genres that no longer seemed possible in the England of the 1700s; and what was most distinctive about the Fielding-Hogarth genre was its mixedness, its tragi-comic organization of inclusiveness, and its melding of past and present, of Biblical and classical allusion (and various other sign systems), of local representation and gestures from authoritative sources such as the Parable of the Good Samaritan, the Life of the Virgin, or the Judgment of Solomon.

A second Shakespeare was beginning to emerge, however, by the time of Hogarth's death. The copious Shakespeare was being replaced by a Miltonic Shakespeare of intense, narrow interpersonal relationships. Milton's Satan-God, Satan-Eve, Satan-Eve-Adam, or Satan-Sin-Death prepared the way for Samuel Richardson's confrontations of Pamela and Mr. B. or Clarissa and Lovelace or Clarissa, her father, and Lovelace. I do not mean to suggest that Richardson thought of his novel as specifically Shakespearean, but he helped contemporaries to see Shakespeare in the other way, allowing them to recognize something in

124

Shakespeare via the immensely popular Richardsonian novel that they had not seen before. This Shakespeare was, of course, anticipated by some of the Restoration's simplifications. Dryden's *All for Love* was to *Antony and Cleopatra* as *Clarissa* to *Tom Jones.*

In this final section I shall follow strands of painting by three English painters—John (originally Johann) Zoffany, Henry (originally Johann Heinrich) Fuseli, and J.M.W. Turner. I am aware that only the last was born English, and that almost as soon as English art asserts its Englishness it is once again infiltrated by foreigners. But then this assimilativeness is itself English if not Shakespearean. When "Dutch William" was called a foreigner by his English subjects, Daniel Defoe replied ironically in *The True-Born Englishman* (1701):

> From our fifth Henry's time, the strolling bands
> Of banish'd fugitives from neigh'bring lands,
> Have here a certain sanctuary found:
> The eternal refuge of the vagabond.
> Where in but half a common age of time,
> Borrowing new blood and manners from the clime,
> Proudly they learn all mankind to contemn
> And all their race are true-born Englishmen.   (ll. 252-59)

The English power of assimilation is related to the Shakespearean comprehensiveness, the ability to create a tragicomic form that gives a deeper, more complex psychological reality than the strict formal coherence demanded by the neighbors across the sea.

Zoffany is the easiest case. His Shakespeare representations followed directly from Hogarth's *Falstaff examining his Recruits.* While Reynolds was painting splendid versions of Hogarth's *Garrick as Richard III* such as *Mrs. Siddons as the Tragic Muse,* Zoffany continued to paint small conversation pictures which omit any indication of a stage. He turns a theater piece into an illustration but with the odd conversation-picture sense of Mrs. Pritchard acting Lady Macbeth or Garrick acting Macbeth. They are clearly contemporary Englishmen in contemporary costumes, but in a real gothic chamber, one that was not to be seen on a stage. Stage scenery, except for operatic drama, was not elaborately developed during this period. The same sets were used repeatedly—the same interiors, rural prospects, and sylvan groves. Critics as late as the 1790s were commenting on a production of Richard III in which "Trinculo's curtain stood for the tower, and Bosworth Field was a delightful little farm-yard."[24] In other words, Zoffany represents a stage performance rather than a text, but it is often an ideal production with the set replaced by an imaginary space, which he structures in the way Hogarth did his emblematic rooms. As symbols or topoi, the actors' gestures may have been part of the stage business, but they conform to the emblematic background.

The change from emblem to expression was already emerging in the critical writings of that weathervane Arthur Murphy in the late 1750s. The Shakespearean performance he saw on the stage, especially in Garrick's productions, centered around four or five intense, crucial moments that reveal the passions—"their turns, and counter-turns, their flux and reflux, and all their various conflicts."[25] In 1768 Zoffany painted his best-known scene from *Macbeth* (repeated in a second version and engraved). He did not choose to portray Macbeth among his retainers at the banquet where Banquo's ghost appears—a Hogarthian subject of the sort Fuseli was producing at the same time, which could have been composed on the lines of Raphael's *Paul and the Proconsul* or *Falstaff examining his Recruits*. Instead he represented a group portrait of *Garrick and Mrs Pritchard in the Dagger Scene* (pl. 72), a scene in which two people are in a close, tangled personal relationship. He chose the moment of Macbeth's indecision when Lady Macbeth takes the daggers away from him and proceeds to the bed chamber to smear the blood on the sleeping guards, in order to blame them for the murder of Duncan. As Stephen Carr has argued, they are probably composed as a Choice of Hercules, with Garrick in the position of Hercules.[26] Lady MacBeth is in the position of an ironic Virtue, who according to Shaftesbury carries a martial sword.

This insight makes some sense, since Zoffany would be alluding to Reynolds' high-flown allegorical portrait of *Garrick between the Muses of Comedy and Tragedy*, shown at the Royal Academy in 1762 (pl. 71). The large figures filling Reynolds' picture space recall the baroque continental histories Hogarth showed in combat with his own more inclusive scenes in *Battle of the Pictures* (frontispiece). Depending on how one reads Reynolds' portrait, Garrick is either unable to decide between his two equal talents for comedy and tragedy (what Joseph Warton, for example, commended in him as equal to Shakespeare), or is inclining toward Virtue-Tragedy in order to explain why he has chosen her rival. Zoffany, however, placing his figures in a more extensive Hogarthian context, makes the choice a Hogarthian (or Shakespearean) non-choice, substituting an ironic figure of Virtue (Industry or Ambition) who incites Hercules-Garrick to success. If so, then we must notice above all else the absence of an alternative to Lady Macbeth—not, as Carr thinks, in the audience to the picture but in the empty space within the picture. Virtue is replaced by the window, gothic in shape, through which we see a moonlit night sky with clouds. The gothic window space presumably has religious connotations, as did Hogarth's equivalent, the clergyman who turns his back when he is needed, in the first plate of *A Harlot's Progress.* This space is balanced by the open door on the left, behind Lady Macbeth, which is also decorated with gothic arches. The doorway is lit with candlelight, an artificial source of light, behind which the murder has taken place; the gothic window opens onto a natural source of light.[27]

The problem is that Macbeth has made his "choice" earlier, off stage, when he took the daggers left him by Lady Macbeth and killed Duncan. Now his problem is only that he cannot go one step further and return to the murder room to bloody the guards: "I'll go no more: / I am afraid to think what I have done; / Look on't again I dare not." Lady Macbeth says, "Infirm of purpose! / Give me the daggers . . . ," and she goes into the room.

Zoffany's point, referring ironically to Reynolds' allegorical portrait of Garrick, is that Reynolds showed Garrick-Hercules between two goods, Comedy and Tragedy, unable to choose because he is equally good at both. Hogarth had used the paradigm as an ironic choice between two evils or between a present evil and an absent good—or as no choice at all, since the good had been removed, all assistance withheld from the Hercules figure who was supposed to be choosing. The last may be what Zoffany is echoing in the empty gothic window and the natural moonlight, as opposed to Lady Macbeth and the murder room. Macbeth's initiative is over, and the choice has been made. The expression of Garrick's face is not one of indecision so much as despair, on the brink of his descent into a more confident evil because there is no turning back.

Zoffany, like Reynolds, and before him Hogarth, has seen that choice is not a Shakespearean paradigm. He attaches what was essentially a Miltonic pattern to Shakespeare, whose form was much less prescriptive, in order to show how poorly it fits. Boydell's Shakespeare Gallery also used this paradigm on its facade and as frontispiece of the first published volume. Here Shakespeare himself is in the position of choosing between Comedy and Tragedy. And as Samuel Johnson had shown, one of his virtues was in not choosing but in combining the two forms.

The Zoffany representation of Garrick and Mrs. Pritchard is still *about* Garrick as Macbeth. Lady Macbeth is merely Vice luring him on, opposed to the empty gothic window on the other side of him. Fuseli's paintings of exactly the same scene and actors eliminate every distraction to focus on the two equal figures. An early version of around 1766 (pl. 73) has them still dressed in eighteenth-century costumes, as Fuseli saw them on the stage. The time is a moment later than Zoffany's: the frantic Macbeth is under the control of Lady Macbeth, and the line written across the floor near Fuseli's initials, "My husband . . . I've done the deed," refers ahead to her return from the murder chamber after having smeared the blood. Fuseli portrays a husband and wife in direct relationship. A later version, of 1812 (pl. 74), simplifies the figures even more, generalizing their costume, stripping Macbeth to what looks like bare nerves and muscles. Lady Macbeth still wears a long, flowing gown, but its lines are less folds of drapery than forces of energy. Both bodies and faces consist of lines of energy that propel them together—energy virtually materialized in Fuseli's brushstrokes which simplify the figures to sheer kinetic force interacting in a darkened space.

Fuseli is the purest example I can summon of the second phase of Shakespeare illustration in the century. With the rise of Reynolds and the notion that a painting must be taken in at a glance—no time for "reading" or meditating—the rights of unity began to assert themselves in English painting. If Shakespeare could represent the copiousness of a Hogarth, the priority of psychological depth and ambiguity to formal unity, he could also represent the psychological depth as a close interaction of characters. Reynolds himself, when he painted Shakespeare, alternated between a clumsily Raphaelesque Cartoon in his *Macbeth and the Witches* and an intensely focused group like *The Death of Cardinal Beaufort*. Neither is a painting for which much can be claimed. James Barry, a close follower of Reynolds' dicta and also of Burke's philosophy of the sublime, found a solution in the importation of Michelangelo or Carracci figures. Another solution was that of his contemporary John Hamilton Mortimer, who boils a Shakespearean scene down to a face caught in the moment of most intense concentration: Lear's face, beard blowing, as he stands on the heath, or Edgar, whose character is expressed in the imagined portrait of the crafty madman, not the actor (pl. 75). There is no longer an actor, let alone a stage—only the essence of Lear or Edgar in facial expression. This is one verison of the intense focus on character which Morgann celebrated so eloquently in the 1770s.

Fuseli's various illustrations for *Macbeth* show how he selected the particular Shakespeare he was looking for. Besides the dagger scene he painted Macbeth and the witches on the heath (pl. 76); the witches by themselves, three sinister profiles and nothing more—the most famous of his *Macbeth* paintings. He painted Lady Macbeth sleepwalking, observed by her ladies in waiting. There were others: the banquet scene with Banquo's ghost and Macbeth, Macbeth's later scene with the witches. But the main groupings appear in the confrontation of Macbeth with Lady Macbeth and with the witches, and in the related scene of Lady Macbeth alone sleepwalking. These illustrate the categories Fuseli outlines in the writings in which he seeks to establish a new hierarchy of art based not on the old genres (history painting, landscape, portraiture, genre) but on categories of emotional response. Burke's *Philosophical Enquiry* is one text behind Fuseli, though by the 1790s he was also familiar with Kant's *Critique of Judgment*. His categories take off from the beautiful and the sublime, but as they move upward to the sublime the criterion is—the opposite of the Hogarthian spreading out in both space and time into prolepsis and analepsis—a concentration on not only the "pregnant moment" in time but the "striking centre" in space.[28]

The Shakespearean dimension of Fuseli's theory lies in the refusal to accept subject matter as the criterion for the highest art; any subject matter can be made sublime by the artist who elicits the expressive character of his figures at the highest level of interpretation. At the bottom of Fuseli's hierarchy is "historic painting," by which Fuseli (unlike his art-historical predecessors) means the merely factual and informative, and he places Poussin, whom he regards as a master of literal narrative, as its proponent. Next higher is dramatic painting, which reveals the springs of action in human passion, and while he gives Raphael as his graphic model (the Cartoons express the passion which Poussin coldly conceals beneath his formalism), it is clear that Shakespeare is the literary figure he has in mind. In his own work the scenes in which a human interaction like that of Macbeth and Lady Macbeth takes place are "dramatic painting." The two figures can be alone or observed by a third party, but it is the interplay of character with character and event with character that he seeks to elicit.

The third and highest category is epic painting, which is the sublime (to the pathetic of dramatic painting), and is represented by Michelangelo's great brooding single figures. If the dramatic is a scene in which an interaction of equals takes place (pathos), an epic scene is one in which a mortal confronts a supernatural force (sublimity): Macbeth confronts the witches, a human against elemental forces of nature. Fuseli's own words will help us to understand what he has in mind:

> The aim of the epic painter is to impress one general idea, one great quality of nature or mode of society, some great maxim, without descending to those subdivisions, which the detail of character prescribes: he paints the elements with their own simplicity, height, depth, the vast, the grand, darkness, light; life, death; the past, the future; man, pity, love, joy, fear, terror, peace, war, religion, government: and the visible agents are only engines to force *one* irresistible idea upon the mind and fancy. . . .[29]

It is obvious that Fuseli is trying to elevate Macbeth and Lady Macbeth, in their primal confrontation, into this "one general idea, one great quality of nature." His idea is to simplify figures into myth, allegory, or symbol.[30] Sometimes he lumps dramatic and epic painting together as "poetical painting" *versus* "historical painting, viz.: matter of fact": "as a torrent gives its own direction to every object it sweeps along, so the impression of a sublime or pathetic moment absorbs the contrasts of inferior agents."[31]

But there is a difference, which can be seen by contrasting *Macbeth and Lady Macbeth* with *Macbeth and the Witches*. In the first, the two equal figures strive to become the "timeless idea," and in the second, one element, Macbeth, contains the "transient moment" and the other, the witches, the "timeless idea," and their conflict is the subject. In the first Macbeth is bending down as if to withdraw from the room (is he entering or retreating from it?), a passive figure against the lines of force that seem to be propelling Lady Macbeth from the source of light, heat, and energy behind her—so that she seems an emanation of that energy source, in other words a supernatural agency like the witches.

Here are Fuseli's words again:

> It is that magic which places on the same basis of existence, and amalgamates the mythic or super human, and the human parts of the Iliad, or Paradise Lost, and of the Sistine Chapel, that enraptures, agitates, and whirls us along as readers and spectators.   (II, 199-200)

What signifies here is the relationship Fuseli sees between superhuman and human as the basis for sublimity and the equation of *Paradise Lost* and the Sistine Chapel as its embodiment. The Michelangelo ceiling is his example:

> Amid this imagery of primeval simplicity, whose sole object is the relation of the race to its Founder, to look for minute discrimination of character, is to invert the principle of the artist's invention: here is only God with man.   (II, 158)

I think we can see what Fuseli is up to by noticing that while he uses Shakespeare as raw material for epic painting, the epic he has in mind is actually Milton's *Paradise Lost,* seen through the eyes of Burke's *Philosophical Enquiry,* where Satan, rising above his legions in Book I is merged with his confrontation by Death in Book II. Death confronting Satan is the "striking centre" of the epic painting. It is a supernatural force—the witches vis-à-vis Macbeth, or the ghost vis-à-vis Hamlet and Horatio (whose interpersonal relations make a "dramatic" grouping). It is also "that transient moment, the moment of suspense, big with the past, and pregnant with the future" (II, 160).

The Shakespearean dimension of Fuseli's art lies not only in the refusal to accept the old assumptions of decorum but in his twisting and complicating the simple (and simply-presented) Miltonic situation. The Fuselian "excesses" were ironically considered by his German compatriots "as symptomatic of English informality,"[32] whereas they probably drew as much on the tradition of Grünewald, Baldung, and Cranach. His peculiarly personal vision was surely German, but it was incorporated into the capacious Shakespearean idiom and used as a way of drawing out unnoticed or secondary implications from the Shakespearean text.

The most notorious example of audacious extrapolation is, I suppose, his drawing of Claudius pouring the poison in old Hamlet's ear as he sleeps in his garden (pl. 77).[33] Fuseli is specifically recalling Hamlet's description of his father in his first soliloquy (I.2): "So excellent a king that was to this [i.e. the present king, Claudius] / Hyperion to a satyr." Fuseli's Hamlet is bathed in light (a Hyperion); Claudius, hunched in the shadow, has the face of a satyr. In the context of the garden, Fuseli is probably also evoking memories of Satan poisoning—literally pouring it into—the ear of sleeping Eve. But he has based his composition not on a Michelangelo Sistine design but on a pederastic incident from a Greek vase (pl. 78). He has made the pouring of poison into old Hamlet's ear a strangely sexual act of filial love/aggression, which also relates through a displacement to the sleeping figure of Gertrude in the background. To say the least, he has elicited yet another dimension of sexual activity beneath the surface of Shakespeare's play.

In a similar way, nudity is not in Fuseli's "illustrations" a celebration of an ideal Michelangelesque form but a way to reduce characters to their most elemental being. At the same time, this can serve as a sign of their human vulnerability, in particular against the voluminously clothed Lady Macbeths who confront and dominate them.

Perhaps we can see more clearly what Fuseli is doing in *Macbeth and Lady Macbeth* and *Macbeth and the Witches* by studying his written comment on Shakespeare's *Hamlet* and what the one general idea, the "one irresistible idea" is in that play and in his *Hamlet and his Father's Ghost* (pl. 79):

> When [Shakespeare], to stamp on power the mark of private virtue, and to consecrate wedlock, thunders law and nature to ambition, tears the womb of incest, and dashes all its horrors into light, they mince passion to a tear for pretty, harmless, blasted Ophelia, and arraign the great instructor of mankind at the bar of Drury Lane.[34]

This is an obscure passage, as obscure but rich in layers of sense as a Fuseli painting. The metaphorical quality of the passage is more important than its direct sense, which has to do with the effect of Ophelia's destruction on an audience that still believes in poetic justice. But the passage is talking about "stamp[ing] on power the mark of private virtue," that is the destruction of King Claudius by the private needs of Prince Hamlet; the large general, mythological end of the play, which is "to consecrate wedlock," produces a natural force that "thunders law and nature to ambition," i.e. sends down a thunderbolt on Claudius' ambition, "tears the womb of incest," that is, his too-close marriage with his brother's wife Gertrude, and "dashes all its horrors into light," the result being a conflagration so terrible that we should not be surprised that one byproduct is the "blast[ing]"—by that same thunderbolt—of "pretty, harmless" Ophelia.

The force that "thunders law and nature" in Fuseli's painting is the ghost: he appears in flashing light, sending out gusts that agitate Hamlet's cloak and hair. In the same way witches appear to be clouds or winds or some other natural force being challenged by Macbeth. But both Hamlet and Macbeth seem almost as threatening themselves as the supernatural figures they confront. Hamlet (in an action in no way substantiated by Shakespeare's text) is barely restrained by his companions, and we realize that the natural force he seems to be confronting is, of course, his own father, now a ghost and so pure spiritual energy, and that later interpretations have brought to light what certainly Fuseli sensed: the "womb of incest" refers as much to Hamlet and his jealousy of Claudius as surrogate of his father who now beds with his mother as to Hamlet's duty to his murdered father. He seems in this painting to be defying the father himself, rather than the easier substitute of Claudius whom he has to deal with in the rest of the play. As in the Satan-Sin-Death relationship, there is hardly any way of telling in pictures like this which is the human and which the supernatural force.

In *Macbeth and the Witches,* we notice that the dominant figure, with whom as our surrogate we associate, is Macbeth himself. Fuseli tells us that horror, as opposed to the sublime, is "only blood-tipped arrows, brain-dashed stones, excoriating knives," "the minute catalogue of the cauldron's ingredients in *Macbeth.*"[35] What renders Macbeth terrible and sublime, he says, is his pose and our perspective on him:

> to render him so you must place him on a ridge, his down-dashed eye absorbed by the murky abyss; surround the horrid vision with darkness, exclude its limits, and shear its light to glimpses.[36]

The other element, of course, is the witches themselves. But the passage I am quoting goes on to stress the importance of "giving to the principal figure the command of the horizon," and this is Macbeth, the human who is challenging the supernatural force. The confrontation is simply a supernatural version of the one between Macbeth-Lady Macbeth, because in the first a figure has "the command of the horizon" against a supernatural force, and in the second the figures are roughly equal.

Fuseli makes his point more than once, that the figure "to be grand, ought to rise upward in moderate foreshortening, command the horizon, or be in contact with the sky." "This art of giving to the principal figure the command of the horizon," he says, "is perhaps the only principle by which modern art might have gained an advantage over that of the ancients. . . ."[37] The figure rising to lone prominence against a bare and low skyline, and even more the leaping up—as of William Tell—is associated with rebellion. In the drawing for *The Oath on the Rütli* the upraised arms go beyond the picture frame (in the painting [359] the group is closed but not contained by the diagonal of the upheld sword); Satan bursts from chaos (893), leaping up and out of the picture space.[38] *The Lazar House* (1023) of 1791-93 adds to Milton's grim picture of suffering on earth a man who tries to escape, bursting out as Satan does from the lower regions.

These were, of course, the years of the French Revolution. It would be nice to think of his diploma piece at the Royal Academy, *Thor battering the Midgard Serpent* (1790, R.A., pl. 80), as a political allegory,[39] especially since Fuseli's own iconography here is so close to what Blake would produce shortly afterward. Fuseli's representation is very different from his source, the story of Thor and the Midgard Serpent: it turns a trick being played on Thor by the giants into a battle between primal forces. The Orc-like figure—not the usually bearded representation of Thor—is sheer energy and youth dragging up this serpent, with its associations of evil and the Fall, from the bottom of the sea, while the aged giant Hymir (the jokester who has laid a wager against Thor's bringing in his fish) cowers at the back of the boat and the equally aged and very Urizen-like figure of Odin huddles in a compact shape watching from a safe distance in the clouds (cf. the title page of Blake's *Urizen* and plate 2 of *America).*

Certainly one could make a case for the revolutionary imagery of such pictures as *Hercules freeing Prometheus* (711) of about the same time; or even *The Death of Oedipus* (1785, 712a), with its Urizen figure in the center as the father, with his disobedient sons gone and his daughters at his knees. *Britomart frees Amoret from Busirane* (1008) takes on additional significance when we see that Busyrane's figure is based on Parmigianino's *Moses*—a father-figure associated with the Ten Commandments, and whom Blake took as a model for his Urizen.

The angle from which we see Thor casts him alone against the horizon. In *The Oath on the Rütli,* we see from the space beneath the rebels' feet; with Thor, from the serpent's point of view: Thor has pulled him up by his chain and prepares to strike; William Tell leaps from Gessler's boat, a leap to freedom recalling the Swiss struggle against Austrian tyranny.[40]

But as in *The Lazar House* these gestures of liberation are often enclosed from above and threatened with compacting or at least restraining, like the figure of Hamlet held back by Horatio. Fuseli introduces a revolutionary gesture and then counters it. Even Thor is constrained—perhaps by formal reasons—by the darkness above the cloud Odin sits upon, which extends over him, and by the shape of his upward-flying cloak, which in any case, with the gesture of striking the Midgard Serpent, force him to lower his head. The figure of Odin and the dark area above the clouds that extends from him functions in much the same way as the arching wings of Death in *The Lazar House,* which cover or canopy the leaping figure, closing the whole upper part of the scene.

The foreshortening of figures, or what the Germans call "the frog's perspective," is related by Fuseli to the escape of Satan or of William Tell; but if it is something like the birth trauma it is seen from the point of view of the parent—for, after all, it is this heroic figure who is rebelling, rising out of the parent, and offering resistance, assuming the parent's own looming presence. But we see him from the point of view of the parent—the "mother," as in *Frankenstein,* whose creation rises up out of her, terrifying because no longer a part of her, now the Other, threatening, and terrible with liberty.

Notice that there is none of this in Blake's Orc or in his *Albion Rose* (pl. 69). No restrictions are imposed on the youth's expansive gesture which has broken the Vitruvian circle. The implications are sexual, the center of gravity being his loins, and his first act—in *America* and other versions of the myth—is to rape the young girl, his keeper's daughter. And yet there is, a few years later, something similar to Fuseli's closure in the complex and shifting relationship Blake shows between Orc and Urizen, as the rebellious son becomes the tyrannous father. Even in *America* the frontispiece, as opposed to the "Preludium," shows Orc now closed and closing the hole he has himself knocked in the wall of tyranny.

In Fuseli there is no interchangeability of roles. The father (or the mother) comes back down on the rising child, cutting him off, radically curtailing him. The examples are legion: the bard looms up but seems pressed down by the force of his own upraised arms, and is in fact about to plunge down to his death (pl. 91). More commonly, Lucifer plummets down as Uriel looms up (1211), and the artist, in *The Artist in Despair over the Magnitude of Antique Fragments* (665), is bent over in the shadow of a huge monument cut off at the ankles. The artistic source for Fuseli's characteristic shape of the bent-over man can be found in his copies of Michelangelo's Ancestors, in the Sistine lunettes who seem to be confined, pressed down by arches (pls. 81, 82). Fuseli uses these figures as the basis for his Shakespeare frontispieces, in particular the one for *Macbeth* (pl. 83). In one of the versions of *Macbeth and Banquo with the Witches*, Macbeth's head is compressed by his over-arching cape, like Thor's (737).

There is a strange detail in the 1812 *Macbeth and Lady Macbeth* painting (pl. 74): a single horizontal line of paint has been inscribed over Macbeth's head, making it appear that his stooping posture as he leaves the murder room is caused by a low lintel. And if we look at a great many of Fuseli's truncated, compacted, or in some way diminished figures, we see that they are all male and that the diminishment often comes from the relationship with a woman. Taking only his Shakespeare representations, we can compare Fuseli's and Hogarth's Falstaffs: Fuseli chooses the scene from *The Merry Wives of Windsor* in which Falstaff is made mock of by the ladies, literally being compressed into the buck basket—arms and blankets over his head (pl. 84). From the *Henry VI* plays he shows Queen Margaret mocking York, who is being held down—in one version she and her soldiers are holding him down, in another he has collapsed into the Christ of a Pietà (441, 1406). Even Romeo, as he descends from Juliet's room, is being covered, pushed down, or held down by Juliet from above (1552-53).

Fuseli puts all his talents into his large paintings of Bottom and Titania in *Midsummer Night's Dream* (pl. 85). The subject is the transformation of Bottom into an ass and of Titania into his doting mistress: the fantasy of an Oberon-husband with the realism of the cynical cuckold who knows both that man is made an ass by love (in whatever guise) and that it is a beast of a man that a woman will fall in love with to the jeopardy of her husband or true love. The image, however (one of his most crowded and fully-realized), amounts to—if we strip away all the accompanying figures—Titania and her assistants preventing Bottom from rising, in one case holding him down with a gentle arm, in the other hovering over his prone body. It is a scene that relates to Fuseli's pornographic drawings of passive spread-eagled men being tortured or in various ways dealt with by terribly active women.[41]

The model here is not Shakespeare, not *Macbeth*, or *The Merry Wives of Windsor*, but Milton's *Samson and Delilah* (pl. 86), from which Fuseli then goes back and finds his theme wherever he can in

Shakespeare. Samson is in his prison cell and Delilah appears in the window with an elaborate coiffure, looking in on her erstwhile lover who sits shorn. Windows are also seen from the outside, while courtesans behind them reveal a comfortable interior—and outside, looking in, is their potential prey. It is obvious that these windows or doorways holding women tend to become vaginal displacements. Fuseli likes to represent fireplaces and other openings before which stand spread-legged women, sometimes with phallic supports to emphasize the meaning (e.g. 1075, 1091, 1092, esp. 1618). Then when holding men, these openings become enclosures, prison cells.

Men are very often stooping, bending under a yoke, under some cramping structure, as Macbeth seems to be stooping under the low door as he returns to Lady Macbeth. They are being held down by some sort of closure above them, often an arch, more often a Queen Margaret. Such compositions run all the way from *Almansaris visiting Huon in Prison* (1228) to *Brunhild with Gunther suspended from her Ceiling* (1381). Fuseli shows Theseus with Ariadne compressing his head (714), and Eve doing the same to (or having the same effect on) Adam—with the angels flying upward, their job done, back to heaven, now that the Fall is a fact. Adam appears with Eve's hands around and over his head, pressing him down, enclosing him in a bower (pl. 87). Even when the husband has imprisoned and punished an errant wife, locking her up with the bones of her lover, it is he who bends down to enter her cell (1493). The ultimate image, I suppose, is that of the maenads guillotining a man: the guillotine is a window-like enclosure, but now it introduces the castration motif, as well as recalling Fuseli's fear, after initial admiration, of the French Revolution (805).

Fuseli applies the situation directly to himself and to the artist. The woman representing Pictura in his *Second Allegory of Painting* (493) is not only bending down over the compressed, indeed squashed figure of the artist, but is preparing to split open his skull (as Jael to his Sisera). In *Caricature of the Artist leaving Italy* (568) the artist is bending back, with his hand protecting his head, and though no immediate threat is visible, the allusion is to the Deluge, for the pose is borrowed from one of the Ignudi adjoining "The Flood" on Michelangelo's Sistine ceiling.[42] Even in Fuseli's self-portraits he is bent over a text, like Tieresias bent over that blood without which he is the merest of shadows, compressed and pensive (pls. 88, 89).

In short, an aspiration to height and power, with consequent constriction, forms a pervasive personal structure of Fuseli's oeuvre—summed up in Coleridge's remark that Fuseli's art is marked by "vigorous impotence" (words that equally apply, among Fuseli's favorite subjects, to Milton's Samson and Satan). Heroism is dwarfed, intimidated, and frustrated: for men heroic pursuits are clearly dangerous, leading, as with Satan, Prometheus, and Adam, to a decline in power. It seems reasonable to relate this constraining, reducing force—the lintel under which Macbeth stoops—to the supernatural force confronting or confronted by a human being in Fuseli's formulation of epic painting. The model for a great many of Fuseli's paintings may be his *Macbeth and the Witches* or *Hamlet and his Father's Ghost.*

And yet the same dangers are not so consistently applicable to Fuseli's women, who (the witches are one example) in many cases carry out the diminishment of the man. This is clear in the nakedness of the hero (for example, Macbeth stooping under the lintel), a sign of his vulnerability, and the overdressed figure of the female; the shorn Samson and the high-coiffured Delilah.[43] As the guillotine image suggests, and also the truncation of the heroic statue in *The Artist in Despair over the Magnitude of Antique Fragments,* the hint of castration is strong. It is the case that in Fuseli not the visible figure of the threatening father comprises the essence of castration, but rather the glimpse of that almost-but-not-quite nothing of the mother, the closure from above.

We can see now, looking back over our cast of characters, that one aspect of Shakespeare has gradually become Miltonic. He was the most powerful of literary models in the first half of the century at least partly because he represented in his plays various points of view rather than one single authoritarian one, as Milton did in *Paradise Lost,* where he cast himself as speaker, epic poet, and analogue of the Son Himself. Hogarth's adaptation of Shakespeare involved painting pictures that incorporated more than one point of view on a subject—both the master's and the servant's, both the patron's and the painter's. Blake, the Miltonic poet, took the single point of view, but it was that of the Other—Adam, not God; the creature, not the created. Fuseli then, we have to conclude, illustrated Shakespeare but focused his scenes on a *Paradise Lost* confrontation, a Temptation in the Garden, Macbeth and Lady Macbeth, or man against a supernatural force. On the other hand, he narrowed himself to a single, overriding point of view—not authoritarian but deeply personal, that of Fuseli the painter, with his own personal preoccupations or obsessions. Looking back, however, we see that Fuseli's pose is not so different from the autobiographical note struck from time to time by Hogarth in his most public modern moral subjects.

Turner: Shakespearean/Miltonic Landscape

Fuseli was a follower of Michelangelo in that he was interested only in the human figure. He suppressed all else. And yet his theory, and to some extent his practice, served to validate the tradition of sublime landscape painting. For one thing, his theory elevated landscape to the highest rank, of epic or sublime painting, and gave it a prominence it never had held in earlier theory.[44] To see how this could be, we must return to Fuseli's Macbeth as both subject and object of terror, as challenger and challenged—with the viewer assuming his position in relation to the witches, but also in relation to Macbeth himself in the vacillating manner of Burke's in relation to Satan and Death. Fuseli places Macbeth on a ridge on which he becomes an extension of the jutting rock; he is appropriated by (or appropriates) the aggressive natural form. In our terms, sublimity consists in the individual's disappearance into a landscape, or his resistance to this absorption—analogous to his struggle in *Macbeth and Lady Macbeth* with the female element (with in this case the witches).

Fuseli puts it this way, discussing the background in Reynolds' portraits: the sublime is "whatever connects the individual with the elements," and the pathetic is "whatever connects it in the same manner with, or tears it away from the species." In other words, in so far as Macbeth and Lady Macbeth make a dramatic painting, a pathetic interchange, they are related as two equal individuals; but, especially in the 1812 painting, insofar as they both dissolve into natural forces, or Macbeth dissolves into a natural force which *is* Lady Macbeth, the effect is sublime, the painting epic.

> For every being seized by an enormous passion, be it joy or grief, or fear sunk to despair, loses the character of its own expression, and is absorbed by the power of the feature which attracts it.

This applies to Hamlet responding to the ghost as well as to Macbeth responding to the witches. "Niobe and her family are assimilated by extreme anguish," he gives us as one example. "The metamorphoses of ancient mythology founded on this principle," Fuseli says, "are allegoric. Clytia, Biblis, Salmacis, Narcissus, tell only the resistless power of sympathetic attraction."[45] Fuseli's sublime metamorphosis is to be contrasted with the ordinary Ovidian metamorphosis in which the nymph is changed in order to escape the destructive passion. Fuseli's nymph is absorbed into a natural force which allegorizes the passion of which she is the object.

It is not difficult to see how this theory could animate landscape painting. It is worth noting that landscape painting in England in the eighteenth century was parallel to history painting in that in both cases there was a native tradition that wanted to portray local English subjects rather than "landscape" or Italian or French scenes, and to do so had to accommodate this desire for the national or provincial to the generic requirements of history or landscape—or just history. There was ideal landscape as a model but also history itself. The solution was most often to paint a fringe of history at the bottom of a landscape, as a kind of emblem attached to the landscape—which could be tempestuous to accord with murderous figures or calm to contrast with them or to correspond to calm figures. The double aim to paint the local and to paint in the great tradition of history found a more immediate solution in scenes of English history, in particular in the rugged, primitive outposts of Wales or Scotland.

An alternative to the fringe of activity along the bottom of a landscape was the Fuselian concept of metamorphosis, which in landscape painting was practiced (independently of Fuseli) by Thomas Gainsborough at the level of *poesia* and the pathetic, but not of the sublime. Gainsborough's figures do seem to dissolve into their natural surroundings, and he manifests this in a history painting of the metamorphosis of Actaeon into a stag in a natural setting with Diana and her nymphs in which everything seems to be merging into natural forms and textures (Royal Collection).

The sublime landscape, in so far as it derives from literature of the period, begins with Thomas Gray's poem *The Bard,* published the same year as Burke's *Philosophical Enquiry.* What Gray shows—literally dramatizes in dialogue—is an encounter between poet and king, the last Welsh bard and Edward I who has conquered Wales and killed all the other bards. The poem presents the bard's retaliatory curse on Edward, followed by his plunge—and by the gradual unfolding of his curse's fulfillment through the Wars of the Roses. This is in a landscape setting with the bard high on the top of a cliff and Edward the king at the bottom. The apparent reversal of status suggests that the bard is in fact spiritually above the king, but also associated with the natural shape and force of the elevation and the mountain. He is in some sense receiving inspiration and power from a higher source. The point of view of the poem—from which we read and see—is from down below, looking up at the bard. The fact that the bard plunges to his death at the end only acts as a final dissolution of the human into the supernatural force from which he has taken strength, the power of prophecy and of retribution.

John Martin's version (1817, pl. 90) conveys this in one way, Fuseli's (pl. 91) in another. Martin shows the confrontation of two widely-separated figures, below and above, closely associated with their spatial and natural positions. One of the things implied by the passage in Burke's *Enquiry* juxtaposing Satan and Death is that the sublime cannot exist without human nature being in some way represented. The human, however, is either resisting natural force (King Edward) or beginning to merge with it (the bard, almost disappearing in Martin's version into the lighter area where mountain top and flashing sky meet).[46] So a painter simply places a bard atop the mountain and the king below, two kinds of power, virtually interchangeable, and he has a typical structure for sublime landscape painting.

Fuseli shows only the bard, but implies the king from whose point of view we see him—as we see the two figures Burke uses from *Paradise Lost,* one at a time, implying the point of view of the other. We are the king looking up at the bard or the human looking up at the transcendent. Moreover, Fuseli's illustration, especially the drawing (pl. 91), uses the graphic tradition of Bible illustration for a contemporary English poem. The figure of the bard is based on figures of Jehovah, Old Testament prophets, and Moses. Fuseli is imitating the Michelangelo figures of the Sistine ceiling rather than the Raphael Cartoons, where the bard would have been Paul preaching at Athens. Here he is a figure of the Father, of authority.

The choice is appropriate. Gray's *Bard* in its literary text is taken from Milton's *Paradise Lost,* Book XII, a filling out of the curse on man following the Fall, presented to Adam on Pisgah, plus a hope for redemption; and it also carries with it something of Pope's *Dunciad* IV, where the bard is destroyed by contemporary corruption but still declaims as chaos and old night close in around him. Gray's bard, looking down on Edward's troops, carries with him quite a bit of Moses (also implicit in Pope's *Dunciad* IV) looking down from Mt. Sinai on the idolatrous, backsliding Israelites. He is the seer, doomed in a fallen world to place prophetic curses and not live to see their fulfillment.

The arms of Fuseli's bard, raised to emphasize his curse, make an arch over his head, as if containing or even cutting off his liberated, rising figure. Given the fact that he is about to leap to his death, we recognize him as the Fuselian conflation of the victorious God of War in Heaven and the plunging loser Satan (pls. 91, 92). Although the bard is challenging the king of England, he is seen from the frog's eye view with which we regarded Macbeth. This is essentially the child's view of his parent, and probably for this reason sublime: the parent is threatening, towering, a rising male principle, apparently tumescent like that mountain that rises behind William Wordsworth's flight in the stolen boat, but closed at the top by his own gesturing, curse-placing arm, which serves the Fuselian role of the over-arching mother containing all her sons/lovers.

An extreme case of sublime landscape is Philippe de Loutherbourg's *Avalanche* (1804, Tate, pl. 92), in which the humans in the foreground confront a huge natural catastrophe—forces that man cannot encompass—and watch fellow men swallowed or absorbed by the avalanche they are barely escaping. Turner's version, *Avalanche in the Grisons* (1810, Tate, pl. 93), simply removes the figures and puts the viewer himself, unmediated, in the position of the threatened human, with no footing, no place to stand, no looming presence, directly confronting apocalypse: the equivalent of Fuseli's witches, or indeed his bard, as natural force.

The reflection of Fuseli's ideas in Shakespeare illustration begins (with no direct Fuseli influence) in John Runciman's *King Lear* of 1767 (pl. 94) and ends in the enlargement of landscape background and subordination of the figures as in Wright of Derby's illustration for *A Winter's Tale: Antigonus* ("exit pursued by a bear") about to be literally devoured by the forces of nature, repeated in the stormy coast (engraved for Boydell in 1794).

Runciman represents Lear on the heath with Kent, the Fool, and others—a scene that takes place far from the ocean, but which Runciman places on the seashore in the midst of a storm.[47] He is illustrating not the scene itself but the metaphor for Lear's state of mind, as transmitted in the Gentleman's speech to Kent (III.i), who has asked, "Where's the king?"

> GENT. Contending with the fretful element;
> Bids the wind blow the earth into the sea,
> Or swell the curled waters 'bove the main,
> That things might change or cease.

In scene iv, on the heath before a hovel, the scene that is supposedly illustrated, Lear relates the storm to the raging sea—"if thy flight lay toward the raging sea," and two lines later disconnects the physical and mental: "the tempest in my mind / Doth from my senses take all feeling else / Save what beats there." That is the image Runciman has painted: Lear and the sea in close conjunction, the sea and the tempest in his mind.

The employment of Shakespeare goes into its third phase in the eighteenth century as a subject for landscape-painting, usually (but not always) of a sublime, tempestuous sort. We only need to recall Samuel Johnson's association of Shakespeare, nature, and the wilderness to realize that the "natural" in contrast to human reason and order can easily become nature itself. This is the case in Turner's absorption of history into landscape, a huge wilderness that resembles a landscape of the mind. But Turner does not let go of the older sense of Shakespearean nature, the people or incident, the copiousness of human types that is the Hogarthian residue in so many Turner landscapes. In Fuseli's terms, however, these people are going to be not so much Hogarthian figures as an Antigonus or a Lear in a starkly simple relationship of conflict or confrontation.

The most interesting of Turner Shakespeare illustrations is, I think, his cityscape *Juliet and her Nurse,* which was exhibited at the R.A. in 1836 (pl. 95). It is not unlike Turner to place the traces of the literary text in the lower right corner, almost out of sight, showing Juliet and her nurse on the Capulet balcony; it is not unlike Turner to set Romeo and Juliet in Venice rather than Verona where Shakespeare set it. This anomaly was immediately noticed by hostile critics; in Verona he could have copied the house itself that is claimed to be Juliet's with its undramatic, easily-accessible balcony. He chose the more dramatic, more readily-recognized Venice.

We shall begin with the small foreground figures and then turn to the larger composition; and begin with the question: Why Juliet and her nurse rather than Juliet and Romeo? The only scene Turner can be referring to is III.v, just after the night spent with Romeo and his departure through the window and over the balcony (the green shutter at the far right edge of the canvas indicates the window out of which he has just departed). The nurse tenders Juliet her prudential advice, that she should give up Romeo and marry Paris. At this point Juliet realizes that she can have no more to do with the nurse or her advice. The nurse in general represents two sentiments in the play: the earthy one, "Thou wilt fall *backward* when thou hast more wit" (I.iii), and the prudential one, "Then, since the case so stands as now it doth, / I think it best you married with the county [Paris]"—to which Juliet responds (solus), "Go, counsellor; / Thou and my bosom henceforth shall be twain."

We should recall, however, that this scene opened with the approach of day, which brings Romeo and Juliet's night of love-making to an end—their last night, their last meeting. No, as Juliet insists, "It was the nightingale, and not the lark"—it is still night, not dawn, and there is no need for Romeo to leave. But, says Romeo,

> It was the lark, the herald of the morn,
> No nightingale: look, love, what envious streaks
> Do lace the severing clouds in yonder east:
> Night's candles are burnt out, and jocund day

Stands tiptoe on the misty mountain tops. . . .
   JUL. Yond light is not day-light. I know it, I:
It is some meteor that the sun exhales,
To be to thee this night a torch-bearer. . . .

This sort of jockeying goes on, until Romeo has reminded Juliet that morning means his detection and death at the hands of the Capulets, and she acknowledges the bird to be a lark. The nurse, however, is the official announcer of the day as she is of real prudential life: "Madam, . . . Your lady mother is coming to your chamber: / The day is broke; be wary, look about."

It would appear then that the picture as a whole, when we look up from the two figures on the balcony, is about that moment at which night and day, desire and reality, imagination and reason, are at interface—when "the lark makes sweet division."

Turner's painting elicited the sort of attack he was receiving in the 1830s, in particular the predictably harsh comments of the Reverend John Eagles:

> This is indeed a strange jumble—'confusion worse confounded.' It is neither sunlight, moonlight, nor starlight, nor firelight, though there is an attempt at a display of fireworks in one corner, and we conjecture that these are meant to be stars in the heavens. . . .[48]

Eagles also refers to such "absurdities" as placing Juliet and her nurse in Venice, but the sky clearly bothers him most, and it is to this that John Ruskin returns in his defense of the painting—the defense which launched him on his massive brief for Turner in *Modern Painters:*

> That this picture is not seen by either starlight, sunlight, moonlight, or firelight, is perfectly true: it is a light of its own, which no other artist can produce,—a light which seems owing to some phosphorescent property in the air. The picture can be, and ought only to be viewed as embodied enchantment, delineated magic.[49]

This is a spirited response, but it hardly meets Eagles' objections. It reminds me of Charles Lamb's defense of Restoration comedy against charges of immorality on the grounds that a world of "embodied enchantment, delineated magic" is not to be judged in terms of the real world, which in this case is the world of Shakespeare's text.

I am suggesting, of course, that the strange lighting effect in Turner's painting is explained by the desire of two lovers for an everlasting night in the face of a cold dawn. Romeo has in fact parted from Juliet, who is left alone with the nurse's voice of commonsense, of the earth—and in fact the nurse is painted in what Turner (through Goethe) designated as material or earth colors, black or negative colors as opposed to the yellow aerial colors of day, of Juliet herself. Juliet is flooded in light, illuminating the side of the nurse turned toward her. Her own head is turned away from the nurse toward the light in the square—but also toward the far side of the Piazza, the façades of San Marco, the Campanile, and the Doge's Palace bathed in sunrise. And yet, as one discerns by a glance at the map, those buildings face west, and the sun rises in the east.

Turner's critics have always noticed these anomalies. W. Cosmo Monkhouse in 1879 pointed to Turner's "strange errors, which no one else could have made, such as putting the sun and moon in impossible positions in the same picture." Before and after Monkhouse, critics have noticed the joining, balancing, mixing, or contending of sun and moon, light and dark, summer and winter in Turner's paintings.[50] But in *Juliet and her Nurse* Turner has gone to Shakespeare's text and found the familiar Turner paradox of light and dark as interchangeable and profoundly ambiguous.

The locus for the congruence of light and dark, blindness and insight, was of course the pair of suns in Milton's apostrophe to his blindness in the invocation to Book III of *Paradise Lost*. Like the bonfire and the true sun in Plato's myth of the cave, Milton's external sun, to which he is blind, is contrasted with "thou Celestial light / Shine inward . . . that I may see and tell / Of things invisible to mortal sight." The sense of duality—of darkness as well as light—is apparent in the sense of the sun as rising and setting. Dugald Stewart, writing of sublimity, discusses a circumstance

> which conspires, in no inconsiderable degree, in imparting an allegorical or typical character to literal *sublimity*. I allude to the Rising, Culminating, and Setting of the heavenly bodies; more particularly to the Rising, Culminating, and Setting of the Sun; accompanied with a corresponding increase and decrease in the heat and splendour of its rays. It is impossible to enumerate all the various analogies which these familiar appearances suggest to the fancy. I shall mention their obvious analogy to the Morning, Noon, and Evening of life; and to the short interval of Meridian Glory, which, after a gradual advance to the summit, has so often presaged the approaching decline of human greatness.[51]

In common parlance, there are phrases attached to declining politicians: "more worship the rising than the setting sun," and so on. These are some of the metaphoric equivalences Turner develops in the sun, which he almost always shows palpable in the middle of the sky, either rising or setting—ambiguously so, for in his terms the rising and the setting are the same, just as the blindness and the insight are one. He does not, of course, show the sun itself in *Juliet and her Nurse* but only its effect on the fronts of the buildings.

Recall the "transient moment" Fuseli imbued with sublimity. Each scene on the Sistine ceiling, he wrote, "turns upon that transient moment, the moment of suspense, big with the past, and pregnant with the future," embodied above all in the single figures of the Prophets who exhibit "in the occupation of the present moment the traces of the past and hints of the future." This is one of the elements of Fuseli's sublime that allows him to include landscape painting, which reveals nature "in the varied light of rising, meridian, setting suns; in twilight, night and dawn."[52]

It is not difficult to see why Turner chose the leave-taking scene from *Romeo and Juliet* for one of his major paintings. As Carolyn Spurgeon noticed long ago, in this play

> the beauty and ardour of young love is seen by Shakespeare as the irradiating glory of sunlight and starlight in a dark world. The dominating image is *light*, every form and manifestation of it; the sun, moon, stars, fire, lightning, the flash of gunpowder, and the reflected light of beauty and of love; while by contrast we have night, darkness, clouds, rain, mist, and smoke.[53]

Turner would have taken note of this imagery. He transforms it into the matter of his painting—into its sky and its lighting system. For the scene which ends with the dialogue of Juliet and her nurse is anticipated by Romeo's earlier words beneath the balcony:

> But soft! what light through yonder window breaks?
> It is the east, and Juliet is the sun.   (II.ii.2-3)

In the darkest night, he tells us,

>   her eyes in heaven
> Would through the airy region stream so bright
> That birds would sing and think it were not night.

The strange lighting of the Piazza and the sky across the Grand Canal recalls all the references to torches at the ball (I.v.28, 45, 88, 126) which erupt in Romeo's lines

> O, she doth teach the torches to burn bright!
> It seems she hangs upon the cheek of night
> Like a rich jewel in an Ethiope's ear . . . .   (ll. 45-47)

These lines may have inspired the displacement of a flaming Juliet to a flaming overflow of light into the Piazza—and to the flare against the dark sky, "Like a rich jewel in an Ethiope's ear." The last words of Romeo as he departs from Juliet's room and the sun rises, just as the nurse makes her entrance, just prior to the scene Turner has painted,

145

are: "more light and light: more dark and dark our woes!"

His departure is a forecast of the end at night in the dark grave vault, Romeo with his torch, the dark vault flooded with metaphoric light from Juliet's apparently dead body ("A grave? O, no! a lantern . . . . / For here lies Juliet, and her beauty makes / This vault a feasting presence full of light"), and finally the coming of day as the mourners gather, and the overcast morning in which "The sun for sorrow will not show his head."

In short, Juliet is of course the source of light in Turner's painting: "It is the east, and Juliet is the sun." She is the surrogate for a sun that is mythically rising in the west and so brilliantly illuminating the façade of the buildings on the east side of the Piazza San Marco.

Why then, given this scheme, did Turner not illustrate the lines I have discussed between Romeo and Juliet rather than the words of the nurse? Because he always chooses the moment of doom—the moment afterward, the moment of Romeo's absence. Juliet's doom is presaged by the blackness, the earth colors, the sunset of the nurse.

The answer to this question is related to the answer to another: Why does Turner place Juliet's story in Venice instead of Verona? First, I should mention the possibility that some details may derive from another text, the story of Giulietta and Marcolini in Samuel Rogers' poem *Italy* (1836, illustrated with designs by Turner).[54] Marcolini's story, which does take place in Venice, is another case of that favorite Turner phenomenon, a "Fallacy of Hope": his marriage with Giulietta just settled, he is mistakenly accused and then executed for a crime—simply because in his moment of exultation he picked up an empty scabbard from the street. Giulietta goes mad, and when the error is discovered

> every night, when the great square is illuminating and the casinos are filling fast with the gay and the dissipated, a bell is rung as for a service, and a ray of light seen to issue from a small gothic window that looks towards the place of execution, the place where on a scaffold *Marcolini* breathed his last.[55]

There are one or two illuminated spots at the far left of Turner's Piazza, and it is possible that Juliet/Giulietta may be looking in that direction. But there is obviously no "small gothic window" on either side of the Piazza, and Juliet is on her familiar balcony and accompanied by her nurse (there is no balcony, no nurse in Rogers' story).

It would, of course, have been characteristic of Turner to place Shakespeare's Verona in Venice and to call a picture *Juliet and Her Nurse* but mean *Giulietta* in an obscure passage in a work by Samuel

Rogers. The only reasonable conclusion, however, is that Turner has conflated the two Juliets as he has Verona and Venice, and he has done this to superimpose on the star-crossed love of Romeo and Juliet, which ends in one sort of tragedy of errors, a story in which Romeo's moment of joy turns out to be another bubble burst by civil law, represented by those state buildings that close the Piazza. The primary sense, as Turner must have known by titling his picture *Juliet and her Nurse,* not *Giulietta,* is of the Shakespeare text. Then, as Turner appropriates whatever text he illustrates, he may incorporate a second text which more clearly (to him at least, since no one, not even Ruskin, until 1980 recognized the second text) makes his point about the destruction of the love affair by external fate.

To continue with our answer to "Why Venice?" we return to another contemporary criticism of the painting, in the London *Times,* that remarks acidly that the *Juliet and her Nurse*

> is nothing more than a second and worse edition of that great colorist's *Conflagration of the two Houses of Parliament.* . . . This is a Venetian Westminster Bridge with a very rough resemblance of a young and an old woman, standing in one of the alcoves, and looking over the Thames, converted into Italian piazzas. . . .[56]

In short, Turner has put Shakespeare's story of doomed love in a composition in which the seat of church and civil government of Venice corresponds, in relation to the side of the Piazza with its spectators (and all the spectators below in the Piazza) to the English Houses of Parliament, Westminster Bridge, and the spectators to the fire in the version now in Philadelphia of *The Burning of the Houses of Parliament* of just one year earlier (B.I. 1835, pl. 96).

In the *Houses of Parliament* paintings Turner's sun has developed certain of its connotations—of power and destruction—until it has become a literal fire destroying the seat of government in the gesture Guy Fawkes had once planned. The French Revolution had turned around the image of the sun as the king, the center of light, warmth, and power, to the sun as force of human reason, justice, and revolutionary destruction. As Thomas Paine put it, perhaps most memorably but echoing many other writers: "From a small spark, kindled in America, a flame has arisen, not to be extinguished."[57]

That is one connotation Turner's sun had assumed by this time in his career. But we still need to see why he chose Venice when he could have found a composition in Verona itself—the castle, the bridge, and the river—which corresponded much more closely to the Houses of Parliament, Westminster Bridge, and the Thames. The story of Giulietta and Marcolini helps us toward an answer, but we also need to look at another Turner—of 1843, but echoing earlier images of Venice in Turner's oeuvre: *The Sun of Venice going to Sea* (pl. 97). The boat carries the sign of the sun painted on its sail, and then in the words "Sol de Veneza Mi Ragi . . . [i.e. Raggia—shine on me]." But to this image Turner adds verses from his poem "The Fallacies of Hope":

> Fair shines the morn, and oft the zephyrs blow,
> Venezia's fisher spreads his painted sail so gay,
> Nor heeds the demon that in grim repose
> Expects his evening prey.

The lines turn the image of sunrise into one of sunset and darken the image into death and not only the demise of this fishing boat but the decline of the Venetian state (fallen in 1797)—a theme as persistent in Turner's work as in his probable sources, Byron, Rogers, and many popular poems and epigrams of the day.[58] It was certainly Byron who gave him Venice as a symbol of lost grandeur, and also pointed out the relationship to London when he addressed Venice in *Childe Harold:*

> and thy lot
> Is shamefull to the nations, most of all
> Albion! to thee; the Ocean queen should not
> Abandon Ocean's children; in the fall
> Of Venice think of thine, despite thy watery wall.   (IV, xvii)

The sun*rise* is of course the rise of the sun painted on the fishing boat's sail, not the real sun (which is behind us, facing or being faced by the artificial, man-made sun on the sail). The situation is not unlike that of Juliet, Romeo's sun, which lights up the Piazza for a magic moment, but like all human copies of the sun, is in fact doomed—Romeo, Juliet his sun, their love, the Venetian state all doomed to the darkness, the sunset of the tomb.[59]

Turner has chosen Venice because, as this painting shows, he—and he feels his contemporaries—regarded it as the prototypical grand city in decline, its sea-challenging and sun-challenging glory fading with the setting sun; and because its great public buildings, now only tourist attractions, were recognizable at once by everyone. Venice allows him to extend the private sunrise and sunset of Romeo and Juliet to the larger disintegration of the Montague and Capulet families, to the public, political, and national catastrophe, with an allusion by way of his graphic image back to the situation in England. *Juliet and her Nurse* is an example of Turner's annexing Shakespeare to his own profoundest concerns, using Juliet and the Nurse as a key to the play of light and shade in a composition of Venice's Piazza San Marco, where he could also bring to bear his political and social worries of the 1830s. Even while ostensibly painting Venice, Turner is portraying local English subjects.

In terms of the so-called epic structure I have drawn from Fuseli, there is a small foothold for the human being in the immediate foreground with Juliet; and there is the great open space of the Piazza in the middle ground, with crowds of tiny antlike people—and as the analogy with *The Burning of the Houses of Parliament* suggests, water and ground, lagoon and piazza, are pretty much interchangeable for Turner: the sublimity of ocean as space he can transfer to a solid piazza, which appears equally unsolid. And finally there is the great bulk of the state buildings that close the opposite end of the Piazza from Juliet. I think we will have the schematic sense of this if we recall the avalanche paintings of Loutherbourg and Turner.

Juliet is another case of the ship, the "Sun of Venice," and the defiant artist who paints his own sun against the real sun which is sunk in darkness. The sail, the artificial sun, or Juliet—or even perhaps that tiny house in Turner's *Avalanche*—is a sign of the human within a natural cataclysm, a tiny surrogate for the spectator that remains as a sign of his human challenge and defeat against the force of nature. In so far as Turner himself is, as I think he is, the artist whose prime landscape subject is the sun—the representation of the source of light itself, the greatest of all landscape subjects (only timidly approached by Turner's great predecessor Claude)—then the Sun of Venice and, above all, Juliet are signs of his own temerity and inevitable failure as an artist to duplicate the aerial colors of light, to duplicate nature itself, with the human matter of pigment.

Looking back on Turner's landscapes, Ruskin argued that modern landscape's greatest contribution was its preoccupation with change:

> . . . whereas all the pleasure of the medieval was in *stability, definiteness,* and *luminousness,* we are expected to rejoice in darkness, and triumph in mutability; to lay the foundation of happiness in things which momentarily change or fade; and to expect the utmost satisfaction and instruction from what it is impossible to arrest, and difficult to comprehend.[60]

One of modern landscape's great contributions was the study of clouds, but also, Ruskin insists, change presented as a moral choice in the face of "Fallacies of Hope": "The universe presents itself continually to mankind under the stern aspect of warning, or of choice," he writes, "the good and evil set on the right hand and the left."[61] These words could have described Hogarth's twelve plates of *Industry and Idleness,* with its balanced left-right groupings of figures corresponding to right and wrong, as well as Turner's landscapes.

In the latter the choice takes the form of light against dark in an agon of chiaroscuro. At its simplest, choice can be carried over from history painting to landscape by having a protagonist within the landscape facing, choosing between, or defying the contending natural forces. In *Hannibal crossing the Alps* (R.A. 1812, pl. 98) the protagonist is located by the figure of an elephant, poised between darkness and light, but also between winter and summer, contraries which are also present and future, victory and defeat, physical and metaphorical rise and fall.[62] This is one example of a landscape showing a pivotal moment of decision or choice, couched in landscape terms of time, terrain, and weather. Moreover, as in the Hogarthian mode the choice is not a choice (for Hannibal's choice has been made) but a defiance: the end is in sight, and "the fierce archer of the downward year" (of Turner's verses attached to the painting) marks the transit from autumn to winter, which tells us that summer in the Campagna is going to be Hannibal's real winter and final defeat.

The hero is indicated as well as the dark and light, the summer and winter, as a separate figure, choosing between or defying them; and this figure can be related to the hero as a surrogate for the artist, another Juliet trying to turn back the night, another Sun of Venice trying to duplicate the natural sun.

Turner has Miltonized his Shakespearean text; but he has aestheticized Milton's moral contrast of light and dark, turning it into a fable about the artist controlling nature—of the sort he could have picked up from the Shakespeare of *The Tempest*. The spectator outside the landscape is Burke's observer of these sublimely contending forces, whether they be day and night, stormy and peaceful skies, sublime and beautiful countryside, mountains and meadows, or allegorized figures of Apollo and Python or Europa and the Bull. The contending forces are light against dark or one source of light or power against another—a natural against a man-made as in *Juliet and her Nurse*—and so ultimately the artist against nature.

Turner's paintings can be seen to derive from both the graphic and literary traditions. In graphic terms, he follows the landscape-painter Richard Wilson's pull toward unity and simplicity, and the comic-history painter Hogarth's pull toward mutiplicity and variety. In literary terms, these sources can be replaced by Milton and Shakespeare.

Turner insofar as he takes off from Wilson and the landscape tradition is trying to create unities out of disparities such as the light and the dark. His prime concerns are more closely related to falling angels, the biblical Flood, and the concerns of *Paradise Lost* than to Shakespearean subjects. On the other hand, the small modifications of the powerful sense of unity through foreground figures (like Hannibal's elephant), titles, epigraphs from "The Fallacies of Hope" or other poems, and the inclusion of tiny emblems and words are the result of Turner's Shakespearean need to complicate and disunify.

Insofar as he derives from Hogarth and Shakespeare (and Morland and Loutherbourg), he works in terms of discrepancies and contraries, including the contraries of foreground detritus and background form. Turner's sense of Shakespeare lay in the words, the images, the puns, which he loved to play with in his paintings—sometimes crudely, too literally, as in the materializing of Juliet's "some meteor that the sun exhales" in a flare in the sky—but ordinarily placed off to the side of the landscape. Upon occasion the figures and the landscape are unified to a high degree as I think they are in *Juliet and her Nurse*. Much of the time to be Shakespearean meant for Turner multitudes of people—a copiousness of incident and invention, what in English art was the "Hogarthian" element. The painting grows more Shakespearean or more picturesque as the detritus in the foreground swells to fill the picture, and the landscape recedes to mere decoration. Underneath all the detail, however, the landscape structure that is Turner's own remains the same. The figures could be removed—the army along the ridge in *Hannibal crossing the Alps* or the crowd in the Piazza, even Juliet's balcony, in *Juliet and her Nurse*—and the basic form, the basic unity would not be disturbed.[63]

Turner demonstrates that from the Shakespeare of "character" and Mortimer's portraits the movement in art is toward landscape and the searching through natural forms for equivalents to the Shakespearean psyche. But he also demonstrates that the anecdotal detail that remains in some of his most sublime paintings is also Shakespearean. He fills in around the edges of his simple vortical forms with Shakespearean humanity.[64] The vast expanse of Lake Lucerne and the Rigi at sunset are humanized by a small dog jumping off a boat into the water. Views of the Bay of Uri show, not traces of the memory of the local hero William Tell, but the daily work of the steam ferry taking passengers from one end of the lake to another. An architectural drawing of the west front of Lalndaff Cathedral (R.A. 1796, BM) includes two girls dancing to a fiddler sitting on a tombstone. In these terms, I suspect that Turner is being something the English regarded as Shakespearean: he is trying to encompass all of life; and he includes a touch of the fallibly human—the Fool in *King Lear*, Mercutio or the Nurse in *Romeo and Juliet*—somewhere within a sublime scene because it was this sort of inclusiveness that Englishmen felt raised Shakespeare's tragedy above any other.

151

NOTES

I. Introduction

1. Paulson, *Popular and Polite Art* (Notre Dame: Univ. of Notre Dame Press, 1979.) The present book also follows from my earlier book on English painting, *Emblem and Expression: Meaning in English Art of the Eighteenth Century* (Cambridge, Mass.: Harvard Univ. Press, 1975).

2. The phrase comes from Nikolaus Pevsner, *The Englishness of English Art* (1956; rpt. London: Penguin, 1964).

3. The book on landscape painting to which I allude (*Literary Landscape: Turner and Constable,* New Haven: Yale Univ. Press, 1982) deals with the related, or complementary problem, of talking about, writing about, or putting into words a picture—a purely visual construct. Constable and Turner are the subject of that book. If the present book is about the prior aspect, of how words impress themselves on visual experience and shape it, the other is about the commentary, the words that follow and help us to understand—in fact to control—this sometimes unruly visual experience; and its example is nature, or "landscape," the human attempt to control nature, which then needs to be further controlled by words. Perhaps these should have been two parts of the same book, but it has not worked out that way. The present one is primarily about history painting, the other about landscape.

4. In Kenneth Williams, *Acid Drops* (London: Dent, 1980).

5. See Brownell's *Alexander Pope and the Arts of Georgian England* (Oxford: Clarendon, 1978); Elias Mengel, "The *Dunciad* Illustrations," *Eighteenth Century Studies,* 7 (1973-74), 161.

6. *"The Rape of the Lock" and its Illustrations 1714-1896* (Oxford: Clarendon, 1980), 9-23.

7. Ibid, 11.

8. Ibid.

9. See Michael Steig, *Dickens and Phiz* (Bloomington: Indiana Univ. Press, 1978), 56-57.

10. I am indebted for this idea to Jenny Mezciems in her forthcoming essay, "Utopia and 'the Thing which is not'; More, Swift, and Other Lying Idealists."

11. The later part of this chapter grew out of my essay, "The Tradi-

tion of Comic Illustration from Hogarth to Cruikshank," in *George Cruikshank: A Revaluation,* ed. Robert L. Patten (Princeton: Princeton Univ. Press, 1974), 35-60.

12. Joseph Burke, *English Art 1714-1800 (Oxford History of English Art;* Oxford: Clarendon, 1976), 96. I doubt if Hogarth was aware of the Renaissance distinction between *istoria*—a historical subject (or *devozione*—a religious subject) and *poesia*—an illustration of myths and legends in Ovid's *Metamorphoses* and other poems. "According to the tenets of contemporary [fifteenth century] criticism," Charles Hope writes, "fidelity to a written text was a prerequisite for a successful *istoria* or *devozione,* but when an artist painted a *poesia* he was permitted the same freedom of invention as Poets" *(Titian,* New York: Harper, 1979), 126.

13. Allen, *Mysteriously Meant* (Baltimore: Johns Hopkins Univ. Press, 1970), 282-83.

14. See Hans Hammelmann, "Eighteenth-Century English Illustrators: John Vanderbank," *Book Collector,* 17 (1968), 285-99; "John Vanderbank's 'Don Quixote,' " *Master Drawings,* 7 (1969), 3-15; and *Book Illustration in Eighteenth-Century England* (New Haven: Yale Univ. Press, 1975). See also Paulson, *Hogarth: His Life, Art, and Times* (New Haven: Yale Univ. Press, 1971), I, 161–67, and *Hogarth's Graphic Works* (New Haven: Yale Univ. Press, 1965; rev. ed., 1970), cat. nos. 146-51, pls. 158-63. The Vanderbank illustrations first appeared in the 1738 Spanish-language edition and were used thereafter in the Jarvis translation (1742 et seq.). Hogarth's plates were issued only after his death (see *Hogarth's Graphic Works,* I, 176).

15. See J. Hillis Miller, "The Fiction of Realism: Sketches by Boz, *Oliver Twist,* and Cruikshank's Illustrations," in *Charles Dickens and George Cruikshank* (Los Angeles: Clark Memorial Library, 1971), 61.

16. The figure of Sancho observing Quixote attacking the puppets from Coypel's "Don Quixote and the Puppet Show" was literally transplanted by Hogarth in *The Mystery of Mock Masonry* (1724) and later in *The Analysis of Beauty,* pl. 2 (1753); *Hogarth's Graphic Works,* pls. 46, 211-12.

17. *The History and Adventures of the Renowned Don Quixote* (1755).

18. Samuel Putnam translation (New York: Viking, 1949), I, 120.

19. Vanderbank does illustrate this scene, but he only shows Quixote taking hold of Maritornes with the mule driver watching suspiciously. Nothing of the Don's confusion of Maritornes with Dulcinea is conveyed.

20. For the insights in this and the next paragraph, I am indebted to a

chapter by Laurel Brodsley, "Hogarth's Illustrations to *Hudibras,*" in her unpublished doctoral dissertation (UCLA, 1970), 92-102.

21. See Paulson, *Fictions of Satire* (Baltimore: Johns Hopkins Univ. Press, 1965), 98-102; and *Satire and the Novel* (New Haven: Yale Univ. Press, 1965), 28-32.

22. See Stuart Tave, *The Amiable Humorist* (Chicago: Univ. of Chicago Press, 1950).

II. Shakespearean Painting

1. George Steiner, "The Graces of Goethe," *TLS*, 10 Oct. 1980, p. 1143.

2. The quotation is from a paper found and quoted by Algernon Graves, "A New Light on Alderman Boydell and the Shakespearean Gallery," *Magazine of Art*, 21 (1897), 143-44. For general background, see Winifred H. Friedman, *Boydell's Shakespeare Gallery* (Ph.D. diss., Harvard Univ., 1974; facsimile, New York: Garland, 1976).

3. Preface, "A Catalogue of the Pictures in the Shakespeare Gallery" (May 1789), in *Collection of Prints from Pictures painted for the Purpose of Illustrating the Dramatic Works of Shakespeare by the Artists of Great-Britain* (London, 1793; facsimile, New York: Benjamin Blom, 1968).

4. Fuseli's *Lear and Cordelia* is in the Kunsthaus, Zürich; see Gert Schiff, *Johann Heinrich Füssli 1741–1825* (Zürich: Verlag Berichthaus, 1973), no. 466.

5. "Remarks on the Shakespeare Gallery," *Gentleman's Magazine*, 9 (Dec. 1790), 1088–90.

6. Boase, "Illustrations of Shakespeare's Plays in the Seventeenth and Eighteenth Centuries," *Journal of the Warburg and Courtauld Institutes*, 10 (1947), 96.

7. "Ancient and Modern History," *Works of Voltaire* (New York: St. Hubert Guild, 1901), XVI, Pt. 1, 59.

8. Steiner, "The Graces of Goethe," *TLS*, 1143.

9. "Ancient and Modern Tragedy," *Works of Voltaire*, XIX, Pt. 1, 137.

10. "English Tragedy," *Works of Voltaire*, XIX, Pt. 2, 45-46.

11. Voltaire, *Lettres sur les Anglais* (Basel, 1734), Lettre XVIII.

12. Walpole, *The Castle of Otranto* (1765; Oxford English Novel text, ed. W.S. Lewis, 1964), 8-9.

13. Pevsner, *Englishness of English Art*, 10-11.

14. "Preface" to *The Plays of William Shakespeare* (1765), in *The*

Yale Edition of the Works of Samuel Johnson, VIII (New Haven: Yale Univ. Press, 1968), 62.

15. "Preface" to *The Works of Shakespeare* (1725), in *Eighteenth Century Essays on Shakespeare,* ed. D. Nichol Smith (Oxford: Clarendon, 1963), 44. See also Nichol Smith's introduction; Arthur M. Eastman, *A Short History of Shakespearean Criticism* (New York: Random House, 1968); René Wellek, *A History of Modern Criticism,* I (New Haven: Yale Univ. Press, 1955), 88-92.

16. Morgann, *An Essay on the Dramatic Character of Sir John Falstaff* (1777), in *Eighteenth Century Essays on Shakespeare,* ed. Smith, 231n.

17. *The Spectator,* ed. Donald F. Bond (Oxford: Clarendon, 1965), IV, 186; also 191, 189.

18. *Yale Edition . . .Johnson,* VII, 84.

19. "Round Table," *Examiner* (1816), in *Complete Works of William Hazlitt,* ed. P.P. Howe (London: Dent. 1930), IV, 76.

20. Cf. Devin Burnell's interesting essay, "The Good, the True and the Comical: Problems occasioned by Hogarth's 'The Bench,' " *Art Quarterly,* n.s. 1, 2 (1978), 17-46.

21. Gombrich, *Art and Illusion* (New York: Phaidon, 1960).

22. That English linguistic theorists were aware of these problems is clear; see, for example, Murray Cohen's survey of the subject, *Sensible Words: Linguistic Practice in England, 1640-1785* (Baltimore: Johns Hopkins Univ. Press, 1977).

23. Bertelsen, "David Garrick and English Painting," *Eighteenth-Century Studies,* II (1978), 308-25.

24. Pevsner, *Englishness of English Art,* 24, 39, 46, 47, 92.

25. Bertelsen, "David Garrick." For Hanmer's instructions to Hayman, see Marcia Allentuck, "Sir Thomas Hanmer Instructs Francis Hayman: An Editor's Notes to his Illustrater (1744)," *Shakespeare Quarterly,* 26 (1976), 288-315.

26. This is not the place for a history of Shakespearean staging as it relates to illustration, except to note that the general progression, indicated by the name Loutherbourg, was from the architectural to landscape settings. See W. Moelwyn Merchant, *Shakespeare and the Artists* (Oxford: Clarendon, 1959), viii.

27. *Autobiographical Notes,* in *Analysis of Beauty,* ed. Burke, p. 209. Hogarth claimed that his "scenes" would be made "intelligible" by the "actor figures" (203). "I have endeavourd to weaken some of the prejudices belonging to the judging of subjects for pictures, by comparing these with stage compositions the actors in one suggesting whats to

the spectator [sic]" (211). For contemporaries' remarks on Hogarth as a theatrical artist, see Aaron Hill in *The Prompter*, 27 Feb. 1736; Arthur Murphy in *The Gray's Inn Journal*, 9 March 1754; and even Reynolds' in his *Discourse* XIV of 1788.

28. *Analysis of Beauty*, ed. Burke, 15.

29. A.P. Oppé, *The Drawings of William Hogarth* (London: Phaidon, 1948), cat. nos. 23, 24, pls. 20, 21. Robin Simon argues, quite unconvincingly it seems to me, for earlier stage decorations painted by Hogarth for Bartholomew Fair ("Hogarth and the Popular Theatre," *Renaissance and Modern Studies*, 12 [1978], 13-25).

30. We know it was Betterton's adaptation because the next revival, by the Covent-Garden Theatre company in 1736, advertised that they were giving the public "the Genuine Play of Shakespeare, and not that altered by Mr. Betterton, and so frequently acted at the other Theatre" (i.e. Drury Lane). For the dates of production, see C.B. Hogan, *Shakespeare in the Theatre* (Oxford: Clarendon, 1952), I, 187n., and *The London Stage, 1660-1800* (Carbondale: Southern Illinois Univ. Press, 1960-68). Betterton's version of *Henry IV*, Pt. 1, was published in 1700, and of Part 2, called *Sequel of Henry IV. with the Humours of Sir John Falstaffe and Justice Shallow*, in 1719.

31. Robin Simon argues in favor of the 1728 performance, and in particular the performance of 30 December because it was especially for the Freemasons, and, as I have shown elsewhere, Hogarth's connections with the Freemasons had been established publicly by the mid-1720s *(Hogarth: His Life, Art, and Times*, I, 128-32, pl. 36). I don't find this a very convincing argument in itself, since at the most it might suggest an occasion for the commission or indicate that the drawing was done on spec; the painting only found a commissioner or buyer in 1730. (See Simon, "Hogarth's Shakespeare," *Apollo*, 109 [March 1979], 214–16, AND "HOGARTH AND THE POPULAR THEATRE," 16–17.)

32. In January 1730/1 Hogarth made a list of the commissions he had not yet fulfilled, including three going back to 1728 (BM Add MS. 27995, f. 1, rpt. in J. Ireland, *Hogarth Illustrated*, 1794-99, III, 21).

33. See *Hogarth's Graphic Works*, pl. 137 (cat. no. 131), and for Laguerre's etching, *Hogarth: His Life, Art, and Times*, pl. 117 (I, 322).

34. Hogarth's idea was picked up in Durno's plate of the same scene for the *Boydell Shakespeare* (II, pl. IX).

35. See *Hogarth's Graphic Works*, I, 137 (cat. no. 116).

36. Letter to Caleb D'Anvers, dated Inner-Temple, 25 July 1727; and again, 19 June 1731 and 23 March 1734. The production itself showed little sense of timing in relation to the occasion, which was in June 1727:

there was one performance in September, and not another until a year later. See *Craftsman* nos. 8, 23, 72, 84, 107, 136.

37. See *Hogarth: His Life, Art, and Times,* I, 30-42.

38. *Analysis of Beauty,* ed. Burke, 181-82; and again, 168. Rowlandson's heroes owe something to Falstaff. His fat old men are subsidiary and blocking characters, and they do not have Falstaff's youth and vigor; the vigor is detached from the fat old people and embodied in young men and women. In short, precisely what makes Falstaff uniquely comic (in Morgann's terms) is broken apart by Rowlandson and returned to its original components, from which Shakespeare presumably constructed Falstaff—joining the figure of the blocking character or the old husband with the youthful vigor of the young lover.

39. See *Hogarth: His Life, Art, and Times,* I, 271-76, and Paulson, *Emblem and Expression,* 38-43.

40. See W.T. Whitley, *Artists and their Friends in England 1700-1799* (1928; rpt. New York: Benjamin Blom, 1928), I, 82-83. I am indebted for this identification to Brian Allen, who has identified at least three versions of the *Falstaff examining his Recruits* by Hayman, and suspects that there were originally more. There is a small version in Birmingham and a larger version in Dublin's National Gallery (pl. 23). The version I reproduce (pl. 23), now lost, may have been one of the exhibited versions shown at the Society of Arts in 1761 (no. 38) and 1765 (no. 49). There is also a drawing of the subject in the Yale Center for British Art (B.1975.4.1237), which is close compositionally to the lost version. The surviving versions appear to date from about the mid-1750s onward, but Hayman first tackled the subject in the early 1740s for the Hanmer Shakespeare, engraved by W.W. Ryland. The larger painting was engraved by Ryland in 1776, the year of Hayman's death. See also Merchant, "Francis Hayman's Illustrations of Shakespeare," in *Shakespeare Quarterly,* 9 (1958), 142–47.

41. Simon, "Hogarth's Shakespeare," 216–19. He believes the lines illustrated are I.ii.422–24, Ferdinand's "Most sure the goddess / On whom these aire attend: Vouchsafe my prayer / May know if you remain upon this island." The original version was only revived in 1757 by Garrick: see George Winchester Stone, Jr., *Shakespeare's 'Tempest' at Drury Lane during Garrick's Management,"* Shakespeare Quarterly, 7 (1956), 1–7. As Simon points out, the *Tempest* painting recorded as hanging as a Vauxhall Garden decoration was based on the opera and was obviously not by Hogarth (220n).

42. Simon notes the resemblance to "religious subjects such as the Adoration of the Magi or Annunciation: at least, the virginal associa-

tions of Miranda seem clear, in keeping with their recurrence in the text" (218). Robert Halsband has also developed this insight in a forthcoming article on illustrations for *The Tempest* in the eighteenth century.

43. See below, pp. 83–85.

44. See *Hogarth: His Life, Art, and Times*, I, 202-5.

45. A striking example is the grisaille narrative of the history of Cyrus on the staircase at Easton Neston. The figures anticipate in many ways the figures in Hogarth's history paintings of the late 1730s onward.

46. The citation of Dryden's *Fables* was in an advertisement for an engraved version. See *Hogarth: His Life, Art, and Times*, II, 274.

47. See below, pp. 106–07.

48. Conrad, *TLS*, March 1975, p. 249.

49. "Confrontation and Complexity in Shakespeare's Scenes," in "Symposium: Shakespeare in the 18th and 19th Centuries," Yale Center for British Art, 25 April 1980.

50. Simon argues that Hogarth's *Garrick as Richard III* does not show Shakespeare's *Richard III* but Colley Cibber's. It illustrates lines from Cibber's, not Shakespeare's play, which were taken from *Henry V* and transposed and altered, introduced just before the climactic moment of Richard's dream, from which Richard is awaking in Hogarth's painting. His lines, "Give me a Horse—bind up my Wounds: / Have mercy, Heav'n!" has been preceded by the Cibber-Shakespeare lines:

> . . . Hark, from the Tents
> The Armourers accomplishing the knight
> With clink of Hammers closing rivets up,
> Give dreadful note of PREPARATION; while some
> Like Sacrifices by their Fires of Watch
> With Patience sit, and inly ruminate
> The Morning's Danger . . . .

Hogarth also follows Cibber's use of a single tent, rather than the two rival tents of Shakespeare's text. See Simon, "Hogarth's Shakespeare," 216-17; and Hogan, *Shakespeare in the Theatre*, I, 378.

III. The Bible

1. The Banqueting House Ceiling's iconography is discussed by Roy Strong in his Neurath Lectures of 1981. For the other monuments discussed here, see John Shearman, *Raphael's Cartoons in the Collection of Her Majesty the Queen and the Tapestries for the Sistine Chapel* (London, 1972); John White, *The Raphael Cartoons: Victoria and*

Albert Museum (London: V & A Museum, 1972); and Andrew Martin-dale, *The Triumphs of Caesar by Andrea Mantegna in the Collection of H.M. the Queen at Hampton Court* (London: Phaidon, 1979). For the whole discussion of the Sistine Chapel—Raphael's and Michelangelo's contributions—as well as the Vatican Stanze, I am indebted to Sidney Freedberg, *Painting of the High Renaissance in Rome and Florence* (Cambridge, Mass.: Harvard Univ. Press, 1961).

2. For reproductions of these paintings, and documentation, see E. Croft-Murray, *Decorative Painting in England,* Vols. I, II (London: Country Life, 1962, 1970).

3. Freedberg, *Painting of the High Renaissance,* p. 4.

4. See below, p. 118.

5. The remainder of the "Raphael Bible" was to be found on the ceiling of the Segnatura and the arched vaults of the Loggia (collected in engraved series). Unlike the elaborate works below in the Segnatura, these small ceiling designs "were meant first of all to tell their story, and it was not expected that they be formal structures of the profound deliberation required for the larger efforts, and for those of more complex content, elsewhere in the Raphaelesque style. Intellectual considerations of order were quite secondary to ease, and where it could be attained, efficacy of narration." And as they were continued in the Loggia, they "became less formally deliberate and more casual: quickly facile, and sometimes strikingly elliptical in their temper of narration" (Freedberg, 413). It is interesting that Hogarth, whose stated aims correspond to that of the popular images of Raphael's Loggia, used as his model the "formal structures" (of "profound deliberation") of the Segnatura walls and the Tapestries.

6. Richardson, "Essay on the Art of Criticism" (1719), in *Works* (1773), 179; Shaftesbury, *Second Characters,* ed. Benjamin Rand (Cambridge, Mass.: Harvard Univ. Press, 1914), 134-36. Freedberg is eloquent on the side of Richardson and the Raphael of the Segnatura and the Cartoons contrasted with the Michelangelo of the Sistine ceiling: the former "are the expression less of man as an individuality than of the community of men: representations of the greatness that men attain and promote in social concourse" (128).

7. Freedberg, *Painting of the High Renaissance,* 268.

8. White, *Raphael Cartoons,* 8-10.

9. In *The Death of Ananias,* the cartoon, as White says, is "the most grandly calm and the most classical of Raphael's mature compositions. The apostles stand at the hub of the still, compositional circle. The eye moves swiftly past the recoiling figure on the left to focus on the tragic grace of the dying Ananias and to be held there by the advancing wall of

figures." In the tapestry, however, there is instead "a steady compositional flow, which culminates in the group around St. John, who no longer appears as the centre of an almost self-contained secondary action. There is new emphasis upon the recoiling figure who is now on the right of the central gap, and Ananias is flung back against the compositional flow with what appears now to be horrifying awkwardness" (9).

10. Freedberg, *Painting of the High Renaissance*, 276.

11. Ibid., 279.

12. See Burke, *English Art 1714-1800*, 101. Thornhill, it should be remembered, was the artist who, as Burke has said, was significant to his contemporaries because he was an "English artist wholly relieved from the drudgery of portrait painting in order to decorate churches and princely buildings with grandiose subjects from the Bible and classical mythology" (98). His end, painting copies of the Raphael Cartoons, is thus doubly emblematic.

13. Freedberg, *Painting of the High Renaissance*, 279.

14. Freedberg, *Painting of the High Renaissance*, 146; Reynolds, *Discourse* VII, in *Discourses*, ed. R.R. Wark (San Marino, Calif.: Huntington Library, 1959), 146.

15. We know he distrusted the Old Testament and Jews, the one minority group he regarded as dangerous. There is evidence that the Jewish keeper in *Harlot*, pl. 2, is also connected with Walpole, who had been recently criticized for his support of a Jewish naturalization bill—and so is parallel with those other Walpole protégés in 1 and 3, the clergyman, Charteris, and Gonson. Presumably Hogarth regarded the Jews not only as representatives of Old Testament cruelty and rigid justice but as City powers—presumably for this reason Walpole was seeking their support. Hogarth seems to see Jews through the stereotype of Shakespeare's Shylock: they rigidly follow the Law, demand their bond, and are bloodily cruel. For Walpole, see British Library Cat. 8132.a.92(2), *Robin's Panegyrick or, The Norfolk Miscellany* (Part I, London, 1729?), p. 111, a poem entitled "On the Bill for Naturalizing Jews"; also p. 121, another poem referring to Walpole and the Jews. Walpole was resurrected in 1753 in the more famous "Jew Bill" controversy (BM. Sat. 3264). For the possibility that the Jewish merchant may have been based on Sampson Gideon, cf. Alan Ramsay's portrait.

16. Cf. Hogarth's source in Dutch Dissolute Family pictures or tavern-drinking scenes in which every person, animal, and stick of furniture is behaving dissolutely. He took one element, the dog—the dissolute dog—from the dissolute family and used it to replace the comfortable family dog, who traditionally symbolized fidelity. But this

is taking a dog who is parallel to the humans and putting him among contrasting humans—a satiric device we might associate with Rabelais or, in England, the earl of Rochester—and in some situations with Swift or Pope. For the aspect of the English dog, see Paulson, *Popular and Polite Art in the Age of Hogarth and Fielding* (Notre Dame: Univ. of Notre Dame Press, 1979), 49-63.

17. My remarks on Hogarth's children are, I hope, a corrective to David Kunzle's essay, "William Hogarth: The Ravaged Child in The Corrupt City," in *Changing Images of the Family,* ed. Virginia Tufte and Barbara Meyerhoff (New Haven: Yale Univ. Press, 1979), 99-140, which argues that Hogarth's children tell us something about contemporary attitudes toward children. Well, yes, I suppose within limits of tolerance this is true: Hogarth could not violate contemporary assumptions. But his children tell us a great deal more about Hogarth than about his times.

Hogarth himself had no children. I used to receive letters from people who claimed to be descended from Hogarth, and I have read of others who have made the same claim. There were no direct descendants, since Hogarth and his wife Jane were childless (his sisters were spinsters). But London was, so to speak, well supplied with Hogarths: William Hogarths and Jane Hogarths were turned out of the Foundling Hospital every few years. The custom from 1740 when the Foundling opened was to name the foundlings deposited there after the Hospital's governors, and when these were exhausted after characters in popular fiction. Thus, with William Hogarths there were also the occasional Tom Jones and Sophia Western. And whenever one William Hogarth "graduated" another could be named. These children were in a nominal and symbolic sense Hogarth's children: he took some of them into his home, and foundlings became increasingly the subject of his art.

18. I am indebted for this point to David Dabydean, with whom I have had conversations on the subject of Hogarth and his representation of blacks. Dabydean is dealing with the subject in a forthcoming study.

19. See Paulson, *Popular and Polite Art,* 157-71.

20. Ibid., 3-23.

21. See *Hogarth: His Life, Art, and Times,* I, 486; *Art of Hogarth,* 38-40.

22. *Hogarth* (London: Tate Gallery Exhibition, 1971), 63.

23. These remarks are based on *The Art of Hogarth,* 50-53, which in turn rely on my discussion of the order of the various versions of *Paul before Felix* in *Burlington Magazine,* 114 (1972), 233-37, and my discussion of Bishop Hoadly and Paul before Felix in *The Art Bulletin,* 57

(March 1975), 293-94. Hoadly's sermon on "St. Paul's Discourse" was not published before it appeared in Hoadly's *Works* of 1773 (III, 735-42). We would have to suppose Hogarth's presence at one of the sermons deliveries or his reading it in manuscript. Although neither is impossible, it is more likely that Hogarth came at his interpretation through other sermons and through Richardson's *Pamela.*

24. *Novels of Samuel Richardson* (1902), IV, 121-22.

25. "Sermon IV. Felix's Behaviour toward Paul examined," in *The Sermons of Mr. Yorick*, III (London, 1766), 104; in later collected editions the numbering is continuous from the first two volumes, and so this sermon becomes no. XIX.

26. Ireland, *Hogarth Illustrated*, II, 92.

27. The documentation is in *Hogarth: His Life, Art, and Times*, II 51-55, 430.

28. See Paulson, *Popular and Polite Art*, 9-23.

29. John Berger, *Ways of Seeing* (London: Penguin, 1972), 103.

IV. The Miltonic Scripture

1. See Roland M. Frye, *Milton's Imagery and the Visual Arts: Iconographic Tradition in the Epic Poems* (Princeton: Princeton Univ. Press, 1978).

2. James Turner, *The Politics of Landscape* (Cambridge, Mass.: Harvard University Press, 1979), 42.

3. See Thomas M. Greene, *The Descent from Heaven: A Study in Epic Continuity* (New Haven: Yale Univ. Press, 1963), 387-95.

4. Hartman, "Milton's Counterplot," *ELH*, 25 (1958), 1-12.

5. See Gert Schiff, *Johann Heinrich Füsslis Milton-Galerie* (Zürich, 1963), 38.

6. Moore, *Milton's Theory of Redemption: Incarnation and Simile in "Paradise Lost" and "Paradise Regained"* (Unpub. doctoral diss., Yale Univ., 1981).

7. See below, pp. 150–51.

8. The illustrations to Books I and II, previously attributed to John Medina, are now believed to have been by Henry Aldrich. See Suzanne Boorsch, "The 1688 *Paradise Lost* and Dr. Aldrich," *Metropolitan Museum Journal*, 6 (1972), 133-50. For the general subject of the illustrations to *Paradise Lost* in this period, see Mary Ravenhall, *Illustrations of "Paradise Lost" in England, 1688-1802* (unpubl. doctoral diss., Univ. of Illinois, 1980).

9. *Explanatory Notes and Remarks on Milton's "Paradise Lost"* (1734), 71-72. There were two earlier illustrations for *Paradise Lost*

made by Hogarth, probably in 1725, one showing the Coujncil in Hell (Bk. I) and the other the Council in Heaven (Bk. III). In the second the Father and the Son are having a lone chat together, though surrounded by a circle of conventional angel-heads (of the sort Hogarth ridiculed the same year in *Kent's Altarpiece*). See *Hogarth's Graphic Works*, pls. 58, 59, and 57; cat. nos. 55, 56, and 54.

10. See *Hogarth: His Life, Art, and Times*, I, 388.

11. We can pass over Francis Hayman, whose illustration of 1750-53 chooses the sentimental scene of Satan's happy departure for earth, with his well-wisher Death waving Bon Voyage.

12. Paulson, *Popular and Polite Art*, 157-71.

13. Quoted in Merchant, *Shakespeare and the Artist*, 67.

14. In Thomas Weiskel's Freudian interpretation of the poem, Fear is a representation of the subject fleeing (i.e. through repression) from the sight of the primal scene—and this is repeated by the poet who addresses/ confronts Fear. See Weiskel, *The Romantic Sublime: Studies in the Structure and Psychology of Transcendence* (Baltimore: Johns Hopkins Univ. Press, 1976), 110-24; and Paulson, "Burke's Sublime and the Representation of Revolution," in *Culture and Politics from Puritanism to Enlightenment* (Berkeley: Univ. of California Press, 1980), 241-69.

15. Epistle II.iii, trans. Smith Palmer Bovie, *Satires and Epistles of Horace* (Chicago: Univ. of Chicago Press, 1959), 271.

16. *Poetics*, XIV.4.

17. Barry's *Satan, Sin, and Death* was one of eighteen illustrations he made for *Paradise Lost*. Barry's six sketches in the Ashmolean, his earliest thoughts, are on paper cut from printed sheets announcing his distribution of the Adelphi etchings on 23 April 1792—and so have to be after that date. The first mention of his series is in a letter of 26 Dec. 1794 (Barry to Earl of Radnor, Barry, *Works*, I, 279-80). Therefore it is possible that Barry's *Satan, Sin, and Death* follows Gillray's of 9 June 1792. See William Pressly, *The Life and Art of James Barry* (New Haven: Yale Univ. Press, 1981), 152-53.

18. *Freud & Philosophy: An Essay on Interpretation*, trans. Denis Savage (New Haven: Yale Univ. Press, 1970), 322.

19. Satan's rebellion took the form of narcissism, as Sin reminds him:

Thyself in me the perfect image viewing
Becam'st enamor'd, and such joy thou took'st
With me in secret, that my womb conceiv'd
A growing burden.   (II, 764-67)

The allegory held deep meaning for the artist who worried over the complementary risks of narcissism and idolatry—both embodied in the Satan-Sin relationship. The whole process of artistic creation was adumbrated in the birth of Sin out of the rebellious idea; the passion of Satan for himself in his offspring; and this narcissistic-incestuous passion producing an offspring that pursues and rapes its own mother and then challenges its father as a king in its own right. (The Sin-Eve parallel [out of "the left side" of Satan's mind and out of Adam's left side] also points to Ambrosio, whose "Sin" is the devil/woman/boy Rosario who is sent by the devil to tempt him.) We could carry the revolutionary-aesthetic analogy even further, noting the relationship Milton establishes between Sin and Scylla, a classical equivalent who is gnawed by her own children (as she was ravished by her son): what originates in Satan's mind and accepts his embraces can expect to be ravished and devoured by her offspring. "The revolution devours its own young" were Vergniaud's well-known words.

20. See *Revolution and Utopia* (London: Macmillan, 1977).

21. For Blake's "copying" of Michelangelo's *Last Judgment,* see Leslie W. Tannenbaum, "Transformations of Michelangelo in William Blake's *The Book of Urizen,*" *Colby Literary Quarterly,* 16 (1980), 19-50; see also Jennijoy La Belle, "Michelangelo's Sistine Frescoes and Blake's 1795 Color-Printed Drawings: A Study in Structural Relationships," *Blake: An Illustrated Quarterly,* 14 (1980), 66-84. See Northrop Frye, "Expanding Eyes," *Critical Enquiry,* 2 (1975), 206-7: "A universe in which God was up there and Satan down there could no longer hold together: . . . . The separation of the mythical spatial categories from the actual world made their reactionary shape clear: what was up in the sky was revealed as what Blake called the ghost of the priest and king, and what was underneath was the ghost of exploited humanity." The old construct, as Frye remarks, "was an intensely conservative and authoritarian construct and had been consistently, if often unconsciously, so used in European culture."

22. Wimsatt, "Laokoön: An Oracle Reconsulted," in *Day of the Leopards: Essays in Defense of Poems* (New Haven: Yale Univ. Press, 1976), 48.

23. Bloom, "The Pictures of the Poet," *New York Times Book Review,* 3 January 1982, p. 4.

24. *Oracle,* 15 Nov. 1792; see Allardyce Nicoll, *Early Eighteenth-Century Drama,* vol. II of *A History of English Drama 1660-1900,* 3rd ed. (Cambridge: Cambridge Univ. Press, 1952-55), 30; Sybil Rosenfeld, *A Short History of Scene Design in Great Britain* (Oxford: Clarendon Press, 1973), 72; C. Hogan, ed. *London Stage,* Pt. 5, 1776-1800 (Carbondale: Southern Illinois Univ. Press, 1968), lxii.

25. *London Chronicle,* Nos. 25 and 26 (24-26 Feb. and 26 Feb.-1 March, 1757), pp. 199-200, 207-8; Murphy, *The Life of David Garrick, Esq.* (London, 1801), II, 179.

26. "Verbal-Visual Relationships: Zoffany's and Fuseli's Illustrations of Macbeth," *Art History,* 3 (Dec. 1980), 357-87, originally written for my NEH Summer Seminar (1979) in "Visual-Verbal Relationships." For some examples of Zoffany's Hogarthian intellectual play, see Paulson, *Emblem and Expression,* 138-48, and "James Ensor, Johann Zoffany, etc.," *Georgia Review,* 21 (1977), 506-11.

27. Cf. the effect of a human source of light contrasted with a natural—the first usually inside, the other outside a room—in the paintings of Wright of Derby in the 1760s and 70s. (See Paulson, *Emblem and Expression,* 184–93, and below, on Turner, pp. 148–49.

28. See Esther Gordon Dotson, "English Shakespeare Illustration and Eugene Delacroix," *Essays in Honor of Walter Friedländer* (New York: Institute of Fine Arts, 1965), pp. 40-59.

29. Lecture III, in John Knowles, *Life and Writings of Henry Fuseli, Esq., M.A., R.A.* (London, 1831), II, 157.

30. For the three categories, see Fuseli's Aphorisms 36-40, Knowles, III, 74-76; also Lectures III (1801) and IV (1805) on "Invention."

31. See Farington's quotation of Fuseli, *Farington's Diary,* 24 July 1805; Fuseli, Aphorism 77, in Knowles, III, 87.

32. This may be called the Hogarthian, an element sometimes included by Fuseli himself. Hogarth is one of those who "informs" rather than "moves" or "astonishes." His "representations of local manners and national modifications of society, whose characteristic discrimination and humorous exuberance" we admire, but which, "like the fleeting passions of the day, every hour contributes something to obliterate, which soon become unintelligible by time, or degenerate into caricature, the chronicle of scandal, the history-book of the vulgar" (Knowles, II, 157). See also William Vaughan, *German Romantic Painting* (New Haven: Yale Univ. Press, 1980), 30.

33. Gert Schiff, *Johann Heinrich Füssli 1741-1825* (Zürich, 1973), I, cat. no. 445 (hereafter parenthetical numbers in the text refer to Schiff's catalogue); *Henry Fuseli* (London, Tate Exhib. 1975), cat. no. 36; Peter Conrad, "The Pre-Romantic Agony," *TLS,* 7 March 1975, p. 249.

34. [Henry Fuseli], *Remarks on the Writings and Conduct of J.J. Rousseau* (London, 1767), 67-68n.; cited, Dotson, 54, 56.

35. *Analytical Review,* 24 (Dec. 1796), 566; Aphorism 58, in Knowles, III, 81.

36. Lecture IV (1805), in Knowles, *Life and Writings of Henry Fuseli,* II, 226.

37. Ibid.

38. Blake is supposed to have ranked Fuseli's *Satan, building the Bridge over Chaos* "with the grandest efforts of imaginative art" (Palmer to Gilchrist, 23 Aug. 1855). In this picture Satan is descending, but if we did not have the title he could as well be rising (Schiff 1821).

39. One learns nothing but the source and the story from Schiff and the Tate catalogue. Peter Tomory adventurously speculates on its relation to the French Revolution: Thor "was the hero of the Norse lower classes, as Odin was of the aristocracy, so democratic Virtue overcomes the strangling coils of hereditary Vice" *(The Life and Art of Henry Fuseli,* London: Phaidon, 1972, p. 105). Something like this may well be the case, but how does Tomory know that Odin was hero of the aristocracy and Thor of the lower classes? He would not have found this in Mallet's *Northern Antiquities* (II, 770, 134 ff.), nor in Fuseli's review of the Edda Soemundae in *The Analytical Review* (Dec. 1788). Nor does it substantiate the speculation to add, as he does, that "Such a reading is indicated by Carl Guttenberg's engraving of *William Tell* after Fuseli and published in Paris in 1787"—which is simply another case, preceding the Revolution, and in no way confirming the Thor.

40. Tomory, who tries to connect Fuseli literally with the theater, argues that this "was the angle of view obtained from a seat in the pit of the actors on stage. This groundling's view of the figures high against a low horizon . . ."—with presumably the same lower-class social comment (p. 71).

41. When Prometheus is being chained in the Caucasus, though Haephestus is doing the work, a woman is also taking part (1780).

42. Tomory, *Henry Fuseli,* 30.

43. Schiff has explored some of Fuseli's obsessions, in particular his hair-fetish, the presence of which is noticeable even in so remote a place as the Achilles on Patroclus's funeral pyre (1359). But the significance of hair to Fuseli becomes clear if we mention only the fantastic hair styles in the portraits of his wife, or of other women, and especially of threatening courtesans; the picture of a woman sitting by a well, out of whose depths reaches a man's hand, grasping for a plait of her hair she is letting down to him (1577); and the picture of Samson in prison completely shorn, and of course blind, and Delilah sitting in the window wearing the usual elaborate and high Fuseli hair style (1414, pl. 86 in this book.)

It is not altogether clear to what extent Fuseli is merely repeating a convention of anti-feminist satire, present in one of his earliest drawings (239) showing a wife with her foot pressing her henpecked husband to the ground ("You fool, your *mare* rides you . . ."—another significant

Fuseli premonition), compacting him into the shape Fuseli later associates with despair or silence (722, 908). Indeed, it is probably not surprising that Fuseli's early works and his allegories of the artist show his iconography at its most basic: sexual and excretory imagery; the woman dominant—necessarily, masochistically so—over the man; and the truncated, compacted, and in some major way diminished male figure. From here a viewer can go off into the many views of a male spread-eagled on the ground, his sexual organs toward us, being transfixed or otherwise mistreated; to the male in the pornographic drawings helplessly being played with sexually by a group of naked women. What writers like Secheverell Sitwell and Ruthven Todd have noticed as the peculiar characteristic of the erotic drawings is the unruffled coiffure (perhaps reminiscent of Cranach nudes but here more elaborate and phallic) worn by these women engaging in coition or the "torture" of the spread-eagled man (1620-26). I would substitute for Schiff's rather complicated Freudian interpretation the simple self-sufficiency of Fuseli's women, summed up perhaps in the phalli that support their fireplaces (1618), appear on their Nazi-like armbands (1440; neckband, 1449) or in the candles on their tables, and parallel the erect member of the man venturing into their rooms (1617).

44. Lecture IV, in Knowles, *Life and Writings of Henry Fuseli*, II, 217-18.

45. Lecture V, Part II (1805), on "Expression," in Knowles, II, 259-60.

46. In Thomas Jones' version the Bard is connected by shape with the blasted tree standing near him, and he seems to be in the midst of a storm, but the confrontation is far off—the troops winding around the mountain.

47. See Merchant, *Shakespeare in Art*, ch. 12.

48. *Blackwood's Magazine*, 40 (Oct. 1836), 550-51.

49. "A Reply to Blackwood's Criticism of Turner," in *Works of John Ruskin*, ed. E.T. Cook and Alexander Wedderburn (London, 1903), III, 639. For Turner's paintings, see *The Paintings of J.M.W. Turner*, ed. Martin Butlin and Evelyn Joll (New Haven: Yale Univ. Press, 1977).

50. *Turner* (1879), 136. For Ruskin a Venetian view of 1844, "with sunlight and moonlight mixed, was, I think, when I first saw it, the most perfectly beautiful piece of colour of all that I have seen produced by human hands, by any means, or at any period" *(Works,* VII, 431). For Turner's use of the sun, see Paulson, "Turner's Graffiti: The Sun and its Glosses," in *The Romantic Image*, ed. Kroeber, 167-88. See also Charles Stuckey, who treats the whole theme of the co-presence of sun and

167

moon in *Temporal Imagery in the Early Romantic Landscape* (unpub. diss., Univ. of Pennsylvania).

51. "On the Sublime," *Philosophical Essays* (Edinburgh, 1810), 384.

52. Knowles, *Life and Writings of Henry Fuseli*, II, 160, 161-62, 217.

53. "The Imagery of Romeo and Juliet," from *Leading Motives in the Imagery of Shakespeare's Tragedies* (London, 1930; in *Shakespeare: Modern Essays in Criticism*, ed. Leonard F. Dean, New York: Prentice Hall, 1961, pp. 73-74).

54. Gerald Ziff, review of Butlin and Joll, *Art Bulletin*, 62 (March 1980), 170.

55. Rogers, *Italy* (1836), 87.

56. *Times*, 6 May 1836. Stephen Pickles, *TLS*, 21 March 1980, p. 322, notices this resemblance but ("Though unremarked, the similarities . . .") does not acknowledge the *Times* critic.

57. Thomas Paine, *Rights of Man*, Part 2 (1792), ch. 5 (London: Penguin, 1971), 232.

58. The Cleveland version of *The Burning of the Houses of Parliament* (R.A., spring 1835) makes its own allusion to Venice by using the same viewpoint, and roughly the same composition as Canaletto's *View of the Thames from the Steps of Somerset House* (Royal Collection and Yale Center for British Art). Two years earlier, his first Venetian painting, *Bridge of Sighs, Ducal Palace and Custom House, Venice: Canaletto Painting* (1833, Tate Gallery), had already made its allusion to Canaletto, who appears on the left painting the scene, and also to the interpretation of Venice Turner was to perpetuate in his later paintings. The painting's title asks us to remember Byron's famous lines that open *Childe Harold*, Canto IV: "I stood in Venice on the Bridge of Sighs / A palace and a prison on each hand." Turner's interests in Venice probably goes back to the illustrations he made between 1832 and 1833 for John Murray's edition of Byron, followed by his visit of 1833. The England-Venice parallel is also made in pendants of 1834–35, *Keelmen heaving in Coals by Moonlight* (on the River Tyne) and *Venice* (both, National Gallery, Washington).

59. Also to be noticed in the Cleveland version of *The Burning of the Houses of Parliament* is the floating fire pump—quite unable to cope with the fire, or even approach it—on whose side appear the words "SUN" and "FIRE," separated by a sun sign (referring to the Sun Fire insurance company). Thus the sign of the sun is ironically opposed to the real consuming fire, and thereby we are given a sequence consisting of the word, the sign, and the sun/fire—just as in *Juliet and her Nurse* Turner gives us the human sun Juliet lighting up the Piazza in conflict with the real sun that is going to wipe out her human pretensions.

60. Ruskin, *Works*, V, 317.

61. Ruskin, *Works*, VI, 416.

62. See Stuckey, *Temporal Imagery*, pp. 155-61.

63. Martin saw that the Turner formula—dwarfing tiny human figures in a huge natural setting—was more appropriate for *Paradise Lost*, where the landscape was a manifestation of divine power, wrath, or love (as in Turner's *Plagues of Egypt* or *Avalanche* paintings).

64. This is the most favorable way I can sum up the effect of the Turner painting. For a less favorable way, see Paulson, "Turner's Graffiti: The Sun and its Glosses," in *The Romantic Image*, ed. Kroeber, and Paulson, *Literary Landscape: Turner and Constable* (New Haven: Yale Univ. Press, 1982), Pt. II.

2

3

2. Illustration for Pope's *The Rape of the Lock:* Belinda on the Thames. Etching. 1714.

3. Illustration for Pope's *The Rape of the Lock:* Frontispiece. Etching. 1714.

4. Hogarth, illustration for *Hudibras:* Hudibras wooing the Widow. Etching. 1721-22 (publ. 1726).

5. Hogarth, illustration for *Don Quixote:* the Adventure of Mambrino's Helmet. Etching and engraving. 1726.

6. Hogarth, illustration for *Don Quixote:* the curate and Barber disguising Themselves. Etching and engraving. 1726

173

7. Hogarth, Sancho's Feast. Etching and engraving. 1726-27?

174

8

9

8. Francis Hayman, illustration for *Don Quixote:* Don Quixote and Maritornes. Etching and engraving. 1755.

9. Thomas Rowlandson, illustration for *Don Quixote:* Don Quixote and Maritornes. Drawing. c. 1800. Collection, Mr. and Mrs. Philip Pinsof.

10

11

10. Hogarth, large *Hudibras* plates: Hudibras meets the Skimmington. Etching and engraving. 1726. Courtesy of the Print Collection, The Lewis Walpole Library, Yale University.

11. Annibale Carracci, Marriage of Bacchus and Ariadne. Fresco, Farnese Palace, Rome.

12. Hogarth, large *Hudibras* plates: Hudibras sallying forth. Etching and engraving. 1726.

13

14

178

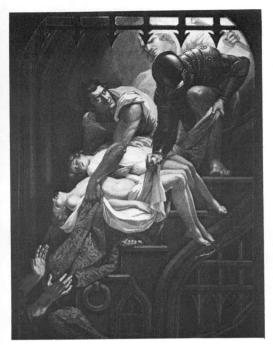

15

16

13. James Barry, King Lear and Cordelia *(Lear,* V.iii.). Engraving, Boydell Shakespeare. 1793. Yale Center for British Art, Paul Mellon Collection.

14. Annibale Carracci, *Pietà.* Painting, National Gallery, London.

15. James Northcote, Burial of the Little Princes *(Richard III,* IV.iii.). Engraving, Boydell Shakespeare. 1793. Yale Center for British Art, Paul Mellon Collection.

16. Caravaggio, The Entombment of Christ. Painting, Vatican.

179

17

18

19

17. Benjamin West, Ophelia, Claudius, and Gertrude *(Hamlet,* IV.v.). Yale Center for British Art, Paul Mellon Collection.

18. James Northcote, Scene from *Richard III* (III.i.). Engraving, Boydell Shakespeare. 1789. Yale Center for British Art, Paul Mellon Collection.

19. Joseph Wright of Derby, Scene from *The Tempest.* Mezzotint, Boydell Shakespeare. 1793. Yale Center for British Art, Paul Mellon Collection.

20

21

22

20. Hogarth, Falstaff examining his Recruits. Painting. 1727-30. Collection Lord Iveagh.

21. Hogarth, *The Beggar's Opera*. Painting. 1728. Collection W.S. Lewis.

22. Hogarth, large illustration for *Hudibras:* The Committee. Etching and engraving. 1726.

23. Francis Hayman, Falstaff examining his Recruits. Painting. 1754.
Present location unknown.

24. Hogarth, Henry VIII. Engraving. 1728.

25. Hogarth, The Committee of the House of Commons. Drawing.
1729. Fitzwilliam Museum, Cambridge.

26. Hogarth, The Committee of the House of Commons. Painting.
1729. National Portrait Gallery, London.

27

28

27. Hogarth, The Denunciation. Painting. 1729. Courtesy of the National Gallery of Ireland, Dublin.

28. Hogarth, The Christening. Painting. 1729. Private collection.

29

29. Hogarth, Scene from *The Tempest.* Painting. c. 1736. Lord St. Oswald Collection.

30. Hogarth, Sigismunda. Painting. 1759. Tate Gallery, London.

31. Paulo de Matteis, The Choice of Hercules. Etching. 1713.

30

31

189

32

33

32. Raphael, Paul and the Proconsul. Cartoon for the Vatican tapestries, Courtesy of H.M. Queen Elizabeth II, Victoria and Albert Museum, London.

33. Raphael, 'Paul preaching at Athens.' Engraving by Nicolas Dorigny.

34

35

34. Francis Hayman, The Play Scene from *Hamlet*. Painting. c. 1740. Present location unknown.

35. Hogarth, The Rake's Progress, plate 1. Etching and engraving. 1735.

36

36. Hogarth, *A Harlot's Progress*, plate 1. Etching and engraving. 1732.

37. Hogarth, *A Harlot's Progress*, plate 2.

38. Hogarth, *A Harlot's Progress*, plate 3.

37

38

193

39

40

41

42

43

44

42. Hogarth, The Cholmondeley Family. Painting. 1732. Collection of Marquess of Cholmondeley.

43. Hogarth, A Scene from *The Conquest of Mexico*. Painting. 1732. Lady Theresa Agnew collection.

44. Hogarth, *Marriage à la Mode*, 1. Painting. 1743-45. National Gallery, London.

45

45. Hogarth, *Marriage à la Mode*, 4. Painting. 1743-45. National Gallery, London.

46A. Hogarth, *Marriage à la Mode*, 5. Painting. 1743-45. National Gallery, London.

46B. Detail of the tapestry. Engraving. 1745.

46 A

46 B

47. Hogarth, *Marriage à la Mode*, 6. Painting. 1743-45. National Gallery, London.

48. Hogarth, Moses brought to Pharaoh's Daughter. Engraving. 1752.
British Museum, London.

49. Hogarth, Paul before Felix. Painting (after cleaning, 1970). 1747. Lincoln's Inn, London.

50. Hogarth, Paul before Felix. Engraving by Luke Sullivan. 1752.

51. Hogarth, Paul before Felix burlesqued. Etching. 1752.

52

53

52. Hogarth, Boys Peeping at Nature (subscription ticket for *A Harlot's Progress*). Etching. 1731.

53. Hogarth, Boys Peeping at Nature (revised state, used as subscription ticket for Paul before Felix and Moses brought to Pharaoh's Daughter). Etching. 1752.

54

55

54. Henry Aldrich, Satan, Sin, and Death. Engraving. *Paradise Lost.*
1688.

55. Louis Cheron, Satan, Sin, and Death. Engraving, Milton, *Poetical Works.* 1718.

56. Hogarth, Satan, Sin, and Death. Painting. c. 1735-37. Tate Gallery,
London.

57. Hogarth, The Western Family. Painting. 1738. Courtesy of the
National Gallery of Ireland, Dublin.

58

59

208

60

61

58. Henry Fuseli, Satan, Sin, and Death. Drawing. 1770. Ashmolean Museum, Oxford.

59. James Gillray, Sin, Death, and the Devil. Etching. 1792.

60. James Barry, Satan, Sin, and Death. Etching. 1792.

61. William Blake, Satan, Sin, and Death. Drawing. c. 1800. Henry E. Huntington Library and Art Gallery, San Marino, California.

62

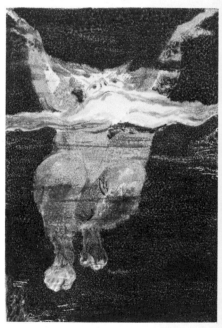

63

62. Michelangelo, God Separating the Light from the Darkness (with Ignudi). Fresco. Ceiling, Sistine Chapel, Rome.

63. Blake, Urizen Floating up through the Water. Engraving for *The Book of Urizen.* 1795. Yale Center for British Art, Paul Mellon Collection.

64

65

64. Raphael, God Creating the Sun and Moon. Fresco. Ceiling, Loggia, Vatican.

65. Blake, Urizen Launching his new World. Engraving for *The Book of Urizen*, plate 23. 1794. Yale Center for British Art, Paul Mellon Collection.

66 (a)

66 (b)

67

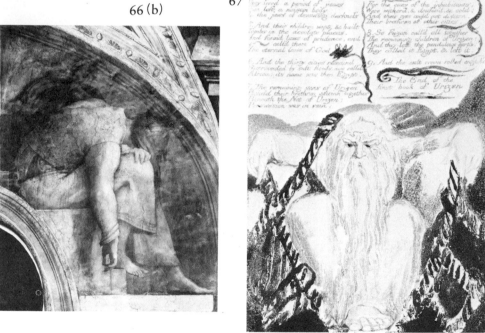

66. Michelangelo, Lunette of the Ancestors of Christ: (a) Aminadab and
(b) a sleeping Figure. Fresco. Ceiling, Sistine Chapel, Rome.

67. Blake, *Urizen*, plate 27. Engraving for *The Book of Urizen*. 1794.
Yale Center for British Art, Paul Mellon Collection.

68

69

70

68. Michelangelo, *The Prophet Zachariah*. Fresco. Ceiling, Sistine Chapel, Rome.

69. Blake, Albion Rose. Etching. Dated 1780 (probably 1790).

70. Blake, *America,* plate 10. Paul Mellon Collection.

71

72

71. Reynolds, Garrick between The Muses of Comedy and Tragedy. Mezzotint. 1762. Yale Center for British Art, Paul Mellon Collection.

72. Zoffany, Garrick and Mrs. Pritchard in the dagger scene from *Macbeth*. Mezzotint. 1768. Yale Center for British Art, Paul Mellon Collection.

73

74

73. Fuseli, Garrick and Mrs. Pritchard in the dagger scene from *Macbeth*. Drawing. c. 1766. Kunsthaus, Zürich.

74. Fuseli, Garrick and Mrs. Pritchard in the dagger scene from *Macbeth*. Painting. 1812. Tate Gallery, London.

75. Mortimer, Edgar. Etching. 1782-86. Yale Center for British Art, Paul Mellon Collection.

76. Fuseli, Macbeth and the Witches. Mezzotint, Boydell Shakespeare.
1793. Yale Center for British Art, Paul Mellon Collection.

77

78

77. Fuseli, Claudius and Old Hamlet. Drawing. 1771. Graphische Sammlung der Eidgnössischen Technischen Hochschule, Zürich.

78. Design on a Greek vase. British Museum, London.

79

80

79. Fuseli, Hamlet and his Father's Ghost. Drawing. 1780-83. Kunsthaus, Zürich.

80. Fuseli, Thor and the Midgard Serpent. Painting. 1790. Royal Academy, London.

81

82

81. Michelangelo, Lunette of the Ancestors of Christ: Josaphat and Joram. Fresco. Ceiling, Sistine Chapel, Rome.

82. Fuseli, Copy of the man writing in the Josaphat Lunette. Drawing. N.d. Kunsthaus, Zürich.

220

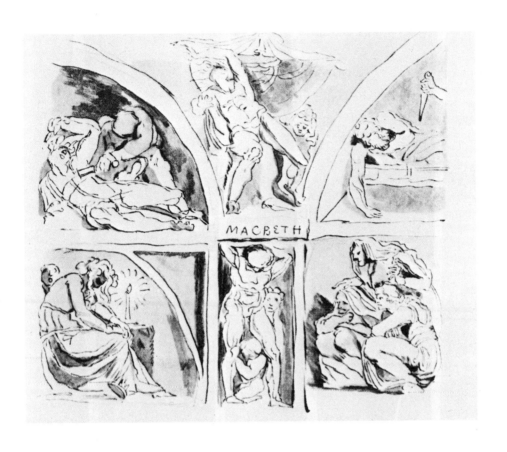

83. Fuseli, Frontispiece for *Macbeth*. Drawing. 1777-78. British Museum, London.

84

85

86

87

84. Fuseli, Falstaff and the Buck Basket *(Merry Wives of Windsor)*. Painting. 1792. Kunsthaus, Zürich.

85. Fuseli, Titania and Bottom *(A Midsummer Night's Dream)*. Painting. [1780-90.] Tate Gallery, London.

86. Fuseli, Samson and Delilah. Drawing. [1800-05.] Kunsthaus, Zürich.

87. Fuseli, Adam and Eve. Aquatint. 1794-97. Milton Gallery.

88. Fuseli, Self-portrait. Drawing. [c. 1777.] National Portrait Gallery, London.

Sketch for Ulysses in Hell. Tiresias &c Zurich

89. Fuseli, Tiresias drinking. Drawing. [1780-85.] Kunsthaus, Zürich.

225

90

91

92

94

90. John Martin, The Bard. Painting. 1817. Yale Center for British Art, Paul Mellon Collection.

91. Fuseli, The Bard. Drawing. c. 1800. Kunsthaus, Zürich.

92. Loutherbourg, Avalanche. Painting. 1804. Tate Gallery, London.

93. Turner, Avalanche in the Grisons. Painting. 1810. Tate Gallery, London.

94. John Runciman, King Lear on the Heath. Painting. 1764. The National Gallery of Scotland, Edinburgh.

95. Turner, Juliet and her Nurse. Painting. 1836. Private collection.

96

97

96. Turner, The Burning of the Houses of Parliament. Painting. 1835.
Philadelphia Museum of Art, The John H. McFadden Collection.

97. Turner, The Sun of Venice. Painting. 1842. Tate Gallery, London.

229

98. Turner, Hannibal crossing the Alps. Painting. 1812. Tate Gallery,
London.

INDEX

231

The Hodges Lectures

THE BETTER ENGLISH FUND was established in 1947 by John C. Hodges, Professor of English, The University of Tennessee, 1921–1962, and head of the English Department, 1941–1962, on the returns from the *Harbrace College Handbook,* of which he was the author. Over the years, it has been used to support the improvement of teaching and research in the English Department. The Hodges Lectures are intended to commemorate this wise and generous bequest.

VOLUMES PUBLISHED

Theodore Roosevelt Among the Humorists: W.D. Howells, Mark Twain, and Mr. Dooley, by William M. Gibson (1980)

Arts on the Level: The Fall of the Elite Object, by Murray Krieger (1981)

THE HODGES LECTURES book series is set in ten-point Sabon type with two-point spacing between the lines. Sabon is also used for display. The series format was designed by Jim Billingsley. This title in the series was composed by Williams of Chattanooga, Tennessee, printed by Thomson-Shore, Inc., Dexter, Michigan, and bound by John H. Dekker & Sons, Grand Rapids, Michigan. The paper on which the book is printed bears the watermark of S.D. Warren and is designed for an effective life of at least 300 years.

THE UNIVERSITY OF TENNESSEE PRESS : KNOXVILLE